UNDUE INFLUENCE

How the Wall Street Elite Put the Financial System at Risk

CHARLES R. GEISST

WILEY

John Wiley & Sons, Inc.

Published by John Wiley & Sons, Inc., Hoboken, New Jersey.
Published simultaneously in Canada.

For general information on our other products and services, or technical support,
please contact our Customer Care Department within the United States at 800-762-2974,
outside the United States at 317-572-3993 or fax 317-572-4002.

Wiley also publishes its books in a variety of electronic formats. Some content that
appears in print may not be available in electronic books.

For more information about Wiley products, visit our web site at www.wiley.com.

Library of Congress Cataloging-in-Publication Data

Geisst, Charles R.
  Undue influence : how the Wall Street elite put the fianancial system at
risk / Charles R. Geisst.
    p. cm.
  Includes bibliographical references.
  ISBN 0-471-65663-1 (cloth)
  1. Stock exchanges—United States. 2. Stock exchanges—Law and legislation—
United States. 3. Securities industry—Deregulation—United States. 4. Financial
crises—United States. I. Title.
  HG4910.G449 2005
  332.64′273—dc22

                                                                    2004011590

Printed in the United States of America

10 9 8 7 6 5 4 3 2 1

For Margaret and Meg

CONTENTS

INTRODUCTION

In late 1999, a Republican congressman held a party in Washington to celebrate the passing of new legislation destined to have a profound effect on Wall Street and the entire financial industry in the United States. Despite the date on the law, the principle upon which it was based actually had been a cornerstone of the Reagan revolution 15 years earlier. The party seemed a bit late.

The centerpiece of the affair was a large cake bearing the message "Glass-Steagall, RIP, 1933–1999." Sipping champagne with one of the new law's sponsors, Jim Leach, Republican from Iowa, were Alan Greenspan, chairman of the Federal Reserve Board, and various Treasury officials and congressmen who had been instrumental in getting the new legislation passed, finally repealing the most talked about law of the twentieth century. After years of failed efforts and false starts, the Banking Act of 1933, as the Glass-Steagall Act was officially known, had been erased from the books and replaced by the Financial Services Modernization Act of 1999, the Gramm-Leach-Bliley Act. The champagne flowed and congratulations were offered by all. Never before had a law had so many detractors yet been so hard to effectively replace. The battle against Glass-Steagall began in the 1930s, revived in the 1960s, and became a major plank in the Republican platforms of the1980s. Ironically, it was not until the end of the century that it finally was repealed.

Since the dark days of the Depression, the Glass-Steagall Act had come to symbolize the fundamental cornerstone of what had become known as the social "safety net" erected by Congress to protect the American consumer. The law provided deposit insurance (left intact in 1999), allowed the Federal Reserve power to control bank interest rates (this power was repealed in 1980 and 1982), and most importantly, separated commercial and investment banking. This last part of the act was the most contentious, at least to the banks themselves. Any institution that accepted deposits from customers was not permitted to underwrite corporate stocks or bonds. The securities markets were considered too risky to use customer deposits for underwriting. The conditions that caused the Crash of 1929 were not going to be repeated again.

Over the course of the next 70 years, the Wall Street securities houses came to love Glass-Steagall because it created a virtually oligopoly among the major investment banks. They could not be owned by, nor could they own, commercial banks so the two sides of the banking business were indeed separated. The most lucrative side of what was known before 1933 as banking in general—investment banking—became the sole province of Wall Street, paying fat salaries and bonuses and fanning the occasional periods of speculative excess. The less lucrative, but steadier side remained commercial banking: taking deposits, making loans, and clearing checks. This was not exciting business and for years it had looked enviously at Wall Street. In a good year, all of those fat fees earned by investment bankers could easily exceed the less spectacular fees earned by banks doing their ordinary, run-of-the-mill business. If only the two sides could be rejoined.

The banking law did not survive the passing of the twentieth century, but other parts of the safety net did. The Securities Act of 1933 and the Securities Exchange Act of 1934 both remain as survivors of the 1930s because they aimed at reforming the practices of the securities industry rather than dividing it in the name of consumer protection. But the 1933 act had some gaping holes in it, acknowledged even when it was passed, that managed to remain plugged until the 1990s. Then, a wave of accounting fraud hit some of the "New Era" companies most conspicuous during the 1990s' bull market, and financial collapse followed. The unfortunate part of the financial meltdown was that it was caused in no small part by the deregulation that preceded it. The plaster had cracked, but it was the banks that were fueling the speculative fires of the mid- to late 1990s. The Gramm-Leach-Bliley Act officially was passed in 1999, but its effects had been felt for several years before since the Federal Reserve had allowed all of the deregulation mentioned in it to already occur on a de facto basis for almost 10 years. The market meltdown and scandals that followed were the most serious since 1929.

A larger question remained unanswered in the post–bear market debris left by a deregulated banking system: How was it possible that another series of scandals so similar to the one 70 years before could occur after decades of regulatory and legal developments? Part of the answer was obvious. Investors were still as gullible as ever, hoping to make a quick killing in the market. It was as if everyone had heard the old stories about the vast amount of wealth created during the nineteenth century and was only waiting for a New Era to begin. Many investors knew about the great American fortunes made in the Gilded Age and the Jazz Age. Now, new technologies were being used that could usher in a similar era of unforeseen riches almost a hundred years later. The frenzy that followed was natural. Cautionary voices were still heard in the marketplace, as they had been in the late 1920s, but not very loudly. The best that the Federal Reserve chairman could do was to call the period one of "irrational exuberance." The major policy tool at his disposal for calming the markets never was used. In 1930, the Fed was loudly blamed for not stopping the market roller coaster. In 2001, the worst condemnation it faced was that it had not seen the problem coming quickly enough.

The market collapse of 2001 was caused by a successful campaign by Wall Street and bankers in collaboration with like-minded individuals in the Clinton administration and Congress, many of whom with strong ties to the Street, to erase the Depression era laws constraining the markets. They inherited the sentiment from the generation of Republicans preceding them who wanted to abolish the banking laws in the name of free market ideology. When Congress passed the Gramm-Leach-Bliley Act in 1999, it represented one of the most successful campaigns by an odd combination of Republicans, New Democrats, and others ostensibly interested in free markets to put their imprint on the financial markets. The move also helped revise American history, adding to the ideological fervor of free marketers, proving that the same capitalist system that defeated Soviet Communism could certainly get rid of some cumbersome Roosevelt era laws. Unfortunately, the result was the market collapse in the new century.

Activists opposed the deregulatory bill, fearing that large banks would ignore minorities and local communities in favor of corporate customers. In addition to Alan Greenspan, the Clinton administration broadly supported it, including Treasury secretary Robert Rubin, along with legislators from the other side of the aisle, including Senator Phil Gramm of Texas. It also had wide support from other parts of the financial services industry, especially among insurance companies and smaller financial companies, which assumed that it would allow them to be bought by larger banks. Once the bill was introduced, the juggernaut began for its quick passing.

While the details were being negotiated, a portent of things to come occurred. A Connecticut-based hedge fund—Long-Term Capital Management—began to totter in the summer of 1998. The fund, which used borrowed money to accumulate massive positions in bonds and stocks, was teetering on the verge of failure when the Fed stepped in to help it shore up its positions. The fund also claimed to have an all-star cast of academic and professional stars on its roster who knew how to mitigate risk while searching for arbitrage profits. They were the embodiment of modern risk management techniques, the kinds that made the old separation of commercial and investment banking "obsolete." The banks had loaned so much money to the fund that a default would have placed all of them under severe pressure. The action was the first by the Fed to help bail out a nonbank, and it attracted wide attention. The Fed's quick actions helped sidestep a nagging question.

In many ways, Long-Term Capital Management was a surrogate for the New Era. It was neither a securities house nor a bank, but because of its massive positions it qualified for Fed attention. Why it actually needed the help was asked frequently. In the new environment, risk management tools were considered adequate to contain the risk that these large institutions acquired. What happened at the hedge fund? Where were the risk managers when traders began accumulating positions so large that a market shock, like the one that occurred in the summer of 1998 prompted by the Russian default, could bring the fund to the brink of insolvency? After the fund was bailed out, the question was no longer asked.

Even in the face of the hedge fund's problems, pressure continued to build for Gramm-Leach-Bliley to pass quickly. There was much at stake. Assuming Glass-Steagall would eventually be replaced, the Fed allowed Travelers Insurance and Citibank to merge, creating Citigroup. The new giant financial services company was on borrowed time since the old law had to be repealed. Regulators assumed that Citigroup was fait accompli and that the repeal was imminent. When it became clear that the bill was about to pass, questions arose about the protections that the Glass-Steagall Act provided.

If banks and other financial services firms now were to be under the same roof, then customers' deposits again were at risk because a firm or individual trader could make an error in judgment, putting the company's assets at risk. It had happened many times before. In the 1990s alone, financial fiascos erupted in Orange County, California, and many smaller communities around the country over the use of derivatives packaged with exotic securities. Baring Brothers in London was destroyed by a single rogue trader accompanied by some very bad management. Often, the instruments that put these institutions at risk were the same ones that were used to prevent risk in the first place. But Wall Street and its regulators always provided the same stock answer to questions about the basic soundness of financial institutions. Modern risk management techniques made failures at large institutions less likely than in the past. The examples just cited were nothing more than statistical aberrations. Risk management reigned supreme in the New Era.

The marketplace would not be dissuaded from "modernizing" despite the spotty historical record. The Financial Services Modernization Act passed in late 1999, sweeping away the restrictive parts of the 1933 law. The Travelers/Citicorp merger was officially recognized as the biggest financial merger of the century. Other significant mergers occurred between financial institutions in its wake, but it was the Travelers/Citicorp deal that marked the high water mark of the deregulatory movement in the United States.

The dismantling of Glass-Steagall, gradual though it was, marked a low point for consumer advocates and traditionalists in banking circles who believed that a little regulation is a good thing. The New Deal penchant for regulating institutions finally gave way to regulation in the form of dos and don'ts. Institutions were now free to engage in activities that in the past had been proscribed because of chicanery, fraud, and amalgamation of financial power. The safeguards remaining were mainly rules proscribing certain kinds of financial behavior. Structural restrictions were swept away. The brave new world merging Wall Street and the banks finally had been attained after decades of failed attempts. And the payoffs for the prophets of the big deal and facilitators of the deregulation trend were substantial.

In the wake of deregulation, much debris has already begun to wash ashore. Many of the large banks suffered serious losses after the Enron and WorldCom affairs because they had loaned the companies money *and* provided investment banking services, a doubling of exposure unthinkable in the old era. Securities analysts were literally caught with their trousers down around their proverbial ankles when their glowing research was shown to be nothing more than sales hyperbole on behalf of less than creditworthy companies that their banks wanted to court. But most importantly, the old firewalls that existed between the different types of banking have fallen in favor of greater efficiency and profitability.

Bankers and regulators embraced lack of regulation as an ideological principle rather than a practical one. They have gathered much support from the free market ideologues, who assiduously have been working for years to dismantle the last vestiges of the New Deal. The breaking down of the barriers also has given those who favor privatizing Social Security much heart and indirect support. Unfortunately for them, the market fiasco beginning in 2001 has helped the issue recede for the time being. But it is clear that deregulation of the banking industry has been by far the most successful part of the overall drive to change the history of the past 75 years.

The history of the deregulation movement begins in the grassroots movements of the pre-World War I years when Progressives were able to make outlandish claims about business and government. Their simple conclusion at the time was that business and finance needed regulation, not the laissez faire attitude that characterized Wall Street and the banks until that time. The reason for their success was simple. Although their claims about the behavior of big business during the Jazz Age were often outlandish, they were also often on the mark. After the Crash of 1929, they appeared to have been proven correct and the ball began rolling for serious reform.

Since the first years of the twentieth century, Wall Street and the East Coast establishment had been at loggerheads with the rest of the country. Wall Street was the home of high finance— "finance capitalism" as it was then known—and the legacy of the robber barons. The workingman and the farmer needed protection against big business and its capitalist masters who were more than willing to extract the best of a man's labor and then toss him aside, as Marx originally had written. Trading securities was not real work in the American ethic; it was simply a way of stealing from others. Labor gave things value, not speculation.

This mixture of mild Socialist thought and American industriousness created many politicians who did not fit the stereotypical East Coast mold. Most hailed from the Midwest and the West, were practically educated, and minced few words about the power of Wall Street bankers, notably J.P. Morgan. During the 1920s, they became particularly upset at a host of American institutions because of the farm depression looming in the agricultural areas. As a result, they took aim at the Federal Reserve, Wall Street, the White House, and any other institution or individual they thought was exploiting the average workingman. In the 1920s they were sometimes successful in Congress, but during the Depression they helped coalesce into a group that supported the first 100 days of the New Deal, producing the major banking and securities laws that survived until recently.

The saga played so poignantly on Wall Street and in Washington over the previous decades has led to a new financial world characterized by fewer barriers than at any time since the 1920s. The old Progressive arguments still reverberate occasionally when financial scandals erupt, but current thinking considers regulation and the safeguards it provided as relics of the past. But the emergence of another major scandal or the failure of a financial institution will quickly bring the arguments back from the dusty archives and position them center stage in an argument that is certainly not at an end. As this story demonstrates, being ignorant of the distant past is understandable. Being ignorant of recent history is unforgivable.

CHAPTER 1

DISTRUST OF WALL STREET IN THE 1920s

My idea of New York and by that I mean the controlling interest there, is that they sit back and look upon the rest of the country much as Great Britain looks upon India.

Senator Henrik Shipstead, Minnesota, 1922

During the first months of the New Deal in 1933, the American banking and securities industries underwent the most radical reorganization in their histories. Led by the new administration of Franklin D. Roosevelt, Congress enacted several new laws that broke the stranglehold bankers had on the economy and the credit creation process. Many Democrats as well as some Republicans believed that the United States was being held hostage by a small coterie of bankers whose influence was out of all proportion to their actual numbers.

The criticism was not new. It had been heard before many times since the 1890s when the Progressive movement first began to be heard. The critics claimed that Wall Street ran the country and often allied itself with clandestine foreign interests intent on sapping the United States of its vitality and its money: at the heart of the matter were bankers and their Jewish allies who controlled the forces of money and credit. Also thrown into the critical mix was big business in general, which had shown a disturbing tendency to form monopolies further designed to enslave the workingman. In fact, anyone who served big business was in the same category—enemy of the average worker and farmer.

The appeal was highly emotional and gained many followers during the 1920s and 1930s. The fact that it did not coincide with reality was never questioned. Most traditional Wall Street bankers such as J.P. Morgan Jr., like his father Pierpont before him, disdained Jews and dealt with them only when it suited their business needs. Many Jews could not gain decent jobs on Wall Street and founded their own banking houses instead. The prominent Jewish banking houses like Lehman Brothers, Goldman Sachs, and J. & S. Seligman often dealt with the older waspish banks like J.P. Morgan & Co. and Brown Brothers Harriman, but conspiracies between them were far-fetched notions not based on reality. Despite decades of Wall Street history indicating the opposite, the ideas remained strong during the 1920s. The 1920s were characterized by conspiracy theories, and bankers' connections proved attractive to the subscribers of vague power connections.

The foreign connection was still vulnerable to criticism because Wall Street had been dealing with foreigners since before the Civil War. For over a hundred years, the country had relied heavily on foreign investment, coming especially from Great Britain, to build its infrastructure, and many Britons knew more about the United States than many U.S. citizens. And the British had a central bank, another bugaboo in the United States because the Bank of the United States had been defunct since the 1830s. Although the United States appeared to be the savior of Europe after World War I, it was clear that many of its financial institutions were still relatively new and required time to develop properly. In finance, the private banking houses filled the historical void. Bankers were the emissaries of the country in the nineteenth and early twentieth centuries. The practice worked pragmatically, but many outside Wall Street and Washington began to openly question the authority of these unofficial emissaries. How could they exercise such far-reaching authority when they were private citizens? Who elected them?

Bankers' relations with their foreign counterparts would be a central issue in the 1920s. When the Federal Reserve was created before World War I, the new central bank was the product of several years of discussion between legislators and Wall Street bankers, some of whom were foreign born. As a result, it was vulnerable to criticism from those who thought bankers were selling out to foreign interests. After World War I the country was thrust into a new international role and the connections only incensed critics further. Soon, the harshest critics would see conspiracies around every corner and a banker beneath every bed. In the 1920s, these critics were both loud and marginal at the same time. The press acknowledged them, but were they a real force in public affairs?

Many of these ideas were directly inherited from the Progressives. Others were inherited from agrarian groups whose appeal became timely in the 1920s. Although the decade was best known for the booming economy, it was also characterized by anti-Semitism, xenophobia, Prohibition, and rough years for farmers. America was divided on many issues, but it was the general sense of prosperity symbolized by the stock market that united many disparate groups. The boom of the 1920s was mainly an urban affair. Outside the urban areas, the suspicions about and distrust of Wall Street and the cities were on full display. The problem for many agrarians was that uniting over a common cause was neither easy nor apt to be readily noticed outside the Midwest.

While Progressives in the 1920s all shared a common political tradition, they also shared a common intellectual one as well. Most supported Theodore Roosevelt and his Bullmoose Party in the 1912 elections and after his loss supported many of Woodrow Wilson's policies. But a common thread among them was the crusading lawyer Louis Brandeis, who in the 1920s was sitting on the Supreme Court, having been appointed by Wilson in 1916. His 1914 book *Other People's Money* had become the bible for the Progressive movement, showing how bankers used deposits to insinuate their way onto corporate boards, seizing a power that was not rightfully theirs. The Morgan banking empire was the motivating force behind the book, and the Progressives had already developed a deep distrust of the financial oligarchy by the time World War I began. Events during and after the war did little to change their collective minds.

On the Back Burner

Causes abounded in the 1920s, but making the public conscious of them was difficult. During the decade of Prohibition, producing spirits was both illegal and highly profitable, earning bootleggers a fortune. Legislators who intended to make an issue of the proliferation of national banks at the expense of state banks found the task was difficult but not impossible. When the spread of the Ku Klux Klan necessitated imposing martial law in some states, making a fuss about policies of the Federal Reserve Board seemed tame if not immaterial. The twenties were full of sensational headlines and behind-the-scenes public policy issues did not usually capture front-page headlines. Those wanting to affect policy were necessarily forced to resort to extremes to make themselves heard.

Congress still had its share of neo-Progressives who did not mind raising hell on behalf of their constituents if the cause suited their agendas. The height of Progressive influence had waned since the heyday of Senator Robert "Fighting Bob" La Follette of Wisconsin, although the torch still was ably carried in Congress by Senator George Norris of Nebraska and La Follette's son and successor Robert Jr. They would achieve some notable successes, culminating in reform legislation passed during the New Deal. The movement managed to carry the conscience of the Progressive movement through various administrations in Washington, and its voice was still heard, although it had considerable competition for attention during the twenties. The booming stock market and a newly discovered consumerism made social issues take a back seat unless they were sensational. The public was much more interested in buying newly mass-produced radios and automobiles than it was in hearing about the ownership of the Muscle Shoals power project in the South.

Against this backdrop, activists toiled in relative obscurity. By the end of World War I, a tradition had been established that was already ingrained in the American psyche. Workers were entitled to decent treatment by employers. Big business had been portrayed by crusading journalists and muckrakers as predatory and immoral. But not all Progressive programs were liberally construed. The individual came first under its practical ideology, and anything that affected the average working citizen bore close scrutiny. Prohibition also was supported by many of the independent-minded legislators who fell under the Progressive banner. The United States did not join the League of Nations after many of the Progressives voted for avoiding the organization. But business was still the dominant power in the United States. The latter-day Progressives were an antidote to the excesses of the trusts and holding companies, but the battle they waged often changed battlefields on short notice. But they did more than simply put their fingers in the dyke. In the interim between the outgoing Hoover administration and the first years of the New Deal, they would achieve their longest-lasting victories. In the 1920s, they were relegated to being voices in the wilderness.

Other than Norris and La Follette Jr., especially after his father died, the best-known Progressive of the 1920s was William E. Borah, Republican of Idaho. More closely allied with the fiery Populist orator William Jennings Bryan than most other Republicans, Borah was born in Kansas in 1865 and attended the University of Kansas before studying law. He moved to Idaho in 1891, began practicing law, and was unsuccessful in his bid for a seat in Congress on the Silver Republican party ticket in 1896. His star rose quickly when he was chosen to prosecute three men charged with killing an Idaho governor in a bomb blast. The defendants were represented by Clarence Darrow, who won the case, but not before Borah had emerged as a major legal talent. His powers of oratory impressed many of the out-of-town journalists covering the trial. He was elected to the Senate in 1907 and served continuously until his death in 1940. In 1936, he failed in his attempt to win the Republican nomination for president. Like Fiorello La Guardia, a Republican congressman from New York, he was the champion of the underdog and directed most of his Senate orations against the establishment forces that dared to tread on the workingman. In his early years, he was a sponsor of legislation calling for shorter working hours and better working conditions. He became so popular in Idaho that he virtually insured himself a Senate seat for life.

Despite his intentions, Borah was not universally admired. An eloquent orator, he became known as the conscience of the Senate. But he often did not follow up on his speeches with action of any sort, becoming known as a talker rather than a doer. Eventually, he acquired the unfortunate nickname "Our Spearless Leader" because of his inaction on many issues. True to the 1920s, the nickname took hold quickly, although it did him no harm in his home state. With his great mane of dark hair, fiery orations, and adoption of underdog causes, Borah became a legend in Washington but never a potent force. His counsel was widely sought but often went ignored. He was a true Progressive of his era and the archetypical Son of the Wild Jackass, a nickname given to Progressives in the 1920s: smart, well-read, Spartan in his personal life, upright, and often unheeded. He often was described as a "party of one." Unfortunately, such parties never achieved many lasting political results.

During the 1920s, this disparate group of Progressives pursued its agenda, occasionally making national headlines. Their one great rallying point was the farm problem. Agricultural prices were flat after the recession of 1920–1921, and many of the gains made by farmers during World War I disappeared. Legislators from agricultural states fought for their constituents in Washington, but it was an uphill battle. The prosperity being created by manufacturing and the stock market created a din above which it was difficult to be heard. Farmers toiled as they always had with little sympathy from officialdom, but their problems only made their legislators even more resolute.

One 1920s' trend unified Progressives more than any other. The rapid expansion of business, prompted mainly by the popularity of the automobile, produced many real and imagined injustices. Retailing began to expand at a rapid clip and stores began to expand, opening many satellite stores across state lines. The great chain store revolution was underway. All sorts of merchants, from grocers to "five and dime" stores, began expanding rapidly. As they grew, cries of "invasion" were heard, mostly from the same states most heavily represented by the Progressives. According to the antiexpansionists, the livelihoods of local folks were being threatened by outside forces. Worse still, they were being invaded by Wall Street bankers, financiers of these expansionist elements bent upon destroying rural America.

To critics, Wall Street meant fancy dressed financiers, oblivious to the needs of the farmer and the average worker. It also implied being a Jew. Although the connection was very tenuous, it was established when Henry Ford referred to both J.P. Morgan and Jay Gould (long since dead) as Jews, despite the fact they were both practicing Episcopalians. According to critics, when a chain store moved into a rural area, the invasion brought with it aliens of all sorts. Local money was shipped out to Wall Street and local businesses were destroyed, all in the name of profit. The argument was similar to the one used later by those opposed to sending American businesses abroad. What good did this trend accomplish? It was only another example of enslaving the common man, according to some politicians.

Despite the complaints, the Progressive movement remained mostly grassroots until 1927 when one of these small-town politicians, Republican congressman Louis T. McFadden of Pennsylvania, sponsored a bill that changed the face of American banking for the rest of the century. Emboldened by his success, he and others would begin to speak up even more loudly in the years that followed. Then, the Crash of 1929 provided them with the results they needed to become even more vocal. The often disparate movement that began with the trustbusters at the turn of the century seized upon the Crash and had an extraordinary opportunity to reconfigure American society. For the previous 30 years, they had been in a vocal opposition. Their adversaries were the scions of Wall Street, many of whom were born to their positions of power and wealth. Others were among the nouveau riche but were not capitulating to a grassroots movement without a struggle. After a decade of successful activism, the early 1930s would become the Progressive movement's battleground.

The Power of Wall Street

The American moneyed elite had been exercising their influence since the War of 1812 and had become thoroughly embedded in society and culture for over 100 years before the 1920s saga began. Originally, wealthy merchants helped finance the war by supplying funds to the U.S. Treasury in return for a commission and interest on their investment. By the late 1820s, merchant banking houses took up the task and made it more institutional. Wall Street became the financier to the states and the federal government, a position it never relinquished. When modern corporations began to emerge, their need for capital was just as great.

Like the early companies they funded, Wall Street investment houses were all partnerships and were managed by families that passed the power and wealth from son to son. Although many of the firms got their starts at different times, simple continuity spelled success for most of them because America's need for capital was intense. The United States was not developed enough economically for most of the nineteenth century to supply the capital necessary to fuel expansion plans; thus capital needed to be imported from abroad. Any banking house able to link the domestic need for money with wealthy foreign connections was ensured of success. Between the early 1830s and the 1890s, most of the moneyed elite were established and became well-known names on Wall Street. Also, their political influence was considerable.

The old names in investment banking were the Browns of Brown Brothers, Enoch Clark of Clark Dodge & Co., Junius Spencer Morgan and his son John Pierpont Morgan of what would become J.P. Morgan & Co., Kidder Peabody & Co., and

August Belmont and his son August Jr. of August Belmont & Co. Other well-known names appeared briefly on center stage but disappeared due to mismanagement or overly ambitious plans, notably Jay Cooke, founder of Jay Cooke & Co. The firm carried on through his son-in-law Charles Barney and would survive into the twenty-first century. These mostly Anglo-Saxon firms, with the exception of Belmont, were joined after the Civil War by a handful of small but influential Jewish-American banking houses, notably Kuhn Loeb & Co., J. & S. Seligman & Co., Lehman Brothers, and Goldman Sachs. Between them, they formed the nucleus of early Wall Street underwriting syndicates. They were so successful that many of them were dubbed the "money trust" in the early twentieth century in the heyday of the trust movement.

Wall Street banking houses created power for themselves and their successors by helping the government fund itself over the years. Enoch Clark became one of the major financiers for the Mexican War by selling bonds and helping the Treasury pay its war bills. Brown Brothers, founded by Alexander Brown in Baltimore at the turn of the nineteenth century, aided the government of Maryland during a financial crisis in 1834. Later, the firm helped establish North Atlantic shipping between the United States and Europe. J.P. Morgan helped the Treasury raise funds many times, with the bailout of the Treasury during the gold crisis in 1894 being the best-known operation. August Belmont & Co. also participated in the rescue after the death of Belmont Sr. Jay Cooke became the best-known financier of his day by capably selling Treasury bonds during the Civil War, but he squandered the goodwill he established with unwise railroad financing ventures after the war. By the end of the nineteenth century, all of the major banking houses were well-established and their family dynasties were already considered part of the American elite.

The Jewish-American banks also recognized the path to fame and fortune. Kuhn Loeb, under the guidance of Jacob Schiff, its guiding light for decades, was a major bond house and financier to the Panama Canal. The Seligmans also participated in Civil War financing and scored heavy public relations points by helping support Mary Todd Lincoln after her husband was assassinated, at a time when presidential wives were not granted pensions. They also participated in the first round of Panama Canal financing. Goldman Sachs made its name by developing the market for commercial paper after the Civil War, but was not a government financier until later in the twentieth century. Lehman Brothers began its business as a commodities trading house in the South and took several decades to win its way into Wall Street underwriting syndicates, notably in an alliance with Goldman Sachs. By the end of the nineteenth century, it was clear that the American financial oligarchy had been able to attain wealth and power by assisting the government directly or indirectly. The formula changed in the twentieth century as more banking houses opened on Wall Street.

As the country grew and the economy expanded, many new investment bankers succeeded by specializing in ventures the more established houses frowned upon. Lehman and Goldman underwrote the new issues of many of the expanding retailers. Charles Merrill did the same at the small firm that bore his name. Occasionally, one of the smaller bankers scored a major coup and entered the ranks of the Wall Street elite, as Clarence Dillon did at the small firm of Dillon Read. Dillon was originally named Clarence Lapowski, whose father was a Polish Jew who emigrated to the United States about the same time as many other Jewish merchants after the Civil War. After enrolling at Harvard under his new name, he went reluctantly to Wall Street to become a bond salesman. Within 15 years, he merged the Dodge brothers' car manufacturing company with Walter Chrysler's to form the modern Chrysler Corporation. He had also beaten J.P. Morgan & Co. to the punch in the process and helped strengthen the presence of the newcomers on Wall Street against the traditional banking powerhouses.

Wealth accumulation for its own sake became a goal for the financial oligarchy. In order to protect it, acquiring political power seemed a natural corollary. But combining the two in nineteenth century America was a potent mix—too powerful for those intent on practicing political power while retaining their wealth. The antimonopoly movement and the anti–big business movement were vociferous enough to keep the political ambitions of the moneyed class at bay. Helping Uncle Sam was as close as most bankers got to political power, although it certainly ensured them of political access. Wealth went hand-in-hand with political power but not with elected power. August Belmont had political ambitions but during the Civil War had to settle for being the chairman of the Democratic Party, which was in a state of disarray at the time. After his father Cornelius died, William Henry Vanderbilt, best remembered for his classic quip "The public be damned," was wise enough to read the prevailing winds of public opinion and invest his $100 million inheritance in Treasury bonds lest someone actually take him seriously and retaliate. Great wealth brought with it a keen sense of avoiding public wrath, which often could be ugly concerning big business and Wall Street.

The banking dynasties created in the nineteenth century had different life spans, but while they were at the apex of Wall Street life was very good. Pierpont Morgan was known for his extensive art collection. On the day he died, the New York art market became very discombobulated, having lost its major buyer. August Belmont and his son became the dandies of New York society, listing "sportsman" as one of their activities. Horseracing was a family avocation and the Belmont Stakes was named after Belmont Sr., who began that racing tradition. Clarence Dillon retired early from his banking career at Dillon Read and became a vineyard owner in France, boasting several labels of wines under the family name. Charles Merrill became the principal owner of the Safeway food store chain before returning to Wall Street to help reorganize Merrill Lynch. Henry Lee Higginson became one of Boston's most prominent citizens after the success of his bank, Lee Higginson & Co., while the Lehmans laid claim to a future New York governor in addition to their sizeable fortune. Jacob Schiff became one of the most influential supporters of Jewish causes in the country before the 1920s and spawned a dynasty of investment bankers in his wake. The Mellons laid claim to a sizeable banking empire in Pennsylvania in addition to a substantial interest in the Aluminum Company of America and the Gulf Oil Company.

The list was extensive, and most of the nineteenth century oligarchy were able to extend their influence well into the twentieth century, with the exception of the Belmonts. They would be joined by future generations of bankers, many of whose parents were not in the country in the nineteenth century.

Progressives also were among the moneyed elite before World War I. Theodore Roosevelt's presidency was a milestone for the movement. Many antitrust actions began during his administration that would eventually reach fruition under Taft or Wilson, notably lawsuits against American Tobacco, Standard Oil, and U.S. Steel. Yet, Roosevelt's ties to the financial community were very strong. Although Pierpont Morgan and his allies were quite sick of Roosevelt after he successfully set out to challenge the formation of the Northern Securities Company during his first term in office, they did not provide any serious challenge to him in the 1904 presidential election, when they were actually asked for, and provided, donations to the Republican Party. For his part, Roosevelt acknowledged his one-time ties to Wall Street, which extended through his family well back into the nineteenth century. But his relations with Wall Street deteriorated during his second term, and when he decided not to run again in 1908, Morgan and Wall Street breathed a sigh of relief.

Robert La Follette did not recognize Roosevelt as a true Progressive, criticizing him for the same trait that many others would criticize the latter-day Progressives in the 1920s—inconsistency. During the 1908 election campaign, he looked back at Roosevelt's achievements in office and declared, "President Roosevelt has crystallized public sentiment, and elevated civic standards. He will live in the history of his time, a unique figure. He will not live in history as the author of any great, constructive legislation." He was also keenly aware of Roosevelt's ties to the New York brahmans in banking, upon whose clandestine support he often relied. La Follette cited Roosevelt's "confidential relations with Morgan, Perkins, Frick, Harriman, and those associated with them, in the interlocking directorates, controlling the Big Business of this country...," and continued, "I could not conscientiously accept him as a leader of the Progressive movement, and there was no alternative for me but to continue as a candidate."[1]

Investigating the Money Trust

The first time the financial oligarchy was put on public display was in 1912 at what became known as the Pujo hearings in Washington, named after Representative Arsenee Pujo of Louisiana, chairman of the House Committee on Currency and Banking. For several years, the term "money trust" had been bandied around Washington by Progressives. In the years preceding World War I, several investigations had revealed extensive Wall Street interests in the life insurance industry, prompting many states to pass individual laws designed to keep investment bankers away from the industry for fear that the assets of the insurance companies would be used for improper purposes. At the same time, several Midwestern states passed "blue sky" laws, intended to serve as a registration process for any securities sold within their borders. But the Pujo hearings put top Wall Street bankers on display and revealed the financial oligarchy for the first time.

The term "money trust" was coined by Senator Charles Lindbergh of Minnesota and was popular in the press. It was something of a misnomer, however, as others quickly pointed out. The power that bankers wielded in the New York market was considerable but was not as tight as the steel, tobacco, or oil trusts because there was no common element of ownership as in a traditional trust. Lindbergh went so far as to claim that it would not surprise him if Wall Street concocted the occasional financial panic just to cover its own tracks. He claimed it had happened before, repeating a popular notion about the Panic of 1907. At that time, it was thought that the panic was created by Pierpont Morgan to deflect interest from his bank during the insurance investigations. But the influence wielded by Morgan and his counterparts at other banks was breathtaking in its scope and breath. Any investigation into that power would have to focus on the de facto power bankers held, because they steadfastly claimed that they held no power beyond that which their positions conferred on them.

A previous House investigation headed by Representative Augustus Stanley of Kentucky into the steel trust was deemed somewhat ineffective because it did not have a chief counsel to advance its agenda. The Pujo committee appointed New York lawyer Samuel Untermyer as its counsel so that it would not make the same mistake. Untermyer also was skeptical about the term "money trust" but had no illusions about the power of bankers. When asked about its influence, he stated clearly, "There is, of course, no such thing as a money trust,...there is no definite agreement or understanding between the few men who wield and control the vast money power of the country. There is certainly nothing illegal in the dangerous community of interest under which they are exercising that power with constantly increasing effectiveness. They are acting, with rare exceptions, strictly within their legal rights but the results are none the less oppressive and perilous for the country. In fact, they seem far more so for that reason."[2] The comment echoed the complaints of many other critics and described the insidious power that the money trust purportedly wielded.

The hearings began after Untermyer was appointed counsel in January 1912 and continued sporadically for the rest of the year. The first witness the committee planned to call was not a banker but the former presidential candidate and Populist leader William Jennings Bryan. He made a statement at the outset that the money trust could control the committee, and he was summoned to explain his remarks. Other bankers who did not relish the prospect of testifying took a more creative stance. The president of a bank trust company in Buffalo, New York, claimed that his institution was a state bank and did not have to reply to the committee since congressional authority only extended to national banks.[3] After a ruling in favor of the Pujo committee, the banker was very unhappy. However, the confrontation that everyone anticipated came at the close of the hearings in December when Pierpont Morgan himself appeared before the committee, questioned by Untermyer. He was interrogated at length about his dealings with the Equitable Life Insurance Company, as well as his views concerning credit and the role of bankers. Wall Street was extremely nervous before his testimony because any slips by its best-known banker could spell doom for the way it did business. But Morgan answered the questions with a simple aplomb, suggesting that bankers knew best about banking and were more than capable of acting without restrictions. His views on credit especially were simple to the point of distraction, which was exactly the point. Untermyer was trying to get to the heart of conspiracy among bankers, but all Morgan would reveal was that he expected his customers to have displayed character in the past; the trait was the criterion upon which he based his credit decisions. He was unwilling to spar with the committee counsel. Wall Street drew a collective sigh of relief.

The *New York Times* likened his testimony to a sermon, delivered after Sunday school. The paper conceded, "The radical element was not ready to present the financier with a halo but there were significant admissions that there must be a readjustment in several respects of previous impressions of the man and his work."[4] All sides claimed victory. Morgan did not appear in full public view often and almost had developed folk status as a result. The usual view of him was as something of an ogre at worst or an avuncular figure at best who helped the country during financial crises, for a price. His performance before the committee helped deflect the ogre image, and Wall Street celebrated by staging a rally, a "Morgan market." But the victory was short-lived at best. Pierpont died several months later. Most of his partners attributed his death to the questioning at the Pujo hearings, which apparently upset him more than his public performance indicated. His son and heir Jack began following Untermyer's affairs closely, while the other partners were convinced that the New York lawyer was nothing more than a scoundrel who caused the death of the most celebrated banker in American history and arguably the most powerful figure in the country for the 20-year period between 1890 and his death.[5]

Among the volumes of testimony was a description of the power that the three top executives of Bankers Trust Company had accumulated in the short time the institution had been in existence. A director of the company, Walter Frew, testified that the company had assets of $168 million and over $200 million in deposits, which was extraordinary considering that it was only founded in 1903. The implications of the testimony were clear to most observers. Without a close tie to Morgan, no bank could have accumulated that much in such a short period of time. Since Benjamin Strong was a top executive and would soon become governor of the New York Fed, the link between the Fed and Morgan control was forged for the next 15 years until Strong's death in 1928.

The hearings provided a useful venue for the Progressives and helped the Federal Reserve Act pass Congress. They also prompted passage of the Clayton Act two years later, the second major antitrust law after the Sherman Act of 1890. The vast number of interlocking directorships held by bankers was revealed, showing strong control over a vast array of companies. When the evidence of the interlocking relationships was presented before the committee, it required a chart over six feet in length. Some of the revelations would also prove useful in demonstrating how the New York underwriting syndicates operated and how power could in fact be concentrated among the top banking institutions. But as Untermyer noted when he was first appointed counsel, there was nothing illegal about a confluence of financial power. It may have been dangerous, but that had not yet been convincingly demonstrated. Another 20 years would have to pass before that connection was attacked more successfully.

When the Pujo committee wrote its final report in 1913, the term "money trust" survived. The definition had become a bit firmer than before:

> If, therefore, by a "money trust" is meant an established and well-defined identity and community of interest between a few leaders of finance, which has been created and is held together through stock holdings, interlocking directorships, and other forms of domination...your committee...has no hesitation in asserting as the result of its investigation up to this time that the condition thus described exists in this country today.[6]

Throughout the hearings, the connections had been put on display, but illegality and corruption had not been proved. Nevertheless, the oligarchy had been put on display for the first time. Such revelations were the last thing Wall Street needed. Financial power depended to a great extent upon operating successfully behind the scenes rather than in full public view. Before World War I, the best that could be hoped for when conducting hearings was what later would be called "transparency." The clearer financial processes appeared, the less chance there was of chicanery and corruption. In that respect, the hearings were successful.

Enter the Fed

Wall Street usually attracted the most attention by critics of business and industry. Banking was usually a distant second, but after the money trust hearings it moved into the forefront. At the same time that the Pujo hearings were being conducted, the Federal Reserve Act was passed and the new central bank went into operation in 1913. After 70 years, the United States again had a banking institution whose activities spanned state lines. That simple fact alone made the old guard extremely unhappy. The Federal Reserve spanned state lines by operating through 12 district banks. Commercial banks could join the new institution by subscribing to its capital stock. By doing so, they could advertise themselves as Fed members. But that distinction was different from that of "national bank." A national bank was chartered under the older National Bank Act passed during the Civil War. National banks could be distinguished by the "N.A." after their names, short for national association. For decades, the United States had two types of banks, those nationally chartered and those state chartered, whose licenses were granted by the state in which they operated. The great irony was that nationally chartered banks were no larger or more powerful than state-chartered banks, with a few exceptions found in the larger cities. Local banking laws kept both types from expanding across state lines.

Much of the opposition to the Fed in the 1920s centered on the governor of the New York Fed, Benjamin Strong. He was its first leader, from the central bank's inception until his death in 1928. Long associated with the House of Morgan, Strong originally worked for the Bankers Trust Company, a trust bank started after the turn of the century and closely allied with Morgan. He was closely allied with Henry Davison, a Morgan partner, and came into Morgan's inner circle when he helped a group of bankers arrange a bailout during the Panic of 1907. From that time, he was considered part of the Morgan coterie. He had strong personal ties to Davison and was his neighbor in Englewood, New Jersey, where several of the Morgan partners had homes. When the Fed was formed, his job at the New York Fed ensured the money trust close ties with the central bank. Several other Fed members also had ties to Morgan, and it was assumed by many Progressives that the Fed was nothing more than a tool of the money trust.

In the 1920s, Strong worked closely with Montagu Norman, governor of the Bank of England, to implement a systematic cur-

rency stabilization for the pound, backed by loans from private
American bankers and Federal Reserve credits. In the mid-1920s
Strong agreed to Great Britain's return to the gold standard at a
high rate against the dollar, requiring American interest rates to
be set lower than those in Britain. The deal set off a general
strike in Britain because of the high level of the pound. International deals of that sort proved nettlesome to the agrarian radicals in the Senate, who claimed that the United States was being
sold out to foreign interests. But while international finance was
prominent in the 1920s, it was still the more mundane matter of
the rights of national banks versus those of state banks that con-
sumed most bankers' time.

Many local, small banks signed up under the National Bank
Act so that they could advertise themselves as national banks.
But in many states, the fancy appellation did not pay public relations dividends because state banks were favored. After the Fed
was created, the problem became more acute because many
local bankers resented interference of any sort from Washington. The local state banks could not gain any advantage from the
Fed because the central bank only dealt with its own members.
And many national banking associations also had to contend
with the Comptroller of the Currency, the regulator created by
the old act. State banks were not under its supervision. Being an
N.A. in a small town actually had disadvantages in many places
where Washington and Wall Street were not trusted but no one
ever imagined that one of those small-town bankers, Louis T.
McFadden, would become the bête noir of American banking
for the rest of the twentieth century.

Sparring Partner

One of the staunchest opponents of the Federal Reserve and Wall
Street was Representative Louis T. McFadden, a Republican from
Pennsylvania. He was joined by a chorus of agrarian legislators
from the Midwest. The target of their collective wrath was the Fed,
but for very different reasons. The agrarians criticized the cen-

tral bank for the farm crisis of 1920, which saw a collapse in farm prices after the heady years of World War I. But it was McFadden who would have the most serious impact on the institution in the 1920s. Born in Bradford County, Pennsylvania, in 1876, McFadden was a local boy who made good. After attending local public schools, he attended a commercial college in Elmira, New York, and joined the First National Bank of Canton, Pennsylvania, in 1892, which was a nationally chartered institution despite its small size. Seven years later he was elected cashier and rose through the ranks of Pennsylvania bankers. In 1906, he served as treasurer of the Pennsylvania Bankers' Association. He was then elected cashier of his bank and finally was made president in 1916. Since his school days, his resume was one of a successful, local banker loyal to his institution.

McFadden's career changed substantially when he was elected to the House of Representatives and took his seat in March 1915. Throughout what was to become an increasingly turbulent career, he served until 1935. In many ways, his career was something of an enigma. Although a financially prudent local banker, he was berated in public by the comptroller of the currency for running a marginal banking operation in Pennsylvania. A strong proponent of national bank reform, his name became forever associated with the McFadden Act, a restrictive piece of legislation that prohibited bank expansion for the next 70 years. Throughout his career, he remained a foe of the Federal Reserve, viewing it as an institution that actually undermined national banks rather than helped them. And after the Crash of 1929, his views were so radical that he was finally stripped of the important House chairmanship that allowed him to introduce the McFadden Act in the first place. His death in 1936 was mysterious enough to prompt conspiracy theorists to conjecture that he had been murdered by Wall Street financiers, who were tired of his rantings against the financial establishment.

McFadden's battle with the comptroller of the currency began several years after taking his seat in the House. McFadden fired off a letter to the comptroller, John Skelton Williams, calling for abolition of the office and an investigation of Williams's administration. The request came at a delicate moment because Williams was due for reappointment and did not appreciate the charges. He responded strongly, accusing McFadden of being motivated by greed and embarrassment. Noting that the congressman never provided facts to support his allegations, Williams took an unusual step and released a statement that McFadden's bank had been under constant supervision for the past 20 years for shoddy banking practices. He also claimed that only the comptroller's supervision had kept it solvent. He noted that its capital had shrunk over the time period while other banks in the area had grown.[7] Most damning was Williams's comment that McFadden and his family had been recipients of loans far in excess of the bank's capital over the years. Regarding First National, Williams stated,

> The bank continues to violate the law; and this feature together with other unsatisfactory conditions seem largely due to lack of proper management. The examiner is of the opinion that the bank will not observe the law or regulations of this office as long as President McFadden is the Managing Director, because the other directors seem to take no personal and active interest in the bank and permit President McFadden to use the bank for his personal interest without due regard for safe and sound banking.[8]

Despite the charges, McFadden remained president of the bank until 1925, when he finally resigned.

The comptroller again was in McFadden's sights a year later when he proposed in the House that the current composition of the Federal Reserve Board be changed. At the time, the comptroller and secretary of the Treasury sat on the board and McFadden took exception. He was now chairman of the House Committee on Banking and Currency, the most important committee in the House because of its role in overseeing banks, the Treasury, and the Fed. He would use it to his advantage, as Arsenee Pujo had done 10 years before. Citing the Treasury's role in helping finance the large Liberty loans sold during World War I, he claimed that the process hurt the small investors who bought the war bonds by paying too little interest. But the problem was more extensive. The huge borrowings had the effect of crowding the market, making subsequent Treasury and corporate financings more expensive than they should have been because investors were demanding higher rates of interest than previously had been the case. The comptroller was included in McFadden's proposal because the office was part of the Treasury. There was little doubt that it had everything to do with Williams's own charges the year before. The proposal did not succeed at the time, and the board maintained its membership for a short time.[9] Nevertheless, the allegations were shrewd and comprehensive, demonstrating that their author was not quite the country bumpkin that he may have appeared.

The incident was not the first involving McFadden that revolved around personal circumstances. Over the years, his crusades indeed had a personal element to them, apparently being fought for self-preservation as well as for principle and politics. Although not unusual, it was nevertheless strange that a small-town banker from Canton with a populist twinge would soon find himself with one of the most sought-after committee chairmanships in the House. Using the chairmanship as a pulpit, McFadden soon found himself in the forefront of the fight against the expansion of retailing across the country. His battle would not involve dry goods or grocery stores but the business he knew best.

Despite his background, McFadden displayed a grasp of national affairs that belied his small-town origins. In 1921, he argued that the federal government would do well to tax the interest on municipal bonds, which had been previously deemed tax exempt. Writing in the *New York Times*, he claimed that the Treasury would collect at least $200,000,000 per year by instituting a tax on municipal bond interest: "It is submitted that it is absurd for a great nation like ours, while taxing incomes from its own bonds, to exempt wholly from Federal taxation incomes derived from bonds of States, counties, cities, towns, villages and other conceivable political subdivision already created or which may hereafter be created in the entire country."[10]

Besides being a lost source of tax revenue, interest on municipals was a favorite tax dodge of the wealthy, who increasingly preferred to invest in small, local issues rather than Treasury bonds that could be used to help build the country's infrastructure.

A similar complaint was lodged by Senator Henrik Shipstead of Minnesota, a newcomer to the upper house in 1922. Charging that the Treasury was paying too much interest on its obligations in the 1920s, he claimed that the high interest was diverting funds from farmers and labor, who also needed funds but were being crowded out by the government. His main adversary was Treasury Secretary Andrew Mellon, a favorite target of the Progressives in the 1920s. Mellon hailed from the Pennsylvania banking family with extensive business interests in western Pennsylvania and around the country. His background alone would make him a target for radicals intent on showing a conspiracy of the financial oligarchy. As far as the agrarians were concerned, Mellon and the Republican administrations were far better at representing the interests of big business than they were those of farmers and working people. Adding fuel to the fire was the fact that Mellon also was considered a Morgan ally, again illustrating the reach of the money trust banks. Fellow Republicans and the press were fond of calling him the greatest Treasury secretary since Alexander Hamilton. He later had impeachment proceedings begun against him in the House by Texas congressman Wright Patman, who established a reputation that clearly would have included him in the Wild Jackasses' group. When Shipstead made his complaint, it also was assumed that he was a simple bumpkin who did not know anything about economics or finance. The assumption proved wrong because the pressure brought to bear by the former dentist finally led the Treasury to issue bonds at substantially lower interest rates shortly after the original flap occurred. However, the problems did not diminish Mellon's ability to reduce the public debt substantially in 1921 and reduce a massive budget deficit.

Competitive Imbalance

McFadden's experience in banking led him to begin introducing changes in the National Bank Act. In 1924, he proposed that an amendment be made to the existing law that would help national banks compete with the state banks. Unencumbered by the National Bank Act, the state banks had wider powers in the states than national banks, whose expansion was actually limited. At issue was the matter of branch banking. Many states permitted state banks within their borders to branch out within the state, a power they denied to national banks. McFadden wanted them to compete equally. On the surface, the proposal sounded fair, but it ran somewhat counter to McFadden's other views on chain stores. But in the 1920s, the differences between national and state banks ran deep, and more than one executive at a state bank often claimed that state banks were immune from any sort of federal banking regulation. The differences between the two types of bank reflected the overall distrust of things federal.

The McFadden bill was cosponsored by Senator George W. Pepper, also a Republican from Pennsylvania. Pepper left the Senate in 1927 and in the early 1930s was named as one of many who benefited from J.P. Morgan's largess by receiving allocations of hot stocks as a member of one of the banker's preferred lists. Pepper displayed a good sense of humor but was largely forgotten as a cosponsor of the banking bill. A year after being elected, he told a group in New York that he thought his profession—the law—was the most unpopular in the world, until he reached the U.S. Senate. After reaching the Senate, he claimed that he realized there were "abysmal depths of unpopularity darker and deeper than anything realized by the legal profession."[11] He was correct in one sense: Citizens of the Midwest were becoming more and more disenchanted with their legislators in Washington as the farm problem continued to worsen.

McFadden's legislation proposed that the two types of banks be put on equal footing by permitting branching by national banks anywhere state laws permitted branching by state banks.

Despite its commonsense proposals, it ran into opposition. One Progressive congressman denounced it as a path to a larger and even more powerful money trust that would completely dominate banking at the expense of the state banks. The language of the act effectively prohibited branching within and between states. It did, however, give the greater powers sought by McFadden to national banks. Supporters, including Senator Carter Glass of Virginia, an author of the original Federal Reserve Act, applauded its passing. However, all the original arguments concerned *intra-state* banking.

Like many bills before it, the McFadden Act was replete with vague and often confusing language, but its effects were well summarized by Charles W. Carey of the American Bankers' Association. He exhorted his members to understand that the McFadden bill "is the first effort of Congress to regulate branch banking. As originally introduced, it would have accomplished that end...it would still limit branch banking."[12] The McFadden Act was remembered by history as prohibiting *interstate* branching, which it did. But as the country grew larger and more complex financially, future generations would openly question what Congress had wrought upon American banking.

Some of the act's most vociferous opponents were Progressives, who saw it as an attempt by the money trust to increase its domination of the financial system. One part of the act certainly filled that bill. It gave the comptroller of the currency the ability to allow banks to underwrite new issues of stocks, something that had been proscribed for decades. A bank that wanted to underwrite had to apply for permission. The measure was seen as a vast expansion of bank powers, and it reflected the positive attitude of the bull market and Wall Street. But for the most part, the McFadden-Pepper Act proved divisive between the Progressives and the mainstream in Congress. Senator Burton Wheeler of Montana attacked Calvin Coolidge, a strong supporter of the legislation, as someone who would sacrifice the interests of farmers and workingmen to those of bankers who benefited from the new banking law. Even the bill's supporters found something to complain about. Carter Glass reacted strongly against the lobbying and letter writing campaign of bankers and the American Bankers' Association in supporting the bill, a charge he would repeat at other times under different circumstances in the future. Supporters of the Fed found something to cheer about in the act, however, since it allowed state banks to join the Federal Reserve System, enlarging its powers in the process. It was perhaps the only time that McFadden would bring a smile at the central bank. In the later 1920s, he was on the attack against the Fed again. The second attack was more vitriolic and personality-centered.

The irascible congressman was opposed to the nomination of Eugene Meyer to the Federal Reserve in 1930. Throughout the 1920s, he maintained his position that the Fed had fallen into the hands of internationalists who did not consider the best interests of the United States. After the Crash, the idea of having a former New York Stock Exchange member sitting on the Fed did not sit well with McFadden, who went to great lengths to point out Meyer's clandestine connections, as he considered them. Both he and Senator Smith Brookhart of Iowa went to great lengths to concoct a conspiracy about how Meyer got nominated to the Fed, but it began to fall apart quickly at his confirmation hearings. The affair did not help either of their reputations, although Brookhart suffered the most fallout. Although it was obvious that Brookhart finally had a real live moneyman whom he could accuse of all sorts of chicanery, the hearing became a "ridiculous exhibition of a Senator at his worst," one commentator said after watching. "For sheer futility and inanity he nearly established a world record."[13] It was only the unfortunate beginning of a rash of charges, some vehemently anti-Semitic, that Brookhart and especially McFadden would utter as the Depression grew worse in the 1930s. Meyer was confirmed to the board in spite of the opposition.

Like many other Progressives, McFadden opposed the expansion of chain stores in the 1920s. The rapid expansion of all sorts of merchandisers was seen as a threat to local communities from

Wall Street and the East in general. In a speech delivered over
WJSV radio in Washington, D.C., McFadden went on record
against the expansion of chain stores. He declared, "We are
indeed today involved in an economic battle between the chain
store and independent merchandising." He added, "In my judgment, it is high time that Congress, as well as the people of
the United States, should give serious attention to what is
unquestionably a vital factor in the living costs of not only
the present day but of the immediate future," suspecting that the
presence of chains would raise rather than lower the cost of
consumer goods.[14] Anti–chain store legislation was introduced
in some states.

Opposition to the chain stores was strong among Progressives. Smith Brookhart of Iowa introduced a resolution in the
Senate calling for an examination of chains by the Federal
Trade Commission in 1928. After an extensive study, the FTC
concluded that chain stores provided more benefits to consumers than harm and that they violated no antitrust laws in the
way they did business. But that did not deter local politicians.
In 1931, a Wisconsin legislator introduced a bill that would
have prohibited stores from owning stock in other stores and
adding a tax on those that operated multiple stores in one
state. Within a decade, Congress would pass anti-chain store
legislation cloaked in antitrust clothing at the instigation of
Wright Patman.

Opposing expansion in one sector, however, did not pre-
clude expansion in another. Clearly, more competition between
state and national banks would lower costs to consumers, but the
immediate argument for making the playing field level between
them was political. National banks were handing in their char-
ters to the comptroller and preferring instead to become state-
chartered banks, allowing them to offer greater services to the
public. Two well-known New York City banks had already done
so—the Irving National Bank (later the Irving Trust) and the
Bank of New York, originally founded by Alexander Hamilton.
In order to prevent the national banking system from becoming

increasingly shaky, Congress would have to act to put an end to the defections. McFadden's bill seemed to address the problem but was facing an uphill fight in Congress. The actions of the two banks would be repeated under a different set of circumstances in the 1970s.

More Radicals

Elections in the early 1920s brought a fresh group of radical Progressives to the Senate. Their inspirational leader was Robert M. La Follette of Wisconsin, the dean of the Progressives along with George Norris of Nebraska. Also elected were a small group of unknowns who would make a varying impression upon officialdom in Washington. They all hailed from the Midwest and had remarkably similar views on the usual foes of agrarians—the Fed and its masters, the Wall Street financiers. Most were also strict prohibitionists, believing that spirits were enslaving the workingman and should indeed be banned.

Political language had become more shrill since World War I. La Follette demonstrated little more than a passing interest in international affairs, stating that he was not in favor of making the world safe for democracy as was Woodrow Wilson. He considered Wall Street the main agent of American imperialism and had been at loggerheads with the agents of American capitalism for years. This radical view was tempered by the fact that the Progressives had no political organization and no unifying structure through which their ideas could coalesce. At the beginning of the 1920s, as at the end, the Progressives were mostly agrarian orators who opposed the Eastern establishment but could do little except complain and occasionally introduce reform legislation. In order for them to be effective, Wall Street would have to present them with a cause.

One of the lesser-known Progressives reaching Washington summed up the collective feelings of the group when asked about how Wall Street viewed the rest of the country. Henrik Shipstead of Minnesota was a dentist from Minnesota who went to Washington after the 1922 election on the Farm-Labor ticket, and reiterated many views of his mentor La Follette. He likened Wall Street's view of the Midwest to how Britain viewed India— as colonial master. Without espousing their mentors' views, most would not have been elected on their own merit. Their main strength in the Senate and House was that they added to the number of Progressives who could possibly unite on certain issues, but they brought no structure or specific plans for a party organization with them. Shipstead variously was portrayed as a Viking from the far north country and a donnish, reclusive figure, but he still proved to be the conscience of official Washington. His opponents originally started rumors that his election would foster communism and "free love." He was sent to the Senate by Minnesotans with a clear message to boot the establishment.

In his successful race, he defeated Frank Billings Kellogg, a Republican who previously served as Senator from 1916 to 1922. Kellogg was a former member of the Republican National Committee, president of the American Bar Association, and trustbuster under Theodore Roosevelt. After his defeat, he would serve as secretary of state to Coolidge, author the Kellogg-Briand peace treaty in 1928, and be awarded the Nobel Peace Prize in 1930. But he also was known as an establishment Republican. His law firm served as counsel for U.S. Steel, a notable Morgan company.

His defeat at the hands of Shipstead was a shock to establishment Washington, especially given Shipstead's local dentist-turned-politician demeanor. But the dentist was much more complex than the advance publicity portrayed him. During his early years in Washington, he never owned an automobile, claiming that having one at home in Minnesota was enough. He was born in Minnesota in 1881 and studied dentistry at Northwestern. He ran for several offices in Minnesota unsuccessfully before winning a Senate seat in 1922, running on the Farm-Labor ticket. He served continuously until 1940, when he was elected as a Republican, finally losing a quest for reelection in 1946. Although often compared to Brookhart, he always knew proper Washington etiquette and managed to charm his host-

esses at social gatherings, where he often was invited as something of a curiosity. When he once appeared at a dinner party
dressed in formal attire, word began to spread that he was actually a false prophet and a traitor to his class. He replied simply,
"When I go into the hayfield I wear overalls. And when I go out
to dinner, I'll wear a dinner coat. By conforming in the non-
essentials—which most people think important—I may get a
hearing here and there on the essentials."[15]

Also traveling to Washington for the first time in 1920 was
Peter Norbeck, a South Dakota Republican who won his seat
after having served a term as governor. An oil driller by occupation, he attended the University of South Dakota and later was
instrumental in developing the Mount Rushmore National
Memorial site. Unlike many of his colleagues, Norbeck was less
flamboyant, preferring to work within the Senate toward his ends
rather than taking to the pulpit to gain exposure, but his aggres-
siveness was still well known. In 1927, President Coolidge was
inducted into the Sioux Indian nation in South Dakota.
Inductees needed an appropriate Indian name and the Sioux
decided upon "Great Sullen Warrior" for the president. Norbeck,
already an honorary member of the tribe, known as "Chief
Charging Hawk," approved of the name as was required by cus-
tom. The Sioux originally planned to call Silent Cal the "Silent
Warrior" but decided upon "Sullen Warrior" instead.

Louis McFadden displayed a distinctly split political personality during his years in Congress. He displayed traits that would
have made him a bona fide Progressive, except for the McFadden-
Pepper Act, which was viewed with suspicion by many traditional
Progressives for giving expanded powers to nationally chartered
banks and enlarging the powers of the comptroller. Otherwise,
his antibusiness views, criticism of the Fed, and tirades against
chain stores put him solidly in the Progressive camp although he
had little political contact with the Midwesterners.

One politician of the 1920s displayed no ambivalence on
social and economic matters. The career of Smith Wildman
Brookhart, Republican Senator from Iowa, was dedicated to

providing a thorn in the side of his party, many members of which wanted him out of office by the end of his first term. Like McFadden, Brookhart was a local boy who found his way to Washington, intent on making a long-lasting impression. Born in Missouri in 1869, he attended local schools and a technical college in Iowa. After graduation, he taught school for five years before studying law and passing the bar in 1892. He served as an officer in both the Spanish-American War and World War I, attaining the rank of lieutenant colonel before returning to civilian life. He also became an expert marksman. From 1921 to 1925, during his first term in the Senate, he served as president of the National Rifle Association. His major break came in 1922 when he was elected to fill the vacancy of Iowa Progressive Senator William S. Kenyon, who resigned from office. Brookhart had lost the previous Senate race from Iowa in 1920. Kenyon was extremely popular among Midwestern Progressives and Brookhart assumed an important seat in the party. Unforeseen at the time was the fact that American politics had just acquired a nettlesome thorn in its side that would endure for the next 10 years. He was universally labeled a blunderer and a fool, uncouth, and a barbarian, a reference to his middle name. There was substantial opposition to his election at the grassroots level in Iowa, but he nevertheless won his seat as expected. His victory was seen as a result of the economic plight among farmers, his main constituents.[16]

Brookhart was a lifelong foe of big business in all its forms, inheriting his antipathy from the earlier Progressive tradition. He once commented that he was against anything Judge Elbert Gary, the chairman of U.S. Steel and a longtime ally of the Morgans, stood for. Like McFadden, he was also critical of the federal government's inability to raise taxes through more diverse sources in the early 1920s. Using data prepared by the Federal Trade Commission, he claimed that over $2 billion was lost in taxes in 1922 because dividends on stock were tax exempt at the time. Topping the list were four Standard Oil companies, each paying over $100 million to their shareholders. By implication, that also meant the Rockefeller interests, since John D. Rockefeller was the major beneficiary of the breakup of Standard Oil when it was divided into smaller companies. The amount paid, along with that paid out by other major corporations, would make a valuable source of tax revenue, especially after the recession of 1920–1921. He promised to introduce a bill in Congress giving the government the ability to tax dividends as soon as possible.[17] The proposal became one of the first aimed at the wealthy that would become a cornerstone of his Senate career. Wall Street soon learned his name and came to dislike him, along with other Progressive senators who constantly advocated the economic rights of farmers and working people while excoriating Wall Street and the Fed for selling out American interests to foreigners.

The Fed also was the target of some sharp criticism from Brookhart. In the 1930s, the agrarians made a distinction between the Depression in the industrialized part of the country and Wall Street versus the one in the agriculture sector, caused by a deterioration in farm prices that began in the 1920s. The agrarians already believed that a great Fed plot had been hatched to deflate the agrarian sector in 1920, and falling prices only added fuel to the fire. When the stock market rally began after 1925, they believed that the Fed began diverting funds to the money market in New York at the expense of the rest of the country. When credit to farmers fell dramatically after 1925, the agrarians blamed Wall Street for diverting funds that otherwise could have found their way into the Farm Credit System, founded after World War I to help stabilize prices and credit. When he first went to Washington, Brookhart first suggested that the Federal Reserve Board be reconstituted to include representatives from agriculture and labor. His ideal board had no bankers or Wall Street people sitting on it.

He later proposed that the Federal Reserve increase its reserve requirement on member banks so that more reserves would be held in the regional Fed banks than those currently required. He reasoned that the tighter requirement would allow fewer funds to find their way into the call money market, which was used to provide margin money for speculators. If the stock market bubble burst, the local Midwestern banks would be protected from any failures by brokers, which were bound to come. When the idea failed to muster interest, Brookhart then retreated to the time-proven method of stopping what he considered excessive speculation: He suggested that state banks that failed to adhere to his proposed Fed regulations be denied use of the mails. He declared, "Unless something of this kind is done we are now headed for the greatest panic in the history of the world."[18]

Not everyone in the Midwest held the extreme view, however. At a speech at a Rotary Club in Illinois, the head of a local land bank in the Federal Land Bank system stated clearly that the reason commercial banks were not making many loans to farmers was because of the high number of bank failures occurring around the country.[19] The failures had little to do with money being sent to the call money market in New York. Bad loans came back to haunt the banks because of real estate speculation in the 1920s, along with bad business loans. The country was in the midst of a massive series of bank failures that would destroy 14,000 banks by the early years of the Depression. The call money controversy was part of a much larger problem infecting banks around the country, although the Progressives only attacked the part that affected farmers in particular.

Despite his flamboyant public comments, conclusions of that nature began to make Brookhart look prescient after the Crash. The radicalism of the Progressives began to ring true. Only a few months before, their conclusions appeared to be nothing more than the rantings of a marginal group of agrarians. The extent of the Crash and the Depression that followed only made them protest even more loudly than before. The tune never changed. Wall Street was aided and abetted by the Fed in creating the greatest bubble ever seen in the United States, and it had wreaked havoc on the farmer and the workingman. When the economy began to contract sharply and unemployment rose substantially, Wall Street would find itself in the position of scapegoat for the country's problems, many of which it had caused. Until October 1929, the scenario that would rapidly unfold after the Crash was inconceivable, however. How could agrarian radicals possibly foretell events that experienced financiers though remote at best? Despite his predictions, however, Brookhart was fighting a losing battle when his intellect was at stake. "If Smith Wildman Brookhart of Iowa had a more active capacity for deductive reasoning," remarked a satirical commentary of the day, "he might really be the significant figure he modestly likes to think he is."[20]

Ignoring the Agrarians

One other trait common among Progressives was their view on Prohibition. It was seen as necessary legislation to prevent public drunkenness, restore family values, and restore the dignity of the workingman, who all too often had caused economic harm to himself and his family by drinking. On this score, their position was a rural one versus an urban one. In the cities, Prohibition was seen as a necessary evil that was enriching bootleggers and gangsters. A movement called the Association Against the Prohibition Amendment (AAPA) began in the early 1920s to push for repeal of the Volstead Act. Its main objective was to legalize spirit production again so that the federal government could levy an excise tax against alcohol. If that were to occur, its backers reckoned that the increase in revenues would help lower personal income tax rates. In short, the AAPA was a rich man's organization working for repeal, whereas the agrarians wanted to keep it to promote public morals. The issue was another example of the sharply divisive differences between rural and urban areas.

As a Prohibitionist, Brookhart took exception to Wall Street's imbibing at social functions. He revealed in a Senate speech that he had attended a party thrown in 1926 by financiers at the New Willard Hotel in Washington, attended by what he called the "big men" of Wall Street. Liquor was served from silver flasks and flowed freely. At the dinner party that followed, he sat between

Otto Kahn of Kuhn Loeb & Co., the traditionally Jewish investment bank that figured prominently in the money trust hearings, and Edward E. Loomis of the Lehigh Valley Railroad.[21] He
recalled that both tried to influence him on financial policy,
while pouring freely. Although resisting their advances, he later
revealed that he felt somewhat out of place because of the manner in which he was dressed. He remarked, "I was the only one
there dressed like an American citizen."[22] Brookhart felt "dressed"
in a business suit, rather than the white tie and tails favored by
financiers at formal occasions. The greater question as to why a
Prohibitionist was invited to a formal affair where liquor was
served was not addressed, but it showed that someone who put
together the guest list had not done enough homework. The
affair caused a public commotion after he made the speech, but
Commonweal noted that he still suffered from a "gross lapse in
good taste" for revealing it after the fact. Both Kahn and Loomis
declined to comment after the affair. Shortly thereafter,
Brookhart was invited to New York to debate Prohibition with
noted attorney Clarence Darrow, who took the side of the "wets"
over the "drys." After a spirited debate, Darrow remarked that
his opponent was "sincere; it's too bad he is uncivilized."[23]

Criticism of Brookhart was not isolated from the other
Progressives of the 1920s. All except Norris were roundly criticized for their lack of conviction for true Progressive principles,
shirking their ideals, or caving in and voting with the right wing
of the Republican Party. The *American Mercury* cast Brookhart as
"gullible and scatter brained," while Shipstead was notable as a
"gas-bag without the gas." Borah was characterized as "the
biggest sham of them all...the principle peddler from Idaho,
the Great God Borah who had undermined progressivism more
than all progressive senators together."[24] It was not difficult to
see why the Progressives in the 1920s were a movement rather
than a unified group. Their love of oratory and the individual
spotlight made unification almost impossible. Yet the longer
they were able to maintain a presence on the public stage, the
better their chances would be of making a collective impression
after the Crash of 1929 occurred.

Brookhart did not help his own personal cause by making vituperative remarks about Calvin Coolidge in 1924. He denounced the president's record as the "Wall Street Bloc" candidate and declared war on the "small group of crooked and irresponsible dictators" set up by the "Nonpartisan League of Wall Street to control and dominate the Republican Party."[25] The remarks drew sharp criticism from the mainstream of the Republican party, whose hierarchy immediately tried to read him out of the party. His right to hold his seat was later challenged, and he was relegated to the fringe of his party, which only served to make him more radical. By his second term, he was a full-fledged opponent of Wall Street and mainline Republicans as well. When he won reelection in 1926 despite his party's disapproval, Wall Street was otherwise preoccupied and barely noticed. The *New York Times* remarked that "the victory of Smith W. Brookhart...caused scarcely a ripple in the financial district yesterday. It was suggested by some observers that possibly all of the political developments will dawn on the market at once."[26]

The market was not taking notice of Brookhart or any of his radical colleagues as the Dow average began to climb. The rally of the 1920s was underway, and agrarian radicals from the Midwest were not factored into the equation that drove the market higher and higher. Speculation was building, and many banks and nonfinancial corporations were helping by loaning funds to the call money market so that brokers could extend margin to their customers. Farmers were suffering low prices, and their agricultural depression had already begun, just as the radicals claimed. No one in the seats of power was taking any notice, however. The average man in the street ostensibly was better off than ever before. He was being marketed automobiles, radios, and consumer appliances and was offered time payments by newly established finance companies to pay for them. Sears Roebuck offered premanufactured homes that could be constructed on a customer's lot, and many banks were extending loans to retail customers for the first time. The cities were well electrified, but less than 10 percent of farms were connected to power, living under substandard nineteenth-century conditions.

Demographics had changed substantially since before the world war, and voters now increasingly lived in cities. Farmers' representatives could still be heard clearly, but they were increasingly being painted as radicals, living outside the new consumer society enveloping America. As 1929 approached, Brookhart saw disaster coming and even well-known Wall Street financiers such as Bernard Baruch, Charles Merrill, and Joseph P. Kennedy agreed with the gloomy sentiment and began pulling their funds out of the market. But they would agree on little else.

Flippancy from the East

The Progressives, radicals, Farm-Labor representatives, and dissident Republicans constantly put pressure on the mainstream Republicans throughout the 1920s. Their constituents held values that were rapidly becoming outdated in American society and when those values collided with policies that were understood to be inimical to the interests of farmers, the result was a new batch of senators and representatives who had a clear mandate to stir things up in Washington. Although branded by Republicans as radicals, the new class of legislators were actually plain-spoken blunt men who had little time for subtlety or Washington politics.

Wall Street and the money elite were aware of the radicals during the 1920s, but business was too good to pay much notice. Pierpont Morgan and his son Jack were constant sources of irritation to the agrarians but were somewhat bulletproof since the Pujo hearings. As the market began to rise after 1925, volume on the stock exchanges increased and new issues of stocks and bonds appeared with great regularity. National City Bank in New York rapidly was becoming the premier investment bank/broker for retail investors as it tried to fashion itself into a financial department store, using the popular concept of the decade. It put an extensive wire system into place so that its correspondents could communicate with the home office quickly in an attempt to sell more and more securities to the public.

Until 1929, this disparate agrarian group appeared headed for political oblivion. They had estranged themselves from Calvin Coolidge mainly because of his strong business bent and support. The agrarians also interpreted his vetoes of the McNary-Haugen bill, passed twice during his administration, as a betrayal of farmers desperately attempting to achieve higher prices for their crops. The two bills attempted to raise the prices farmers received for their crops, but Coolidge vetoed them on the grounds that they fixed prices and abused the power to tax. The farm bloc could not override the vetoes but continued to push for relief until they were finally heard in the 1930s during the New Deal.

When Herbert Hoover was nominated to succeed Coolidge, many more dissidents supported him, seeing him as an antidote to the laconic Coolidge. As a candidate, Hoover appealed to a broad array of Republicans because he had previously been a successful businessman, food aid administrator to the Allies during World War I, and secretary of commerce under Coolidge. Many of them were soon to be disappointed, coming to understand Hoover's policies as too probusiness and against agriculture. Despite the efforts of Republicans to bring them into line, the dissidents continued to nettle the administration and rail against Wall Street and the Federal Reserve as often as possible. But suddenly in 1929, they were given a new lease on life as a group and became renowned around the country.

Their celebrity came from a speech given by Senator George Moses of New Hampshire, who coined a term that was to prove enduring through the 1930s. At a speech before a meeting of New England manufacturers, Moses dubbed his western dissident colleagues as the "Sons of the Wild Jackass." The name reverberated throughout the meeting and the country like the proverbial western wildfire. Moses was president pro tempore of the Senate and chairman of the Republican Senate Campaign Committee and his acerbic remark was not well received. The speech also referred to Smith Brookhart's revelations about the Washington dinner party at which liquor was served, stating that "all Senators now attend dinners with trepidation." After hearing the remarks, Brookhart replied that it was clear that "we do not need booze at these dinners to lift us to a high plane of eloquence." Senator Burton Wheeler of Montana added, "Of course, we cannot tell what he might have said if the dinner had not been dry."[27]

The flap would not end quickly. Conjecture swirled around what exactly a "son of the wild jackass" was. Moses did not elaborate and interpretations ran from the obvious to the biblical. Most thought that it was meant to imply that the radicals were offspring of the Democrats more than members of the Republican Party. Will Rogers commented that "this Moses, like the one in the original cast, is a kind of amateur prophet and every once and a while...he brings forth a wisecrack. So next week I can see the Senate passing a resolution to have his form again enveloped in some distant bull rushes."[28] Despite the controversy, some good was to come of the remark as far as the radicals were concerned. The flap came, however, during the aftermath of the worst stock market collapse in American history, giving some indication of the mood the country was in. Politics still reigned supreme, but soon the Jackasses would combine the Depression with their dislike of the Republican establishment to bring about a radical transformation of American society.

The term was so potent that a book soon appeared with the title *Sons of the Wild Jackass*, by Ray Tucker and Frederick Bartley, both experienced journalists. In an effort to give the group a personality, they included senators and a congressman in their list, immediately immortalizing them. Named from the Senate were Brookhart, Shipstead, La Follette Jr., Borah, Wheeler, Hiram Johnson of California, Thomas J. Walsh of Montana, Bronson Cutting of New Mexico, James Couzens of Michigan, Clarence Cleveland Dill of Washington, Gerald Nye of North Dakota, Edward Costigan of Colorado, and Fiorello La Guardia of New York. All were well-known thorns in the side of the establishment at large. There were also some notable exceptions, namely McFadden. As anger faded into pride, many of the dissidents would welcome the attention despite the less than flattering name. The only one who took his omission badly was McFadden.

Little Flower

Sons of the Wild Jackass was published in 1932 and soon became extremely popular. It was the number one nonfiction bestseller in Washington during the summer and quickly became required reading. The only member of the House included in the list was the irrepressible Fiorello La Guardia of New York. In 1932, he had not yet been elected mayor of New York City and his inclusion was based solely upon his career in the House of Representatives.

Born in New York City in 1882, La Guardia served in the consular service in Austria-Hungary, worked as a translator, and then attended New York University School of Law. After his introduction to the Hapsburgs, he returned to New York and served as an interpreter on Ellis Island from 1907 to 1910. Following a stint as a deputy attorney general in New York, he was elected to Congress in 1917 as a Republican. He then served during World War I and was returned to Congress in 1923, serving until 1933, when he lost his seat. In 1928, he ran for mayor of New York but lost the election to Jimmy Walker. But his popularity in Congress and the vast amount of press he received propelled him to the mayoralty in 1932, and he served until 1945. It was his career in Congress that earned him the dubious distinction conferred by Tucker and Bartley. In many ways, it paralleled that of Brookhart, although they were on opposite sides of the political spectrum.

La Guardia earned his entry into the honorary group of Jackasses early in his career. At age 22, he was a United States consul working in Austria-Hungary when he first tangled with Maria Josefa, a Hapsburg archduchess, over a polite request to hide some 500 immigrants from her empire who were bound by boat for the United States. Her request was simple. While she visited the town from which they were to embark, she asked that local officials keep some of them out of the way so that their presence did not offend her. Preferably, they could be loaded onto the ship early. La Guardia objected, telling the ship's captain that the order would violate American ship health laws and that the entire journey could be jeopardized. The Hungarians balked and threatened La Guardia with expulsion if he offended the archduchess in such a manner and began looking for him, presumably to arrest him. He avoided capture by hiding out at the home of the official who was actually hunting him, having tea with his wife while the local constabulary sought him. He revealed later, "I was having tea at his home with his wife. I think a complaint was filed against me in Washington but I never heard anything on that one either. But I did miss meeting Her Imperial Highness."[29]

On another occasion after World War I, he objected to a grand duke of Russia being admitted to the United States. He wrote to the secretary of labor, "I believe the same rigid application of the immigration laws that is generally applied to arriving aliens should be applied to these unemployed and shiftless dukes and archduchesses, who come here to collect funds to destroy organized governments and to prey upon the credulity of social climbing dupes."[30] Remarks of that sort immediately made the "Little Flower" an immediate candidate for the Wild Jackasses. Even as mayor in the 1930s, he continued the tradition. When a Nazi delegation visited New York in the 1930s, he arranged to ensure that their chauffeurs were Jewish. But it was his no-nonsense politics that earned him the enmity of everyone from J.P. Morgan to Andrew Mellon and the trusts. Smith Brookhart breached Washington protocol by discussing the dinner party serving liquor after the fact, but one of La Guardia's revelations made it look tame in comparison. Unlike the agrarians with whom he shared much in temperament, La Guardia was a wet on the Prohibition issue. And he combined it with a penchant for embarrassing federal officials as often as possible.

He drew vast press coverage when he declared in the House that the government was running speakeasies and breweries with government funds, despite the Volstead Act. He then mixed an alcoholic brew in his House office and another in Times Square in New York City, defying the authorities to arrest him. The press could not get enough of him. But he made a more serious point in a radio debate with Brookhart over Prohibition. Speaking over WJZ radio to a national audience, Brookhart declared that Prohibition was in danger from "high finance." Financiers and industrialists wanted to revoke it so that they could put an excise tax on alcohol production, taxing the workingman even more and reducing their own tax rates in the process. Although the argument was vintage Brookhart, the point was well taken since the AAPA avowedly was in favor of repeal and was financed by a strong Wall Street contingent and the Du Ponts of the chemical company.[31] Ironically, they had a hard-line policy at their Delaware plant of immediately firing anyone whom they suspected of coming to work inebriated. La Guardia recognized the problem as well but took a slightly different tack. He said in his speech that the wets and the drys should accommodate each other and work in unison rather than remain at loggerheads. He said that the country could not continue "as it is today, with a deficit in the National Treasury, while racketeers are operating with a surplus."[32] In traditional fashion, he was preaching unity among dissenters while Brookhart, although correctly, was preaching conspiracy.

Yet, the similarities to Brookhart continued. By the end of what would be his last term in Congress, La Guardia had been attacked on several occasions by the mainline Republicans, being called everything from a radical to a Socialist. He too had been read out of the party several times, only to return stronger than ever. He won the mayoralty because of his dogged defense of the man in the street and the underdog. As mayor, he became a spectator to the events that unfolded later in 1933 that led to Wall Street's downfall, but in many respects Wall Street was happy to have him in New York rather than Washington.

Not all of the legislators named by Tucker and Bartley were Republicans. A few of the Progressives were Democrats. One of the best-known was Senator Duncan Fletcher of Florida. Not as irascible or stubborn as his Republican colleagues, he was not named to the famous Tucker and Bartley list but would become a nemesis to Wall Street within two years of the Crash. Born in Georgia in 1859, Fletcher studied law at Vanderbilt and was admitted to the bar in 1881. After dabbling in local politics, he was elected to the Senate in 1909 and served continuously until his death in 1936. During his tenure in the upper house, he served on the commerce and transportation committees. He was also part of a delegation sent by Woodrow Wilson to study farm cooperative banks in Europe, which later became a model for the Farm Credit System. He also fortuitously sat on the Banking and Currency Committee for a crucial four-year period. It was this latter assignment that earned him the most notoriety during his career.

Fletcher was known as a reluctant Progressive, although he became more famous for reform than most of his more flamboyant colleagues. Another noted Progressive was Arthur Capper, Republican Senator from Kansas. Acknowledged as the leader of the agrarian bloc in the upper house, Capper seemed to be purely in the Midwestern vein and not much of a threat to Wall Street. Born in Kansas in 1865, he attended public schools and became a newspaper reporter and then the publisher of several newspapers and magazines, including *Capper's Weekly*. He also owned two radio stations and was a trustee of a local agricultural college. He then served as governor in 1915 and was elected to the Senate in 1918, serving until 1949. On the surface, he was not an economic firebrand like Brookhart nor as ubiquitous as Peter Norbeck of South Dakota. But his experience in agricultural committees in the Senate made him a vocal foe of the futures markets, which traded only agricultural commodities at the time. That experience alone would make him a thorn in Wall Street's side.

Hailing from Kansas was another of his anti–Wall Street qualifications. The state was the home of the first "blue-sky law" passed. Kansas passed the first state law in 1911 requiring companies selling securities to divulge their finances, something of a radical innovation at the time. The term "blue sky" supposedly originated when a state banking commissioner realized that many worthless securities were being sold in the state. In order to prevent promoters from selling worthless securities, or "capitalizing the blue sky," the law was passed. By 1920, over two-thirds of the states had passed their own versions of the blue-sky laws, but no federal legislation had yet been passed.[33] Capper extended the tradition into futures trading when he and fellow Kansan, Representative J.N. Tincher, sponsored the first federal law regulating the grain futures exchanges. The law, the Futures Trading Act, was passed in 1921 but was struck down as unconstitutional by the Supreme Court. It was replaced by the Grain Futures Act a year later, and it stood for 14 years before being replaced by the Commodity Futures Act in 1936, an important but little-known New Deal law passed to keep the futures exchanges in check. Capper was part of the Midwestern tradition that considered short selling and speculation as activities requiring close regulation because of their potential to do harm to farmers. In the 1920s, extending the sentiment to Wall Street was not a great stretch.

One Democrat who made the list was Senator Thomas Walsh of Montana. His background was very similar to the other Progressives. Born in Wisconsin in 1859, he was educated at the University of Wisconsin and graduated from its law school in 1884. He then moved to Montana in 1890 and failed at several bids to elected office until elected to the Senate in 1912. He served for the next 20 years, and his service was mainly on committees overseeing mining and pensions. His record was perhaps the most distinguished of all the Progressives because he was closest to Woodrow Wilson during his presidency. His law-writing credentials were impeccable. He helped write the Federal Reserve Act, the Woman's Suffrage Act, and the Prohibition Act. In the early 1920s, he was prosecutor at the Teapot Dome hearings, an advocate of the League of Nations, and later chairman of the 1924 Democratic convention in New York City. Unlike his Progressive contemporaries, Walsh always proceeded from carefully reasoned positions rather than from the hip or the heart. As a result, he was one of the most admired of the Wild Jackasses.

While a young attorney in Montana, he did legal work for the Anaconda Copper Company, the state's major company, and was offered the post of its general counsel. His future as a wealthy attorney would have been ensured, but he refused the job because it would have required him to refuse cases on behalf of the less fortunate and the workingman, from whose ranks he had risen. He incurred the company's wrath as a result, and it opposed him in succeeding elections; however, this did not impede his career as a legislator of the people. When FDR was elected president, Walsh was his choice for attorney general. However, he died suddenly of a heart attack while on a train bound for Washington to accept Roosevelt's appointment. On hearing of his death, FDR noted, "He was one of my oldest and most trusted friends and one on whose calm judgment I could always rely... to fill his place in the circle of my friends will be impossible."[34]

Walsh was the embodiment of the radical Progressives of his era, although he was hardly flamboyant or a great orator in the tradition of William Jennings Bryan or William Borah. He had been on the side of liberal-minded causes throughout his career, although not all were successes. When he was first appointed to investigate the Teapot Dome hearings, he was sent so much documentary material that the Harding administration hoped he would drown under the weight of it all. But he did not and proceeded to sort it out. As a result, the hearings proceeded. A similar incident would occur after the Crash and Walsh's counsel would prove crucial in the outcome of those later hearings.

Tucker and Bartley wrote what would become a prescient first chapter of *Sons of the Wild Jackass* in which they stated that "a brood of pugnacious Progressives who have been only so much political protoplasm, and might have remained in that quiescent state for generations," were transformed by Moses "into the nucleus of a new party, even though it may yet be years before it functions more than fitfully."[35] Their assessment was correct, but the years would become a matter of months. The stock market crash and causes of the Depression were topics tailor-made for the dissidents since they were the outcome of all the complaints they had lodged over the years. Too much short-term money had been funneled into the stock market, fueling speculation, and now the banking system was in trouble along with investors. The question facing them as a group and the country as a whole was the same that had been asked throughout the 1920s in different contexts.

Congressman Emanuel Celler, a Democrat from Brooklyn, looked back over the years leading to the Crash and the period immediately following. He concluded that "Congress began to skip, first in this direction, then in that. There were no leaders. Congress had not yet begun to feel the measure of its responsibility and the tragedies that rose from the 1929 crash. There was no plan, no direction."[36] Now, after the Crash of 1929, the problems were more clearly identified. What would be done about them? Would the remedy for the Crash and the Depression result in meaningful reform legislation or more long-winded oratory? The answer would come quickly in 1933.

CHAPTER 2

THE ASSAULT
ON WALL STREET

Many of the abuses in investment banking have resulted from the incompetence, negligence, irresponsibility, or cupidity of individuals in the profession.

The Fletcher Report, 1934

A s the Depression worsened, many fingers were pointed at the stock market as the culprit that had destroyed so many jobs and livelihoods. The winter of 1932 was particularly extreme, only adding to the hardship of the unemployed. Hoovervilles were springing up around the country. They were named because many of their inhabitants blamed their plight on the president, who seemed incapable of reviving the economy. They even appeared in places of relative wealth. Central Park in New York City boasted its own encampment, as did other locations on the West Side of the city, not far from where expensive yachts were moored on the Hudson River.

In the months and years following the Crash, complaints about market speculation were rampant. In the 1920s, that was as much an indictment of human nature as of the stock exchanges. But the speculative urge was not on trial as much as the mechanics for letting it express itself, whether on the stock or futures exchanges. In this respect, the complaint was similar to that about drinking. The urge to imbibe could not be deterred unless the production of alcoholic spirits was curtailed, so the Volstead Act was passed. In the early 1930s, a movement was gathering momentum to pass similar legislation against the financial markets in order to prevent ruinous speculation from wiping out savings and investment.

The public had a great many alternatives for speculation prior to the Crash. Many more stock exchanges existed in the 1920s before the securities and banking laws were passed in 1933 and 1934. Several futures markets also traded, or planned to trade, stocks that otherwise traded on one of the larger exchanges. This made speculation easy since the amount of margin required to be used on a down payment varied from exchange to exchange and broker to broker. The New York Produce Exchange announced that it traded over 14 million shares, mostly of New York area stocks, in 1929, leading up to the Crash in October.[1] The Chicago Board of Trade (CBOT) was establishing stock trading facilities to compete with the Chicago Stock Exchange in the early 1930s. Bucket shops still existed in the 1920s, willing to accept bets from the small bettor who wanted to make a quick killing in the market. There was no shortage of ways for the little guy to get involved in the market.

Blaming the Fed

In the months following the Crash, the Federal Reserve came under criticism for its role in the months leading to October 1929. The general complaint was that it had waited too long to raise interest rates to discourage speculation. On the surface, the issue was correct, but structural problems within the Fed itself played a role in the market collapse. The problems were the first example of tension within the system constructed in 1912 and 1913. Originally, New York bankers wanted Congress to adopt a European-style central bank that would issue money and be located in New York City. Contemporary thinking held that the concept was not feasible since it was an attempt by the money trust banks to maintain power in New York rather than shift it to Washington. The Federal Reserve bill, introduced by Senator Carter Glass, a Democrat from Virginia, was seen as a compromise, allowing the new Fed some central banking powers but splitting the system into 12 banks located around the country.

Problems within the Federal Reserve began to mount as the 1920s' bull market continued unabated. In March 1929, the board decided to raise interest rates in an attempt to reduce specula- tion but was thwarted by the New York Fed bank, which added more funds to the market to offset the board's actions. The old tension between parts of the Fed came to the surface, and the New York Fed, dominated by money trust bankers, reasserted its primacy in the system. The Fed Board in Washington did little to offset the actions of New York. Andrew Mellon remained mostly silent on the issue and would eventually step down in disgrace as a result. The chairman of the system, Daniel R. Crissinger, took almost no notice of the problems mounting in the stock market. He assumed the seat on the board left vacant by John Skelton Williams after his death in 1926, leaving Louis McFadden in an irascible mood as a result. The original compromises made when the Fed was created were coming home to roost.

When the market crashed in October, it did not take long for the Fed to be blamed. Its operations during the 1920s had added a vast amount of money to the call money market in New York, where nonfinancial companies often loaned money at two or three times their own cost to speculators. The original warnings made by Brookhart and McFadden seemed to have been cor- rect. The Fed helped cause the market crash and since the board operated in consort with foreign bankers, the United States appeared to be at the mercy of Wall Street and its foreign allies. This was a combustible argument that would not serve Wall Street well. The same money boom could also be respon- sible for the massive bank failures occurring in the 1920s that would continue into the 1930s.

Louis McFadden continued his attack on the Fed in the months after the Crash. Beginning in early 1930, he started a campaign against the Fed and foreign bankers, the same theme he began 10 years before. After 1929, the attack became increas- ingly shrill. His speeches in the 1920s criticized Wall Street for its foreign connections. While nettlesome, his comments still remained within the bounds of acceptable behavior on the part of a Wild Jackass, although he was never mentioned as part of the group. During a decade of inflammatory oratory, his remarks were standard for Progressives and their sometime allies. As the Depression grew deeper, however, McFadden turned up the volume and began making comments far outside the realm of acceptable behavior. Perhaps not being considered a Jackass offended him, but his career in the House began to spiral downward after 1930.

His first fusillade against the Fed after the Crash came in February 1930, when he went on the record in a House speech showing links between the Fed, the Bank of England (with whom he thought the Fed shared guilt for the Crash), and the Bank for International Settlements, being organized at the time.[2] As far as he was concerned, they formed the nucleus of an economic elite acting for its own best interests, ostensibly in the name of American economic policy. McFadden's problem was not with foreigners in general, but with foreign bankers who acted with a small coterie of New York bankers who exacted their wishes upon the United States. In his view, Eugene Meyer, formerly of the Fed and recently of the Reconstruction Finance Corporation, was the main culprit. The charge had some merit because a deal between the Fed and the Bank of England over the value of the pound and American interest rates was thought to be behind the stock market bubble. Later in 1930, he made another speech before the House stating, "The forces which are now making themselves felt in our daily lives come in large measure from without." The war reparations exacted on Germany were still a lingering question in 1930, and he saw them as the cause of many of the current economic troubles. He added, "The financiers and economic experts have had their turn. It is time for them to retire and relinquish the responsibility of determining the policy of the United States Government to the representatives in Congress, where it belongs."[3]

While McFadden made his charges in the House, activity on the stock market dwindled to a fraction of its pre-1929 activity. There were still smart operators on the floor of the New York

Stock Exchange (NYSE), however. A good deal of short selling was taking place as prices moved lower, and the shorts were able to capitalize by buying back their shares at lower prices. The activity was frowned upon by the general public but was considered ordinary business by the floor traders, who saw nothing wrong with the practice. Market conditions in 1931 and early 1932 were only the most recent chapter in a long litany of complaints that dated back to the War of 1812. Short selling was considered unpatriotic because the shorts were taking advantage of poor market conditions to make a buck, as they had so many times in the past. The issue was a burning one in the stock and commodities futures markets, although no clear resolution had ever been reached. Agrarians in the Midwest had tried unsuccessfully to have the practice banned in the Chicago futures markets and even tried to have the exchanges abolished, all to no avail.[4]

Although an accepted practice, short selling in times of distress showed the ugly side of capitalism. It was unclear from the criticisms whether its detractors understood the process or simply criticized it because it had been criticized in the past. Defenders of the NYSE took the position that only they fully understood its economic benefits and that the public had only a distorted view. The technique was not proscribed but did finally get some rules two years later when the Securities Exchange Act was passed. However, it was clear that agrarian radicals and those representing the workingman firmly believed that selling something one did not own and buying it back at a lower price was definitely illegal and should be banned.

Gold Bugs and Conspirators

The Depression helped place the Progressive Republicans and their agrarian allies in more substantial positions of power. In 1931, the Jackasses held no less than nine important Senate committee chairmanships. They were Borah, Foreign Relations; Norris, Judiciary; Couzens, Interstate Commerce; Howell, Claims; Johnson, Commerce; Frazier, Indian Affairs; La Follette Jr., Manufactures; Nye, Public Lands; and most importantly, Norbeck, Banking and Currency. Norbeck was chairman of the committee for four years. At the same time, McFadden was the chairman of the House Banking and Currency Committee, an uncomfortable position for Wall Street. Between them, they held the reins of power over banks, although not the securities business. Political cartoonist Clifford Berryman recognized the value of the movement for his repertoire. He said in 1932 that Borah and Norris were among his favorite subjects and that he was going to have more fun "than a barrel of monkeys" with the New Deal.

An inquiry into short selling in the futures market began in 1930, as commodities prices plummeted and farmers began to feel the pinch. Hoover began that investigation by asking agriculture secretary Arthur Hyde to investigate activities on the Chicago Board of Trade to determine the reasons behind the price drop in many agricultural commodities. Prices had been falling since the late 1920s to lows not seen in decades. One of the products of the investigation was the revelation that the Soviet Union, through its American agents, had sold short a large number of wheat futures for reasons that were not totally clear. The investigation brought measures for reform on the futures exchanges, but the revelations only added fuel to the fire about foreign influences on domestic American markets. Smith Brookhart of Iowa remarked that the situation "proves that the price of wheat is in the hands of gamblers and the complaint should be made against the system and not against those who use the exchanges and employ methods permitted by law."[5] The comment was chilling for the exchanges. If the system proved rotten, then major reform could be expected.

That did not stop speculation, however. Short selling in the stock market increased dramatically as the market averages declined, and old criticisms rose again. But in 1932, it became more of a cause célèbre, especially as Hoover searched for a way to restore some luster to his failing presidency. In the winter, the president disclosed that he had initiated discussions with the NYSE over short selling in an attempt to control the practice.

If the exchange did not comply, Hoover intimated that he might seek legislation to control it. Wall Street was surprised when sub-poenas were sent out within a few months. Although the notion seemed plausible but improbable, it did illustrate the "top down" attitude of the Coolidge and Hoover administrations. In parlance of the 1920s, the "big men" controlled politics and finance, so it was plausible to Hoover to investigate the big men of the stock exchange to see if anything was amiss. Value was clearly eroding on the exchanges, but the real cause appeared to lie somewhat deeper in the economy—although Wall Street was clearly exacerbating a bad situation.

The matter of short selling was closely linked to gold since the dollar was still on the gold standard at the time. Short selling by foreigners was seen as a double threat since stocks would decline in value and then gold flows would change as a result. The British were on the verge of abandoning the gold standard to protect themselves against capital outflows, and there was an increasing fear that the United States would do the same. Louis McFadden wrote a spirited defense of the metal in which he urged the United States to continue mining gold so that there would be enough of it to support financial claims. But the cause of the developing Depression was clear to him. "The failure of our own Federal Reserve system to act judiciously with reference to the control of the total volume of credit," he argued, "based on its enormous and excessive gold holdings, is a real cause of our present difficulties as they are attributable to gold."[6] Operations of the Fed in the late 1920s were criticized for causing an outflow of gold to foreigners, and the fact had not been lost on McFadden, who continued his criticisms of the central bank. The criticism would be one of the last measured ones by him; in the future his attacks would turn more vitriolic and emotional. The gold problem was thought solved in the summer of 1932 when Congress passed the first Glass-Steagall Act, enlarging the powers of the Fed to deal with the gold problem. Unfortunately, it only would be in effect for less than a year.

Journalist Clinton Gilbert added a note of intrigue that further complicated matters. He later wrote that Hoover believed a fantastic story that Europeans were conspiring through a bear raid to pull the United States off the gold standard, thereby wrecking the economy. Accordingly, Hoover asked his friend Frederic Walcott, new to the Senate, to look into the matter; as a result, Senate hearings began to take shape.[7] At the heart of the alleged conspiracy was financier and former stock market operator Bernard Baruch. This already famous Wall Street figure and head of the War Industries Board during World War I added the vaguely foreign element to which many Republican Progressives and agrarian radicals pandered since he was Jewish, wealthy, and had "foreign" connections.

The reformers' cause owed a great debt to George Moses of New Hampshire for labeling them although the conservative Republicans would not yet realize the fallout that would occur in the November elections. As a token of their appreciation, the Jackasses presented Moses with a large wooden club given to them by a group of North Dakota farmers. It was presented to him in the Senate by Gerald Nye in April 1932, bearing the inscription "Regards from the Sons of the Wild Jackass." It would be one of the last official gifts Moses would receive, since he lost his reelection bid in November.

As the hearings were being organized, conspiracy theories began to swirl in all directions. The foreign threat became more imminent when a French newspaper reported that the National City Bank had failed. After some fast telegrams noting that the bank was in no danger, the story was retracted. But the damage had been done. The radicals were always ready to entertain conspiracy theories, and the hearings were called. There appeared to be evidence that the foreigners were acting in consort with New York traders and speculators. In April 1932, Norbeck promised to disclose the names of short sellers on the NYSE, regardless of how prominent the names might be. Members of the Senate Banking and Currency Committee also disclosed that they realized some of the names were fictitious and would search out the short sellers' real identities. The committee was able to show that many short pools were named after the initials of the leaders of the pool or were acronyms for their wives' initials.

Also sitting on the committee were Brookhart and Frederic C. Walcott of Connecticut, a Republican newcomer to the Senate, elected in 1928. A one-term senator, Walcott was a businessman whose background was much different than those of his Progressive colleagues. Born in upstate New York in 1869, he attended prep school and graduated from Yale in 1891. However, he then went into the textile and banking business in Connecticut before running for the state senate. Strong business ties to a Wall Street firm, Bonbright & Co., put him in the Wall Street camp, and suspicions arose that he was put on the banking committee to keep a watchful eye on the radicals. He also served on some commissions that made him closer to the Progressives, notably the state water commission and the fisheries and game board. Upon entering the Senate, he became a vocal opponent of short selling and was responsible for prodding the banking and currency committee into its investigation, helping perpetuate the conspiracy theory. The short sellers came from a list of those who had sold short on April 8 of that year, at a time when market prospects were gloomy. Foreign names were also on the list.

William Gray, counsel for the committee, planned to call Richard Whitney, president of the NYSE, to testify about the practice. The committee then subpoenaed 10 securities firms to disclose their short seller lists. The American Federation of Labor at the same time released a statement claiming the market had lost over $70 billion of its value and that it must be protected from further short selling. "We need protection against speculation that destroys wealth and business structure," it stated.[8] The committee tried to comply, but Richard Whitney proved a difficult witness.

A Standard Defense

Whitney was the first witness called when the Senate began hearings in April 1932. Peter Norbeck was temporarily absent from Washington, and some of the more radical members of the committee decided to begin hearings without him. The marketplace was full of rumor at the time, mostly that the large-scale bear raid was being planned by unnamed speculators. At the same time, Fiorello La Guardia declared in the House that the same unnamed speculators were threatening a panic if the investigation proceeded. He was clearly reacting to the old refrain that occasionally charged Wall Street with creating panics to blackmail the country. But the real fireworks were reserved for Whitney's testimony.

Under close questioning by committee members, Whitney vigorously defended the NYSE against criticism. It was clear that he was speaking for the exchange alone, not for the other 78 stock exchanges he claimed existed in the country at the time. One of his first comments defended floor traders against the charge that they often execute orders before executing those of their customers, benefiting from small price movements in the process. Whitney claimed that strict exchange rules prohibited the practice. It was a charge that would he heard again many times over the next 70 years, always with the same defense. But the real fireworks began when Smith Brookhart questioned him, again claiming that Wall Street was responsible for the Depression and the country's woes. "You brought this country to the greatest panic in history," he charged Whitney, who became indignant. He replied, "We have brought this country, sir, to its standing in the world by speculation," he retorted, countering Brookhart by asking, "You think you can affect the world by changing the rules or regulations of a stock exchange or a board of trade?," the latter a reference to the Chicago Board of Trade.

Challenging Brookhart's assumed naiveté brought a quick response from the Iowa senator. "Yes, we can change them by abolishing the board of trade and stock exchange as far as speculation is concerned." Whitney snapped, "And then, the people of the United States will go to Canada and Europe to do those very things and pay their taxes there."[9] The defense also was standard at the time. If Americans did not do the business then foreigners would. The actual number of small investors capable of sending their orders abroad was minimal, so it was clear that Whitney was referring to professional investors and traders. But Whitney was not out of the woods because he had not yet faced Norbeck.

A week later when Whitney reappeared, the questioning was even more terse than before. After eliciting almost no information from the NYSE president, Norbeck began to show clear signs of irritation. Returning to the question concerning the behavior of floor traders with public orders, Norbeck asked if the small investor was simply not getting "skinned." "I don't agree with that," Whitney replied. "Oh, but you don't agree with anything," snapped the senator, clearly agitated. "We haven't had factual answers to many questions we have asked you," Norbeck responded, "But we will try to develop our own case." He then adjourned the meeting, leaving Whitney sitting at the witness table, clearly distressed. He stayed for the next several hours, dictating facts to a stenographer that he wanted added to the record the next time he testified.[10]

Whitney vigorously defended the old guard of the exchange and the process of short selling, which he claimed was natural and necessary for floor traders. Norbeck was frustrated because the 350 names on the full short-selling list were mostly unknown. Walcott claimed that they were probably dummies designed to hide the real identity of the bears. Walcott's presence in the actual hearings was more muted than expected, especially since he had been such a harsh critic of the shorts when the hearings were first called. Whitney's adamant stance did not do the exchanges any good in the end because, as Norbeck said, the committee decided to frame its own case and the results would not please the old guard. Fiorello La Guardia then entered the fray, stating that he had documents relating to the sale of foreign securities to American investors that were so sensitive that they had to be locked up over night in a police vault until he could bring them to the committee's attention. It was becoming apparent that the hearings were not on a sound footing and were in danger of collapsing early. They needed a strong guiding hand other than Norbeck's.

Despite what appeared to be a good start, the committee began to fizzle in the summer of 1932. Critics in the Senate maintained that it was toothless and that its findings would likely only hurt any chance of an economic recovery. Reactionaries tried to protect Wall Street by claiming that the committee members did not understand the workings of finance and therefore were in no position to be critical. Other committee members were mostly silent during the summer, realizing that the investigation was floundering. One was James Couzens, a Republican from Michigan, and the Senate's only confirmed multimillionaire. A Canadian by birth, Couzens was one of the official Wild Jackasses named by Tucker and Bartley, although his background appeared to imply the opposite. Born in 1872 in Ontario, he held a variety of jobs before going to work for Henry Ford in Michigan in 1903. Rising quickly through the ranks, the irascible Couzens finally left the company in 1919 when he became mayor of Detroit. At the time, his fortune was estimated at approximately $50 million. He was appointed to the Senate in 1922 and elected to a full term two years later. His most important committee job was chairman of the Interstate Commerce Committee. Despite his credentials, he was one of businesses' harshest critics in Congress and had little time for Wall Street financiers. Like Henry Ford, he shared a distaste and a distrust of people who earned vast amounts of money but never produced a tangible product.

New Blood

The elections of 1932 displayed wide discontent with Republicans and ushered in a Democratic Congress. The new faces brought with them a new attitude toward economic conditions and an even harsher view of Wall Street than existed before. Many of the radicals in the Senate and the House lost their committee jobs as the Democrats swept control of both houses. Norbeck was replaced by Duncan Fletcher, a long-sitting Democrat from

Florida, on the Senate Banking and Currency Committee, while McFadden was replaced by Henry Steagall of Alabama as chairman of its counterpart in the House.

The Republican loss and the revelations of the Senate banking committee were followed by a brash move by Louis McFadden in the House. Although his critics were numerous, the congressman never wavered when attempting to press his point about nefarious international interests working against the United States. After Hoover declared a moratorium on debts owed the United States from World War I, McFadden moved to impeach him. Introducing his resolution to a House less than full and an empty gallery above, the congressman read his charges, which were totally unanticipated. Those congressmen in the building but not in attendance quickly entered the lower chamber to witness the proceedings. After reciting a long laundry list of complaints in his House speech, he called for the president's removal. Of the many charges listed were two of his old favorites. He accused Hoover of high crimes and misdemeanors by failing to fill the vacancy left when Roy Young resigned from the Federal Reserve Board in 1930. He was also incensed by the fact that Eugene Meyer was named to the Reconstruction Finance Corporation, which he considered an illegal body because of its emergency status and ability to make emergency loans to banks. Hoover's refusal to pay World War I veterans their promised bonus in 1932 after the Bonus March on Washington also was mentioned as a serious shortcoming of the president. The crux of the charges, which carried on for 14 pages, was that Hoover had usurped the role of Congress:

"Whereas Herbert Hoover, President of the United States, has in violation of the Constitution and laws of the United States, unlawfully attempted to usurp and has usurped legislative powers and functions of the Congress of the United States, which make him guilty of high crimes and misdemeanors and subject to impeachment."[11]

After he finished, utter confusion reigned in the House for about half an hour until a motion to table the motion was intro-

duced by a Democrat. In a hastily called vote, it was tabled by a
vote of 361 to 8 with 60 abstentions. What possibly could have
motivated the irascible congressman was not immediately clear,
but recent history gave a clue. When the debt moratorium was
first announced the year before, McFadden severely criticized
Hoover. Pennsylvania Republicans reprimanded him at the time,
and he lost his power to name federal appointees from the state.
After the impeachment was announced, the party quickly again
moved to reprimand him further, only adding to his discontent. A
local New York newspaper quickly dismissed him as a disgruntled
legislator, still smarting from the reprimand a year before. "That
not all legislators elected by the people are shining examples of
tolerance and breadth was shown in [McFadden's] recent asinine
attempt," it wrote two days after the affair, "The shafts of the cha-
grined Pennsylvania legislator rebounded only to his own utter
defacement."[12] Unfortunately, it was not the last charge the congressman would make. Adding to the excitement, a rogue gun-
man wielded a handgun in the House gallery on the same day,
demanding to be heard. He surrendered without incident. And
the House also managed to pass a bill in favor of beer production
on the same day as well.

If the congressman from Pennsylvania was employing an
unknown stratagem, more serious events during the first 100
days of the New Deal hobbled Wall Street with a speed no one
would have imagined just months before. Within days of taking
office in March 1933, FDR and Congress immediately set out to
tackle the banking problem. All of the issues raised by Progressives, farm advocates, and dissenters over the previous 10 years
had been festering and needed attention quickly. Hearings continued in the Senate, but the banking issue could not wait for resolution. At the time, the issue was not divorced from Wall Street
because many banks were in the securities business and vice
versa. But the securities markets had to wait for remedies while
the banking question was settled, and J.P. Morgan & Co. was
foremost on most legislators' minds. The conspiracy theories
were not as important as the fact that the country was mired in

a severe depression and bankers showed little willingness to offer any constructive ideas on how to alleviate the situation. Ideology had taken the place of constructive bipartisan efforts to remedy the situation. McFadden, as many others, prematurely bemoaned the fact that the New Deal had abandoned the ideas of Jefferson in what apparently was shaping up as a strong dose of statist interference in the economy. But it was still very early to judge what direction the New Deal was going to take until the emergency banking and securities laws were introduced, followed by even tougher measures on bankers.

The Senate committee also hired a new chief counsel early in 1933. Previous counsels had quarreled with Norbeck, claiming that they did not have a free hand to proceed. Aware of the role that special counsels played in previous investigations, the committee selected a New York lawyer, Ferdinand Pecora, to head the inquiry. Highly recommended for the job, Pecora was the opposite of many of the bankers and brokers he examined. Born in Sicily, he was brought to the United States by his parents and went to work in a law office in his teens. After saving money for several years, he attended law school at night. He was also affiliated with Theodore Roosevelt's Progressives in 1912 and became vice chairman of the New York Progressive Party. Several years later, he switched allegiances and became a Democrat because of his admiration for Woodrow Wilson. The affiliation enabled him to become a deputy assistant district attorney, making his mark investigating bucket-shop operators in New York and closing down more than 150 of them. He also served on several New York commissions on banking and abuses in the bail-bond business. His new job with the banking committee paid him the princely sum of $255 per month, a fraction of what some on Wall Street made in a day. When asked by Norbeck whether he would work for that amount, Pecora indicated that money was not the primary motive in his life. One newspaper in Montana noted, "Pecora means sheep in Italian, which probably explains why he has been such a champion of the lambs shorn in Wall Street."[13] As a result of his appointment, Wall

Street was outflanked by Progressives and Democrats on both sides, all intent on reform.

The stock exchange practices committee wanted to interview Charles Mitchell, the president of the National City Bank of New York. The bank had been one of the largest promoters of new bonds and stocks during the 1920s through a securities subsidiary, the National City Company. Charley Mitchell had been one of the cheerleaders of the New Era, tirelessly promoting his company's underwritings to retail investors. National City had established a wire service between its branches, allowing branches to communicate orders directly to the home office. National City was the first large "wire house," a term that would later be applied to retail-oriented brokers who sold securities to the small investor. When so many small investors were hurt by the Crash, Mitchell was the one Wall Street individual most closely associated with retail brokerage.

Although aggravating, selling securities of dubious value to the public did not violate any federal laws in the absence of meaningful legislation. What was more troublesome was the ownership of the securities affiliate by the parent bank. At a dramatic point in the early hearings, a 20-year-old report of former Solicitor General Frederick Lehman was produced. In it, he expressed an opinion that the National City Company's holding of stock in its parent was illegal. The report was written at the time of the Pujo hearings but then mysteriously disappeared, with only a carbon copy of the typed report left in the files. When it was discovered, it was read into the record by Pecora. Mitchell claimed to have been aware of it but claimed to have forgotten its contents long ago. Its opinion was found to have been supported by the sitting attorney general at the time, and its mysterious disappearance was never fully explained.

Also working against Mitchell was his part-time job as a director of the Federal Reserve Bank of New York. The New York Fed had already been blamed for reigniting the fires that fueled the bubble by adding funds to the market when the Federal Reserve Board tried to raise interest rates. When subpoenas were issued in February 1933, after Pecora assumed the job of chief counsel, Mitchell was one of the first to be called. Norbeck pulled no punches when discussing the reasons why: "When the stock market boom went wild, the Federal Reserve Board at Washington made an effort to slow it down and sought the cooperation of Mr. Mitchell who was then director in the New York Federal Reserve Bank...he defied the board and speeded up the boom. He took a 'go-to-hell' attitude toward the board and got away with it."[14]

When the Democrats took control of Congress, Duncan Fletcher became the Banking and Currency Committee chairman, displacing Peter Norbeck. The hearings became known as the Pecora hearings, named after their chief counsel, but Fletcher was firmly in charge. Much to Wall Street's distress, he was also a close confidant of FDR. With Fletcher assuming the reins, the role of the Wild Jackasses began to diminish. The New Dealers were now actively committed to reform through regulation of banking and Wall Street and would not be deterred in their quest to apply strict rules. Although banking had seen some federal regulation over the years, Wall Street had never experienced any federal laws regulating its behavior. When the Senate hearings began, some senators openly questioned whether they had any authority to make laws affecting the New York Stock Exchange since it was a self-governing board empowered by New York law. The New Deal would have a quick response to those sorts of misgivings.

Duncan Fletcher was persuaded by FDR to take the job as chairman of the Banking and Currency Committee in February 1933, before his inauguration. At the time, Fletcher was the third longest-serving Senator behind Borah and Reed Smoot of Utah. Part of their agreement required the committee to fulfill FDR's wishes and investigate the private records of bankers, including their tax records.[15] This sort of intrusion would earn FDR the label "traitor to his class" for daring to intervene in the personal records of financiers. The new committee included Norbeck, Couzens, Carter Glass of Virginia, Edward Costigan of Colorado,

Alben Barkley of Kentucky, and John Townsend of Delaware, in addition to Fletcher. Costigan was also an honorary member of the Jackasses. Of the group, Carter Glass was the most conservative, often disagreeing with the others. The senator from Virginia was the oldest member of the committee, born in 1858. A former newspaperman, he was a major architect of the Federal Reserve Act and served Woodrow Wilson as secretary of the Treasury from 1918-1920. But the committee composition still reflected a strong penchant for reform. Brookhart and Walcott were gone, both having lost their reelection bids. Joining them in the return to private life was George Moses of New Hampshire, also defeated.

Consistency was supplied by Fletcher, who took his new job seriously and worked very long hours on the details of the interrogations that took place in Washington. Wall Street came to realize that the Fletcher committee, unlike its predecessor, was a threat to the established order. The ideological veil descending on the Street began to fall quickly. Morgan and his partners already feared the influence of former crusading Progressive lawyer Louis Brandeis, who was privately advising FDR, despite serving on the Supreme Court. Now, they had reason to fear the banking committee, which was resurrected after beginning slowly the previous year. After the Republicans lost the election and the New Deal Democrats started to assume jobs of greater importance in Washington, Wall Street recognized its problem and began spending money on lobbying to keep the potential nuisances at bay. As far as the Street was concerned, the idea of federal regulation of the securities markets was still far removed. Washington had occasionally intruded in its affairs before, as in 1912, but little direct regulation of Wall Street had ever materialized. The Morgan tentacles were still substantial, extending into all aspects of business life, so there was little reason to be alarmed at the changes in Washington. But Wall Street misjudged the extent of discontent over the Crash, bank failures, and extremely high rates of unemployment. For the first time in

American history, an angry public refused to forgive financiers for their transgressions. The changes that were coming were deceptive, however, since they were piecemeal rather than neatly arranged in one sweeping bit of legislation.

The gold issue was finally resolved in early March 1933 as soon as FDR took office. The Emergency Banking Act passed on March 9, five days after the new administration was sworn in, took the country off the gold standard. As part of the act, no individual could own gold or transport it, an attempt to ensure that capital did not flow out of the country. Anyone violating the law was subject to a $10,000 fine and up to 10 years in prison. Small savers and investors had been hoarding their savings as the banking crisis deepened, and the U.S. money supply contracted as a result. In theory, the currency was still backed by gold until the act was passed, so the loophole had to be closed. If ordinary citizens started demanding gold for their cash, then the crisis would only deepen. The country never returned to the gold standard after 1933. The banking holiday ended, and the country's stock and futures exchanges, which had been closed since March 3, opened again on March 15.

The gold suspension measure was not popular among hard money advocates who maintained that currency not backed by gold was worthless. There was also some confusion about the motive behind the law because the United States had an ample supply of gold at the time and held a substantial portion of the world's reserves. The flip side of the law was also puzzling because not many people actually held gold for investment purposes, especially small investors. One Midwestern newspaper observed that the problem was not the supply of the metal but "if, in a period of excitement people try to hoard it, they take away our standard of value. As the nation's financial and business structure is now organized, it needs its gold as much as a tailor needs his tape measure."[16] Hard evidence of whether any of the early New Deal measures would actually be effective was wanting, but the public confidence issue was paramount. The United States only had become self-sufficient in supplying most of the capital needed by government and industry since World War I and could not afford to have the process interrupted by a crisis of confidence.

Compromise and Reform

After the emergency banking legislation restored some confidence in the banking system, Congress went to work on a securities law. The Pecora hearings revealed that a large number of investors bought new securities solely on the word of their brokers. Many of the issues, especially bond issues, had never been vetted properly and were literally worthless when issued. After a massive round of defaults began in the early 1930s, Congress was outraged and decided to work on a bill requiring investment bankers and the securities issuers to divulge full financial information to investors at the time of initial sale. What became the Securities Act of 1933 had never been proposed at the federal level before, although the concept was embodied in the blue-sky laws passed by the states.

Unexpectedly, Wall Street reacted mostly favorably to the law, although it was clearly seen as an intrusion by the federal government into business. But the reputation of the Street had been hurt since the end of World War I by fast-talking securities salesmen selling worthless securities, just as land developers sold scrub pine land in Florida to unsuspecting investors. Much of the problem was laid at the feet of Charles Mitchell at National City Bank, who was among the most aggressive of the senior bankers in the securities business. Those activities were giving Wall Street a bad name. As George Bovenizer, a partner at Kuhn Loeb, lamented, "We have sat back for 12 years and watched the dragging down of the name of what has been called an investment banker because of some who should never have been in the business." Vividly illustrating the class divisions within the industry, he further stated that the policy at Kuhn Loeb "never employed a high pressure sales campaign to force securities on the people."[17] His remarks vividly illustrated the divisions on

Wall Street at the time. The older white shoe firms managed to
stay above the fray of getting their hands dirty selling securities
directly to the public. What he forgot to mention was that they
employed brokers to do that work for them.

Forcing securities on the public through faulty information
had become an art in the 1920s. At the hearings concerning the
proposed securities legislation, estimates were made that over
$25 billion of the $50 billion in new securities floated since 1920
were worthless. Of that amount, about $12 billion were foreign,
mostly bonds. The scandal caused by the many defaults, not to
mention the outright frauds, was too large to gloss over. It
required immediate attention since the stock and bond markets
had lost most of their integrity and future investment was certainly under a cloud. New capital issues had already dwindled to
a trickle, and the rise in unemployment was a consequence. If
the markets were not given a strong dose of medicine soon, the
Depression would be even more severe. Both Congress and Wall
Street understood this perfectly well. It was why the Securities
Act was passed before permanent banking legislation. In 1929,
over $9 billion in new corporate securities were sold in the
United States; by 1933 the amount dwindled to $380 million. A
significant rebound would not be seen until the mid-1940s.

Illustrating the simple relationship between new capital
issues and economic growth, a former senator and president of
a trust company, Howard Sutherland, remarked, "The national
blue-sky law will divert millions of dollars from the hands of
unscrupulous promoters into the channels of legitimate investment and will do as much to bring money out of hiding as the
establishment of the banks of the country on a sound basis."[18]
The basis for what would become known as the "safety net" was
beginning to appear and was recognized as such. The job of the
New Deal would be to restore faith in the financial system to
the millions of unsuspecting investors who had been fleeced or
victimized by bankers. Since no deposit insurance yet existed
and state blue-sky laws could easily be circumvented, the new

securities bill was crucial to restoring faith in the system, as was the Emergency Banking Act before it.

The new law was modeled on the British Companies Acts, which were considered to be more stringent than the version that passed Congress. The thrust of the law was simple and embodied in the slogan "Let the seller beware." The law called for all companies selling new securities to the public to file a registration statement outlining their financial position and stating the purposes for which the funds would be used. The statement was to be filed with the Federal Trade Commission since the Securities and Exchange Commission (SEC) was not yet founded. When the bill was first discussed, some in Congress wanted it extended to all securities existing, not just new ones. That idea was full of problems, however. Besides being an enormous undertaking, there were problems with the legality of the proposal. In the final version of the bill, disclosure was limited to new securities only or those already in the pipeline to be issued.

Some of the harsher language was toned down in an effort to compromise with Wall Street. The most significant compromise concerned the amount of liability that directors of companies filing disclosure statements were expected to make. After the act was passed, Adolph Berle, one of FDR's economic advisers and a professor at Columbia, commented that the language of the act had been toned down. "An analysis of the act indicates that it is conservative rather than extreme," he stated, "the protection it gives is minimum rather than maximum."[19] Although the language of the act held issuers of securities, their underwriters, and their accountants liable for false disclosure that might lead to investor losses in the future, there were mitigating circumstances that company directors could claim when confronted with charges of wrongdoing. One of these circumstances was the reliance on "experts" by company management and directors. The act required a company's directors to verify its financial reports, but if they deferred to experts then it was the experts' problem if misleading statements were made in the filing statement. And the experts could claim that they were acting with due diligence (best available information) when certifying a company's results, opening the door for dispute concerning who knew what about a company's financial statements and intents. As Berle noted, it was not the business of the government to pass on the quality of securities being issued, only to require full and honest information to be filed so that investors could judge for themselves. Although the explanation sounded plausible, it was clear that the conservative nature of the act and the discussion of directors' liabilities would reappear again in the future. The inevitability of the act was not seriously questioned, even by Wall Street. A well-known periodical remarked that "the intent of the act is admirable. In protecting the investor it may have placed an undue responsibility upon directors of new companies, but that directors of corporations have been permitted to take their obligations too lightly is beyond dispute."[20]

The act was drafted by Roosevelt advisers well-versed in securities laws. Felix Frankfurter, its main architect, was a professor at the Harvard Law School and an expert in administrative law. He was assisted by two younger colleagues, James Landis and Benjamin Cohen, both of whom later would become prominent in the New Deal. Landis provided a link with Brandeis, having served as his law clerk in the past. Despite their efforts, many experts believed that the new law was watered down and not tough enough. This was one reason why Wall Street appeared to support it. Frankfurter characterized it as a "modest first installment of legislative controls to assure commerce and industry a continuous flow of their necessary capital . . . strong insofar as publicity is potent; it is weak insofar as publicity is not enough."[21] His characterization was understated. The law was revolutionary since it finally came to grips with Wall Street for the first time. More importantly, it was only the first link in the safety net being constructed to restore integrity to the financial system. But the vagueness about due diligence and corporate reporting was still a back door left slightly ajar.

One of the prominent accounting firms at the time also recognized the problem. Putting the new law into perspective,
Arthur Andersen & Co. later stated,

> Under this act, a corporation issuing securities, its offi-
> cers and directors, the underwriters, and the experts who
> had expressed an opinion with respect to the fairness of the
> financial statements...could be held liable to make good
> any loss suffered by an investor who had purchased the
> securities in reliance upon the financial statements.[22]

But then it added its own interpretation of the law, based upon
the same looseness that Berle spotted years before. The firm
continued

> At this time, an important change occurred with respect
> to the concept of an accountant's responsibility for the
> financial statements which he certified...the new concept,
> which soon became universally recognized, was that the
> financial statements were the representations of the com-
> pany...under this concept, the company has the original
> responsibility for the fairness of the financial statements,
> but in signing his certificate with respect to those state-
> ments, the public accountant places his professional opin-
> ion on the line that the statements are fair and that they
> reflect accepted accounting principles.[23]

Who was liable for these potential problems was a potential
time bomb that the accounting firm would find worked to its
own destruction almost 70 years later.

After the Securities Act was passed, brokers began to take a
"wait-and-see" attitude, at least initially, making sure that every
bit of information was given to investors concerning investments.
But officials in Washington went to great lengths to explain that
the new law did not guarantee their investments, only provide
better information. Since the SEC was not founded yet, the job
of disclosure fell on the Federal Trade Commission, until the

following year. "The commission's only function," stated one of its members, "is to see that complete and accurate information concerning a security is made available to the public."[24] Investors were confused at the time, with some thinking that their investments would be fully guaranteed, but a drive began to ensure that they were properly informed. After the 1929 debacle and the defaults that followed, it was also clear that many of them were no longer interested in the markets.

Despite the language used about liabilities, Wall Street was still worried about the potential ramifications. A lawyer for the Investment Bankers' Association remarked, "The obligations which this act undertakes to impose upon underwriters are very great and it seems to me not unreasonable to expect that private bankers may hesitate to accept the hazards of these obligations...It may be doubted whether such dealers would be willing to pledge their individual fortunes to such an unknown liability."[25] Reservations were lost in the euphoria surrounding its passing, however. The bill passed Congress with almost no discussion. After the vote, Sam Rayburn, a Democratic congressman from Texas, commented that he did not know whether the bill passed so easily because "it was so damned good or so damned incomprehensible."[26] It made little difference, it was now the first securities law passed in the United States.

As the New Deal gained momentum, some of the Wild Jackasses began to sound more and more like Democrats and actively supported the principles of the New Deal. Roosevelt actively courted them although everyone recognized that their support came in degrees. And sometimes principles were confused with public issues. Smith Brookhart of Iowa still used strong moral arguments in criticizing segments of American society that he found wanting. One problem was Hollywood, which he accused of being immoral in its depictions of life and having a negative effect on the young. His argument practically extended to the spread of cinema chains around the country, part of the larger chain store argument still raging in the 1930s. But the moral point was too tempting to be ignored. His criticisms earned him one of *Vanity Fair*'s "Impossible Interviews," in which he and Marlene Dietrich, a reigning Hollywood queen, were "interviewed," complete with hypothetical dialogue provided by the magazine. This interview was published in a series, the others occurring between Stalin and John D. Rockefeller and Al Capone and Chief Justice Charles Evans Hughes. After his article appeared, Brookhart appeared somewhat nonplussed, asking his son who Marlene Dietrich was.[27]

McFadden Again

In 1931, a satirical book called the *Washington Merry-Go-Round* described the House of Representatives as the "greatest organized inferiority complex in the world." Soon, there would be at least one example that the assessment may not have been far from the mark. Not to be outdone by events in the Senate, Louis McFadden launched an attack on the Federal Reserve in May 1933. Instead of listing his usual charges of consorting with foreign bankers and central bankers, he mounted a broader attack and took the floor of the House to formally impeach the sitting members of the Fed along with some former members as well. At the top of his list for impeachment were Eugene Meyer, who left the Fed by the time charges were made, and Andrew Mellon, who as treasury secretary was an *ex officio* member. His charges were so broad, as they were against Hoover the previous year, that they were almost meaningless by the time he finished his summation. Dutifully, the House sent the charges to the Judiciary Committee. The impeachment motion was never heard from again, dying an obscure death as most members hoped it would.

Journalist Clinton Gilbert summed up the McFadden problem on a light note. "Those who have made a study of Tiny's various mental attacks during the last few years... trace his gall-tinctured idiosyncrasies to his experience in a primary campaign. His opponent was Mrs. Gifford Pinchot... he like some others who have come into contact with the flaming haired effervescing mate of the Governor of Pennsylvania, has never quite recovered his equilibrium."[28] McFadden's election battles were always difficult and having to do battle with Mrs. Pinchot, the wife of Pennsylvania governor Gifford Pinchot, was especially difficult since she was as prone to hyperbole and overstatement as he was. Washington was confused about McFadden's behavior, and no one had a plausible explanation for it. And he did not stop his increasingly vituperative attacks. The next round of slurs would gain him infamy and a House investigation into his activities.

His next attack again came in the House in May 1933, directed against FDR, Jews, and the American gold supply. The tirade was extreme, especially in light of his more measured argument in favor of gold just two years before. Claiming that the country was being held hostage by a group of Jews intent on running the world's finances, he blamed FDR for playing into their hands. He claimed that the Jews held gold reserves in their possession while the rest of the population held virtually worthless paper assets. Citing both the *Protocols of the Elders of Zion*, an anti-Semitic diatribe originating in czarist Russia via Great Britain 20 years before, and Henry Ford's *Dearborn Independent* articles of the early 1920s, he cited events in 1933 as proof that these earlier "prophecies" had indeed come to pass. Both claimed an international Jewish conspiracy designed to enslave the world. Cutting any ties he may have had with the New Deal with his bombast, he finished his speech by pleading with Congress, "Do not allow the great Democratic Party to steer it [the country] onto the rocks while the world waits for it to founder and go down so that the international salvage crews may set to work on the wreck of it."[29]

McFadden played on the conspiracy theory that had been a prominent part of Progressive thinking since the turn of the century. It had been employed before by those who believed that bankers caused panics for their own nefarious ends. His recent use of it took the theory to the end of the road by attributing the plot to Jews. When it was employed against bankers, it carried some appeal to those in the middle who could at least see some plausibility in it. But his extreme use of it showed the theory for what it really was—anti-Wall Street certainly, but anti-Semitic as well, assuming that Jews had their collective hands on the throttle of financial power. When generalized into criticisms of the New Deal, it still played well to those opposed to taxes and strong central government. "Under the New Deal," he was fond of saying, "you pay taxes you did not authorize for purposes you have not approved."[30] In the election held in November 1934, voters in his district disagreed and voted for a Democrat, ending his career in the House, in the same election that also sent Frederic Walcott home from Washington after only one Senate term.

McFadden's attacks against Jews in his speech were remembered long after he was gone from the House. Almost 70 years later, the *Jerusalem Post* marked the anniversary of his comments by noting that on that day years before, "Louis T. McFadden, congressman from Pennsylvania, attacks Jews in Congress, the first act of political anti-Semitism in the United States, 1933."[31] Coupled with attacks he made on the New Deal, he effectively read himself out of political life in 1934, although his constituents in his rural corner of Pennsylvania sent him to the general election after a primary the previous spring. But in his last term, he was generally ineffective, although he continued his rhetoric in Congress whenever he could. In his last year, the House Un-American Activities Committee began looking into his comments because he sent some of them to his constituents under the congressional franking privilege.

Separating Banking

The new federal securities law was generally well received by Wall Street, considering its historical importance and intrusion into the private realms of finance. Clearly, investment bankers thought that the worst was over after the bill passed, but there was more to come. The hucksters who sold worthless new securities to the public may now have been handcuffed somewhat, but the top investment bankers were on the minds of Congress and the New Dealers. When one mentioned the upper echelon, the foremost bank was clearly J.P. Morgan & Co., an empire that had been vilified and begrudgingly admired since the nineteenth century. The money trust had not been forgotten. Nor were the revelations of the Pujo committee 20 years before. The Pecora hearings added enough new material to the long litany of complaints against investment bankers to compel Congress to act decisively against their concentration of power.

Other problems remained among the banks. The strength of commercial banks had been a problem since the mid-1920s, when many began failing at an alarming rate. The soundness of the nationally chartered banks as compared with the state and private banks was striking. The majority of casualties were among state banks, which failed at a ratio of about 6 to 1 over national state banks and had a ratio of deposits of almost 4 to 1. Ironically, the businesses Louis McFadden wanted national banks to enter in the 1920s were the ones causing the failures of many state banks, mainly real estate and personal lending. The largest state bank failure came in 1930 when a bank in New York City, the Bank of United States, failed taking with it over $300 million of customers' deposits. The institution had 59 branches throughout the city and catered mostly to workers and recent immigrants. The bank was a fraud, used by its principals to lure immigrants' money into its vaults. The money was then used to buy the bank's stock, which reached historic highs before the Crash. Its senior directors also engaged in much fraudulent real estate lending, and the bank began to wobble. New York State banking officials and those from the Fed tried to work out a merger to save the institution, but the attempts failed. Finally, word leaked to the public, and a run on the bank began. One commentator described the scenes: "From all over the Bronx, the East Side, Brooklyn, and the upper West Side, people rushed frantically to get their money. Wild-eyed with wonderment and bewilderment, they stood in long lines and worried or pushed... armored trucks brought more money, but the demand was greater than the supply."[32]

After police and troops were called in to restore order, the bank was placed in receivership. Depositors eventually recovered some of their funds from a settlement. But the allure of using other people's money to dabble in real estate and the stock market had become painfully obvious.

Ironically, on the same day the bank failed, two members of the financial oligarchy joined in a merger when Brown Brothers, a private bank in New York City, announced merger plans with Harriman banking interests to form Brown Brothers Harriman. It was the last example of two old banking houses attempting to merge before the Glass-Steagall Act was passed. The contrast between the two was striking. A workingman's bank had failed, the largest failure of its type in American history, but two old private banks were announcing a merger to consolidate their capital and seek new lines of business as the country slid into the Depression.

Morgan Testifies

Meanwhile, the Senate hearings continued in Washington. Jack Morgan appeared before the Pecora committee in May 1933. The appearance was well publicized and much anticipated. While his father appeared nervous before the Pujo committee 20 years before, Jack Morgan displayed no signs of being ill at ease. He was accompanied by his lawyer, John Davis, a former Democratic presidential candidate and a former ambassador to Britain. Most of the committee's questions centered on the exact nature of the bank partnership and its taxes, something that Morgan did not want to disclose. The number of corporate board seats held by the partners also was discussed, much as it had been during the Pujo hearings. The hearings were cordial for the most part, although it was clear that Morgan was not voluntarily giving away any information unless pressed to do so. He indicated that he was more than willing to answer questions concerning banking, but that information about him, his partners, and their arrangements was considered personal. But that was a difficult point to make considering that his bank and its affiliate Drexel & Co. of Philadelphia held more than $250 million in deposits and was the most influential banking organization in the country. Morgan noted that since his was a private banking organization, he believed the committee did not have the authority to pry into its affairs. Pecora quickly dispelled that notion.

The most revealing testimony from the House of Morgan had to do with what were known as "preferred lists." During the 1920s bull market, Morgan and other well-known investment banks offered new issues of stock to preferred customers and friends at the new issue price, which was often much cheaper than the current market price. Many of these new issues were investment funds, similar to mutual funds, established by the Wall Street firms. They would buy shares of other investment funds or stocks, which the investment banks had previously underwritten, helping to create a pyramid of interests. Paper empires of this sort were not uncommon in the 1920s. The Chicago utilities empire of Samuel Insull was another example of a paper pyramid that would not survive the Crash and Depression, but the investment fund pyramids were constructed solely to have one company hold securities of another. The collapse of the Insull utilities empire was a major headline for much of the early 1930s along with the Pecora/Fletcher hearings.

Samuel Insull was Thomas Edison's former assistant in the Edison Electric Company before it was sold to Morgan interests. Insull later removed himself to Chicago, where he created enormous utilities holding companies, including the Commonwealth Edison Company and Middle West Utilities. Constantly fighting off outside pressure from an early corporate raider named Cyrus Eaton, Insull constantly leveraged his companies with borrowed money in order to retain control. The heavy borrowing eventually cost him dearly.

One of the final loans Insull contracted was with a consortium of New York banks, which took his stock as collateral. As the market continued to slide, the value of the stock decreased as well, prompting the bankers to ask for more cash to top up the value of the collateral. There was also strong suspicion that many brokers on the floor of the NYSE began selling the stock short at

Morgan's behest in order to achieve precisely that effect. When Insull could no longer provide further collateral, the empire collapsed and was reorganized by the consortium. The accounting firm that aided in the reorganization was Arthur Andersen & Co., which clearly stated that it was not involved with the construction of the Insull empire, only fixing it.

The paper empires were impressive on the surface but were built on a foundation of other funds or stocks. If there was a serious loss in the pyramid, the whole structure was capable of collapsing quickly. After 1929, many of them did, leaving once proud and reputable investment houses with a serious mark on their reputations. But as the hearings demonstrated, the losses were almost all among investors. The investment banks organized and sold funds and stocks to others, never to themselves. When someone on the preferred lists was allowed to buy the stocks of the highly leveraged companies, it was clear that they should monitor their investment carefully lest it deteriorate quickly.

The immediate reaction to the lists released by Pecora ranged from anger to incredulity to simple disappointment. The *New York Times* was in this latter category. Reflecting the absence of securities laws at the time, it concluded: "The favors which [Morgan] it passed out to friends and customers had no taint of illegality. Things of that kind have been done for years by many brokerage houses and promoting syndicates...here was a firm of bankers...practicing the small arts of petty traders."[33] However, it was clear that practice was considered below the dignity of an institution that held itself above the fray on Wall Street. Even the venerable House of Morgan was behaving like a stock huckster when it should have been leading Wall Street.

There was some evidence that the preferred lists actually were secret operations of the banks involved. Morgan partner Arthur Anderson told the bank's lawyers, "It probably is unnecessary for me to add that I hope you will not make any mention of this operation."[34] J.P. Morgan & Co. was not alone in the practice. Other notable investment banks like Dillon Read and Goldman Sachs were also handing out cheap stock to cronies. Since the revelations came during the worst years of the Depression, the image of self-aggrandizing bankers was even more vivid than usual. The bankers also realized their plight and tried to burnish their image as much as possible. Clarence Dillon, the principal behind Dillon Read & Co., appeared before the Pecora committee with Ivy Lee, the well-known public relations man who had once advised John D. Rockefeller.

One of the problems underlined by the lists was that of confidence in public officials. One beneficiary of Morgan largess was William Woodin, an industrialist who also sat on the advisory board of the Federal Reserve. A Morgan partner offered him 1,000 shares of the Alleghany Corporation, the brainchild of the Van Sweringen Brothers of Cleveland and aided by Morgan, at $20 rather than the market price, which was already above $30. In the absence of any specific laws forbidding the practice, he gladly accepted the bargain. Calvin Coolidge also was offered bargain-priced stock along with General Black Jack Pershing of World War I fame and former senator George Pepper of Pennsylvania. Sentiment at the time held that these public figures should not have been accepting gifts ensuring immediate profits while the country was mired in the Depression. Still, there were no clear conflicts of interest, but the door was left open, especially to the conspiracy theorists believing that this was payback for unnamed past favors. Other critics, like Fiorello La Guardia, saw the revelations as an opportunity to impose new standards of conduct on public officials to force them to live within their means. Will Rogers, never at a loss for words concerning the scandals, commented that those who held the preferred gifts rather than sell them probably were not so smart after all.

Glass–Steagall

Banking legislation designed to reform the banking system was being debated in Congress. The emergency legislation of March was not the end but only the beginning of a revolution for banks. The separate banking hearings being held in Congress prompted

Samuel Untermyer to recall his warning to the country at the time of the money trust hearings 20 years before. He noted that Pecora personally was being treated as harshly as he was then but remained convinced that the recent counsel would remain above the fray and the attacks upon him. Remaining confident that legislation would be passed limiting the actions of the NYSE, he also turned his attention to the securities affiliates of banks, which he blamed for much of the country's economic plight: "After twenty-one years during which inconceivable havoc was created by these unlawful affiliates, the Glass Bill, which I hope is about to be enacted, at least severs these affiliates from the banks. It is about to lock the stable door after the horse has escaped and to do what should have been done two decades ago."[35] Separating the securities activities of banks from their usual banking business was a priority since so many of the worthless securities had come from these affiliated companies.

Untermyer's wish came true on June 13 when the Glass bill, also known as the Glass-Steagall Act, passed both houses of Congress swiftly. The House vote was 191–6 in favor. Louis McFadden was one of the few dissenters. The Senate passed it by a voice vote, without record. At the time, the most controversial part of the Glass-Steagall Act was not the separation of investment banking from commercial banking but the introduction of deposit insurance. In order to shore up the banking system, the bill created insurance on accounts in a clear attempt to win back the confidence of depositors. Although deposit insurance had been used in some states before, it was nevertheless controversial because some critics maintained that it smacked of socialism. It was as important politically as it was financially since the vast majority of deposits in national banks were small, less than $2,500.[36] The president of the American Bankers' Association called the deposit insurance provision "a drift toward Socialistic theories and government control of, and the interference in, business will affect our whole course." Not all bankers agreed, however. The president of the state bankers' association said the act marked "the greatest revolution in banking since the passage of the Federal Reserve Act and perhaps the greatest in the history of bank legislation."[37] His position clearly reflected state bankers' relief that the national banks had been constrained from expanding by the new law.

Roosevelt was very pleased with the new banking act and commended Carter Glass for his efforts in drafting it. Other politicians followed suit. Frederic Walcott stated that it was a rare privilege to work with Glass on the bill, while congressmen claimed that Steagall's name should be enshrined prominently for posterity. Glass was less pleased. The deposit insurance provision was the only part that he approved, but the act passed easily when he and his Senate colleagues realized that there was no way that they could oppose it, since it proved so popular in the House of Representatives. Throughout the country, newspapers focused almost entirely on the deposit insurance side of the law. The *Helena Daily Independent* marked the occasion of the bill's passing by also anticipating the repeal of Prohibition, which finally occurred in December, by stating, "Missoula is now going to furnish the keg beer so all we have to have is the ice and picnic ground."[38] But Wall Street and the banking community were slow to appreciate the provisions of the act, adopting a wait-and-see attitude. Washington pressed ahead with a rigorous interpretation.

Not all parts of the new law were engraved in stone. After the bill was passed by both houses, Adolph Berle still maintained that bankers should have only one responsibility—banking. All other sidelines and part-time jobs should be banned because bankers worked as a public trust and conflicts of interest were natural. "A banker has to be a banker," he told the New York State Bankers' Association, "He cannot be safely or honorably anything else at the same time. In New York not so long ago a vice presidency in a first-rate bank was quoted at so much for salary and five times the salary for perquisites on the side."[39]

Forced to Choose

The Glass-Steagall Act defined banking for the rest of the century. It listed the activities in which bankers could legitimately engage. Investment banking was no longer one of them. When the law was first announced, many commentators passed over this provision as secondary. It stated that commercial bankers could not be "engaged principally" in corporate securities underwriting or trading. Exactly what "principally" meant was the source of some confusion, but the implication was clear. National banks had to divest of their securities affiliates, and the private bankers, like Morgan and Brown Brothers, had a year to divest of either their investment or deposit business. Bankers had to decide what was going to be their principal activity. Most of the private bankers chose investment banking. J.P. Morgan & Co., on the other hand, chose commercial banking, probably under the assumption that the entire issue would fade from view shortly. The bank created Morgan Stanley & Co. to continue its investment banking tradition. The new investment bank had its headquarters next to the Morgan headquarters at the corner of Broad and Wall Streets, and its preferred shareholders were all Morgan partners. The assumption proved incorrect, however, as the bank would discover over the next several years.

The relationship between banks and their securities subsidiaries was more than a simple conflict of interest. It was, as the Senate committee described it, "A prolific source of evil . . . these affiliates have been employed as instrumentalities by commercial banks to speculate in their own stock, to participate in market operations designed to manipulate the price of securities, and to conduct other operations in which commercial banks are forbidden by law to engage."[40] The affiliates were clearly being used to circumvent existing law and were also used as references by many commercial banks. Bank customers asking for investment advice were referred to the affiliates and then sold inappropriate securities by salesmen they thought they could trust as much as their commercial banker. The element of trust between banker and customer had been broken. Many bank customers testified before the committee about being fleeced by salesmen who assured them that the securities they purchased were of good quality, when many in fact were those of companies near bankruptcy.

Within a year of the Glass-Steagall Act being passed, a new wall of separation had been erected on Wall Street. Commercial bankers took deposits and made loans, while investment bankers dealt in corporate securities. But there was a flaw in the banking act that was similar to the Securities Act. While the Securities Act was fuzzy on corporate directors' liabilities for misleading registration statements, Glass-Steagall was fuzzy on what was meant by "engaged principally." The Fletcher/Pecora committee recognized this problem between the intent of the act and its language. It stated that "The banking Act of 1933 is an expression of the legislative policy of complete divorcement of commercial banking from investment banking." But it also noted that "further legislation may be required to completely effectuate this policy."[41] Sixty years later, these semantic oddities would again come to light in unimagined ways.

The distinction between investment and commercial banker previously was very clear in some cases, while not so clear in others. The private bankers were the best example of the latter. Money trust firms like Morgan and Kuhn Loeb, along with other relative newcomers like Dillon Read, accepted deposits, made loans, and underwrote securities. Others, like Lehman Brothers and Goldman Sachs, were more involved in the securities side of the business. Still others, like National City Bank, participated in the investment banking side through subsidiary companies so that the bank itself could claim not to be in violation of the old banking act passed during the Civil War. Regardless of their pre-1934 profiles, they now found themselves in the uncomfortable position of having to give up a lucrative part of their business. Since most of the Wall Street investment banks were partnerships, the choice was particularly difficult since the partners' funds were at risk in whatever side of the business they chose. Yet for the most part, those firms predominantly in securities remained in that business, while the banks chose commercial banking. The one odd choice was Morgan, which chose commercial banking. If many of them had known that more securities regulation was on the way, they indeed may have chosen commercial banking because banking laws tended to protect banks with a panoply of regulations. Securities laws tended to restrict investment banks and securities dealers on a more adversarial basis.

Fallout

The hearings also had two unintended casualties. First, Ferdinand Pecora ran for district attorney of New York County in the November 1933 election. He assured the Senate committee that his work would continue as long as necessary, regardless of the outcome. In the wake of the two new laws, interest in the market scandals may have waned temporarily because he lost his bid for the seat.

Second, the preferred lists put one Hollywood studio in an embarrassing position. The RKO studio had a script waiting for production entitled *The Preferred List*, based upon Morgan and the Senate investigation. It was described as a Gilbert and Sullivan–style comedy, and it was regarded as one of the funnier plays to come to Hollywood in some time; the problem was with its financiers. The studio had been in the hands of Wall Street financiers for years. Charles Merrill, Joseph P. Kennedy, and Otto Kahn, among others, all were involved with it at one time. The film would have been timely and had a huge potential audience, but it could not overcome the potential embarrassment for its financiers. Despite its potential, it was never made.

After the securities and banking acts were passed, and in the wake of the revelations of the Pecora hearings, Wall Street's reputation and standing sank to an all-time low. In some quarters, financiers and bankers were viewed as little better than organized crime. For example, a Montana newspaper in Burton Wheeler's constituency remarked: "Shocked as we are by the crimes of underworld gangs and their allies higher in the social scale, they are but the natural product of the times which produced preferred lists of stock purchasers...the moral fabric of the American people has been determined by economic sappers...there is no place in American society for gangsters, whether they work with a sub-machine gun or a rigged market."[42]

A patriotic organization called the United States Flag Association organized a national conference on crime. Its board of directors was a star-studded group including Chief Justice Charles E. Hughes and Al Smith. One of the topics it discussed was the racketeer in business, which naturally looked mainly toward the stock market. Naturally, Wall Street refused to recognize the criticism and remained characteristically aloof, a position that would cost it dearly in the year ahead.

Despite the new laws, continued revelations before the Fletcher/Pecora committee led many to believe that even more regulation of the markets was necessary. After the Glass-Steagall Act was passed, more information about pools and investment bankers' compensation came to light that clearly disturbed members of the committee. Duncan Fletcher remarked that "the present Federal Securities Act, to a certain extent, will accomplish [its] purpose, but it is only reasonable to assume that, during the course of these hearings scheduled for the future, there will be additional developments and these will enable the Congress to determine whether or not the present Securities Act is sufficient."[43] Fletcher sounded almost prescient, because it was only a matter of weeks before the next scandalous bit of information surfaced.

In October 1933, the committee interrogated the former president of the Chase National Bank, Albert Wiggin. Reports about his activities before and after the Crash made him a more valuable witness than even Charles Mitchell of National City Bank. Investigators focused on him because of his unbanker-like activities. The first topic of interest to the committee was his compensation. He had received a salary of $100,000 per year for life after he resigned his position in mid-1933. In the years preceding his departure, he had received over $1 million in salary since 1928 and a $275,000 bonus during a time in which the bank was losing money. Under questioning by Pecora, Wiggin acknowledged that his compensation was fixed by his colleagues and that he helped determine theirs in return. Furthermore, Wiggin sat on 59 outside boards and that each had received a loan from Chase. Each loan proved to be a loss for the bank. By the time Wiggin testified, the practice had already been out-lawed—the Glass-Steagall Act prohibited banks from loaning money to their officers.

Wiggin and his family also were involved in pools that traded Chase stock in the previous five years. Pools were private amounts of investment funds, usually entrusted to a floor trader on the NYSE, who would trade them, both long and short, in an attempt to make a profit. Wiggin offered a unique justification of pool-ing—to protect the bank's stock. Chase voluntarily was delisted from the NYSE in 1928 and subsequently traded in the over-the-counter market, which was much less formal and had fewer reg-ulations than the NYSE. Wiggin claimed that was done to protect against violent fluctuations in the stock price. The claim was something of a stretch since the stock had declined from a 1929 high of $1,325 per share to $88 in 1933. Under close question-ing from Pecora and Couzens, Wiggin maintained that the price was more stable in 1933 because it was not listed. Then in a clas-sic exchange, the discussion became semantic. After being asked whether he believed in speculation in bank stocks, Wiggin replied, "First I should like to know what speculation is." To which Pecora replied, "That seems to be a term that nobody in Wall Street is quite able to define." Wiggin then answered, "An investment that is unsuccessful is usually called a speculation." Pecora responded somewhat incredulously, "Have you heard of persons operating in the stock market for speculative purposes right at the outset?" Wiggin admitted that he had.[44]

Further testimony showed that executives of the bank traded the stock with some regularity, and employees were encouraged to buy its stock but without the same price protections afforded executives. The bank's securities subsidiary also was a regular trader of its stock, an activity that would not be tolerated under the new Glass-Steagall Act because of the separation of powers. Committee investigations showed that dozens of accounts were established by the bank at other securities dealers and that all had been used to speculate in the stock. Since the stock declined precipitously, any trading loss was charged to the subsidiary, having a negative effect on the bank's earnings and capital. More damning, however, was the finding that Wiggin sold the stock of Chase short in order to profit on the way down. He claimed that he did it to stabilize the stock, which had risen too high in the market. Revelations of that sort only confirmed what the Progressives feared three years before: that a massive bear raid was being conducted to force down prices. But this shorting did not come from foreigners. It was much closer to home—at the bank's corporate headquarters in this case.

Wiggin and Chase were not alone in the practice. Other prominent New York banks, including National City, were mentioned in the report about the pools, and Wiggin and Charles Mitchell were also on Morgan's preferred lists. Wiggin's successor at Chase, Winthrop Aldrich, disagreed with the practices of his predecessor and became a vocal champion of stock exchange and banking reform. He was one of the few senior bankers on Wall Street actually favoring the separation of commercial and investment banking. In lengthy testimony before the committee, he recognized the concerns that had been voiced since the Pujo committee 20 years before. His support of the divorce left Wall Street "gasping," according to one Midwest newspaper. When Aldrich took the witness stand after Wiggin's testimony, he sought to quickly separate himself and the bank from its former president. After the hearings concluded, Pecora noted that Chase, "this great standard bearer, behind its imposing façade of unassailable might and rectitude, was not a whit better than the National City Bank itself. The earlier examination of the latter institution had certainly proved a shocking disclosure of low standards in high places."[45]

Seeds of the NASD

Critics of the New Deal were not entirely discouraged by events during the summer of 1933. Although the new securities and banking acts had Wall Street rocking on its heels, other developments gave it some hope that the new rays of sunlight cast on financial practices had some sunblock, despite the revelations. The Roosevelt administration attributed some of the economic problems of the Depression to excessive competition in industry, which was having a ruinous effect on society. During the 1920s, that competition had led to overcapacity in many industries. Following the Crash, the downturn in consumer demand caused inventories to shrink in the early 1930s, in turn causing unemployment to rise exponentially. The Hoovervilles were seen as a product of the intense social Darwinism that characterized American business for years. The administration reckoned that if industry could act in a concerted way rather than in the predatory fashion for which it was famous, then economic recovery could be achieved.

In June 1933, Congress created a new federal agency, the National Recovery Administration, through the National Industrial Recovery Act of 1933 (NIRA). The agency was designed to reduce the intense and destructive competition between American businesses and replace it with a consensual self-government of business and industry. As part of the program, the Roosevelt administration suspended the antitrust laws for two years and authorized industry to form government-recognized trade organizations, which would reduce internecine competition, devise codes of competition, and dictate fair labor practices. Over 500 codes were drawn up, although many did not pan out. One positive byproduct of the codes was the elimination of child labor. More important for Wall Street, a new organization was created by the securities industry under the guidelines. The main industry association for securities dealers was the Investment Bankers Association (IBA), founded at the time of the Pujo hearings. Following the guidelines of the new law, the existing dealers began to organize into an industry group that would extend its reach beyond that of the IBA. It was known as the Investment Bankers Conference and was separate from the older group. Within several years, the group would be transformed into the National Association of Securities Dealers (NASD), destined to become the largest securities association in the country.

Looking the other way as far as the antitrust laws were concerned gave Wall Street some heart. The problem was that deteriorating economic conditions effectively put a damper on new deals since investor interest had evaporated since late 1929. But even in 1933, Wall Street was not convinced that the country was in the midst of a severe depression. As far as it was concerned, the new laws were the problem.

Underwriting of new securities, always a risk for the investment banks involved, was still a sore point. A spokesman for the IBA noted: "Under the new Glass Banking Act banks may no longer act as underwriters or distributors of such securities, and the question is still: How could the general business of the country procure the necessary investment funds from the public? This question awaits an answer under this act."[46] As far as the IBA was concerned, removing the large commercial banks from the underwriting equation meant that there was not enough capital among the smaller securities dealers to support corporate America. Perhaps the new codes from the NIRA would help settle the problem. The ambiguity gave Wall Street some heart.

By late 1933, there was a general feeling that most securities losses were attributable to fraud on the part of bankers who had sold them to the public. Revelations from the Pecora/Fletcher hearings had confirmed the general suspicion, and the passing of the new laws seemed to confirm the fact. Wall Street naturally tried to defend itself from the allegations by putting the blame squarely on the laws that were passed to prevent more fraud in the future. But the punch/counterpunch strategy did not create any sympathy for Wall Street. The arguments sounded somewhat disingenuous. The president of the IBA told a group of state security commissioners: "It is equally evident to those in intimate contact with prospective issuers [of securities] that the unusual liabilities of the law constitute hazards which officers and directors of corporations decline to assume."[47] But extending the argument a bit further showed the futility of the argument. Accountants would not accept the liability either nor would the other "experts" the law mentioned, such as investment bankers or engineers. No one wanted to assume a financial liability for a company's potential lies that could lead to investor loss. Clearly, more accommodation was needed if the new issues market was to resume its job of raising corporate capital when the economy finally resurrected itself.

While the Progressives' influence could be felt in the hearings and the new laws being passed, they had one more distinct triumph during the first days of the New Deal. For the previous 10 years, there had been much fuss about a dam on the Tennessee River at Muscle Shoals, Alabama. A large government project begun during World War I to provide nitrate and electric power had been discontinued, and the facility sat idle. An attempt by Henry Ford to buy the facility from the government at a substantial discount had been rejected. At issue was the matter of supplying cheap electric power to rural parts of the South that were in serious need of economic development. The reputation of big business was partly to blame for Ford's unsuccessful bid. Private enterprise could not be relied upon to provide serious infrastructure improvements without exacting a heavy toll in return.

The battle over Muscle Shoals was a classic confrontation between Progressive and reactionary forces, which portrayed it as an example of a great public works project versus a socialist nightmare designed to destroy the free enterprise system. George Norris led the charge for it in the Senate at the behest of Franklin Roosevelt, and the bill finally passed in May 1933. The Tennessee Valley Authority was created and owned by the government, and the hope was that it would provide electric power at cheaper rates than those provided by private utilities companies around the country. The legislative victory was the greatest of Norris's career and provided at least one instance of the Progressives' siding effectively with the New Deal to effect social change.

Reaction

As the Fletcher/Pecora hearings resumed in the fall of 1933, more revelations concerning investment banker behavior made headline news. At the same time, news leaked that federal regulation of the stock markets was imminent but probably would have to wait for the next congressional session to be enacted. The committee was studying the behavior of several investment banks during the heyday of the bull market, especially that of Dillon Read. After Pecora's loss in the election, the committee did continue and began investigating the financing of many motion picture companies and their cinema chains. Some of the companies had been borrowing money from the banks and using the funds to pay dividends, when they were actually losing money. The direction of the inquiry had moved from stock market practices to the more esoteric world of corporate finance, which did not have the same newsworthy qualities as the revelations about traders' behavior and investor losses. Nevertheless, the revelations showed a close relationship between bankers and their corporate customers that cut across traditional lines, suggesting improper behavior on the part of both. But improper in 1933 was not necessarily illegal.

The close questioning of some bankers brought a reaction from others. Winthrop Aldrich succeeded Albert Wiggin as the president of Chase National Bank after the revelations about Wiggin's behavior in previous years. The son of Senator Nelson Aldrich, a former senator from Rhode Island, and a force behind the original Federal Reserve Act, Aldrich was an advocate of stock market reform and had publicly supported many reform measures. But in the committee session after Thanksgiving in 1933, he was sternly rebuked by Couzens for interrupting the interrogation of a Chase official concerning the ties between Chase and a cinema company. Aldrich had been critical of investment banking and brokerage in the past but was less critical of commercial banking, his bank's main business. A week after being rebuked by Couzens, he testified before the committee and criticized the Glass-Steagall Act and the Securities Act. Like many other commercial bankers, he had problems with the deposit insurance provision, echoing a criticism that would be repeated thousands of times over the course of the following decades. Guaranteeing deposits "puts a premium on bad banking," he stated, and "is very dangerous from every point of view."[48] By "bad banking" he meant the tendency of bankers to take guaranteed deposits and then make potentially bad loans, realizing that the insurance eventually would bail them out of poor decisions. The criticism had been heard many times before, but it was no coincidence that it was also accompanied by extra costs to bankers, who had to pay a small premium to the Federal Deposit Insurance Corporation for every insured deposit they took from the public. To the committee, one of Wall Street's supporters of reform was only justifying the status quo.

Aldrich's position on the new Securities Act was similar. He reiterated Wall Street fears that the potential liabilities imposed by the law were having a chilling effect on the capital markets for new issues, which had diminished to a trickle. Many underwriters refused to subscribe to new issues under the ambiguities of the new law and attributed the lack of new issues to government interference. "What excites anxiety are some of the civil liabilities imposed upon issuers and underwriters of securities, as well upon the directors and officers of corporations," he remarked, also echoing statements uttered many times since the law passed earlier in the year.[49] But the separation of commercial and investment banking was still supported, perhaps only as a matter of practicality.

Aldrich appeared to be the last person who would have supported the divorce. His father, Nelson, a Republican from Rhode Island, helped call the secret meetings on Jekyll Island, Georgia, that eventually led to the formation of the Federal Reserve. While he was a moving force behind the meetings, he retired from the Senate in 1911 before the Fed was formed and during his lifetime had shown more support for the Morgan style of banking than separating the two functions, the position adopted by his son. He was integrally involved in banking and politics since childhood, having come from an old American family. He also happened to be the brother-in-law of John D. Rockefeller Jr. The connection would serve his son well in later years. A book reviewer for the *New York Times*, reviewing a chatty social portrait of the Stillmans of National City Bank, remarked, "Today we see Winthrop Aldrich, son of the Senator Nelson Aldrich, who believed in the old Morgan conception of banking lining up with Justice Brandeis in the matter of separating investment and commercial banking. Time indeed has its little jokes." But Nelson was also considered a rock in politics and finance, not to be moved by fashions of the day. One commentator remarked, "He was not baited by the sons of the Wild Jackasses or forward looking men. There was nothing of the rough-and-tumble politician about Senator Aldrich."[50]

Winthrop Aldrich took the helm of the Chase National in 1930 after it was acquired by Rockefeller family interests. Wiggin remained with the bank until forced out. A lawyer by training, Aldrich represented the old money contingent of American society. But he was able to successfully read the trend toward regulation. Chase divested its securities affiliate and returned to a solid if unspectacular banking business. Although possessing a lawyer's penchant for caution, Aldrich was well suited to lead the financial community at a time when it desperately needed leadership. His family wealth and background positioned him to lead at a time when someone of high visibility was needed. Journalist Clinton Gilbert, a keen observer of financial affairs, wrote, "The American propensity to genuflect before great wealth and to accept its dictates as dogma, may in time, as the result of Mr. Aldrich's leadership, compel other bankers and so-called captains of industry to give up the glorified, if veneered, ways of the underworld."[51] This was something that Carter Glass or the Sons of the Wild Jackass could not accomplish. They simply were not rich, although they were well intentioned. Ironically, meaningful reform would often be led by the wealthy.

Although it is questionable whether Wall Street supported the New Deal measures to regulate banking and the securities business, it is clear that some of its leaders were more farsighted than others and recognized the writing on the wall. But it was clear that the country was in no mood for any more revelations about banker shenanigans. An Ohio newspaper reported that 34 percent of the people living in South Dakota were on the public dole, while 27 percent were in New Mexico. Similar figures could be found in Arizona and Florida. One point had become clear very quickly. Reform was not ephemeral, and it was to become a permanent fixture in the markets. The argument that the cure was worse than the disease still prevailed on Wall Street, although an even more severe test was coming for investment banking and the economy. When the Glass-Steagall Act was combined with the new Securities Act, Wall Street had been effectively curtailed. In a short space of less than two years, more meaningful reform had been introduced and passed than at any other time in American financial history. And there was still more to come.

CHAPTER 3

CONTINUING THE ASSAULT

*Unemployment was caused by J.P. Morgan and Co., which seeks
to control the world.*

Louis T. McFadden

In the early months of 1934, Wall Street began to realize that
reformers were not finished tampering with the markets.
The Pecora/Fletcher hearings continued and the press continued its assault, never allowing financial irregularities to fade
from the headlines. Many investment bankers thought that the
reforms would stop and that they could return to business as
normal. The New Dealers and Progressives still had enough fire-
power left to complete the job they began in 1933, helping to
shape American society for the rest of the century. But the
reforms were not entirely the work of Progressives and middle-
class legislators. Several wealthy men would also aid in the effort,
helping prove that wealth could be on the side of the average
man in the street.

The Pecora hearings also demonstrated that a new histri-
onic was entering American politics—what the *New York Times*
dubbed the "inquisition drama." Congressional hearings had
taken on a whole new dimension by adding an element of show
business to the usual dull, technical proceedings. Galleries were
opened wide, and the press was kept informed of the proceedings while cigars and cigarettes were distributed to the gallery

and witnesses alike. The influence of Hollywood, itself the center of congressional investigation, had finally come to Washington. Pictures taken of witnesses conferring with their interrogators were common. Jack Morgan even suffered the indignity of having a midget sit on his lap at the hearings in a clear attempt to embarrass him (he took it well, proving unflappable). The newspaper concluded, "Congress gets away with it, of course, because the lofty and the mighty, since the Depression, have been neither lofty or mighty. They are either stubbornly on the defensive or unabashedly on the run."[1] Businessmen one day were at work. The next day they could find themselves in the unaccustomed spotlight, answering questions from legislators who knew a lot less about their businesses than they did about politics.

A substantial amount of testimony had been taken at the hearings since the Securities and Banking Acts were passed in 1933. A great deal of it had to do with the behavior of floor traders on the stock exchanges, something neither act could regulate. In addition to the preferred lists kept by the major investment banks, there were also revelations about pools operating on the exchange floors that would clearly manipulate the prices of stocks to their own advantage. The exchanges permitted the pools, claiming they were integral to doing usual business. Ordinary investors disagreed. Why should the wealthy have privileges that the rest of the investing public did not? In order to correct these problems, it became clear that the exchanges themselves would have to be regulated. Wall Street was annoyed by the Securities Act in 1933, but it would be livid when a complementary piece of legislation was introduced a year later.

More Regulation

The longer investigators kept digging at Wall Street and banking practices, the more dirt they seemed to uncover. After 1933, it was clear that the money trust needed to be dismantled and the 1933 laws did not complete the job. The Glass-Steagall Act proved to be a very effective piece of antitrust legislation, although it appeared on the surface as only a banking act. Morgan and his colleagues were prohibited from practicing old-style banking, but their influence was still felt in other areas not covered by existing reform legislation.

For example, the giant utilities holding companies they formed in the 1920s were still a sore point with the New Deal because of the vast amount of electric power generation provided by only a handful of power companies. After the fall of Samuel Insull's Midwest power empire, New York bankers held extensive control over 50 percent of the country's power generation capabilities. Empowered by the creation of the TVA in 1933, reformers had the utilities industry in their sights in early 1934 and would not be satisfied until legislation had been passed to regulate it in a fashion similar to the securities industry. And James Landis, one of the drafters of the Securities Act, had a meeting with President Roosevelt to request permission to draft stock exchange regulations. The tide was turning against the NYSE and the giant power companies, and Roosevelt recognized that conciliation between the two factions would not succeed and that he would have to side with the reformers.[2]

Although Louis McFadden was gone from the House of Representatives, he was heartened by banking legislation passed to further regulate the Federal Reserve. As the role of the Fed in the Crash of 1929 became more clear, structural defects had to be corrected if it were to be an effective monitor of the banking system. It needed more effective central banking powers than it possessed in the early days of the Depression since it was not a full-fledged central bank, at least in the European sense of the word. Its ability to intervene in the market bubble had been seriously compromised by the New York Fed Bank, which counteracted the system's desire to raise interest rates by flooding the market with additional call money in early 1929. The new funds kept interest rates low and fueled the boom even more, effectively dashing any hopes that government intervention could prevent the inevitable bust from occurring. It was that inability that well-known speculators and investment bankers recognized in 1929, prompting them to withdraw from the market before the Crash.

Despite all of the fast-moving events in finance, financial news still had to compete with Depression news from other parts of the country as economic conditions worsened. Unemployment continued to rise, conditions on the farms worsened, and a whiff of revolution was in the air. The poor blamed the rich and well-born for their troubles, while the conservatives began accusing the Roosevelt administration of socialist leanings as government intervention in the institutions of the economy became the norm. Populists and demagogues were out in force, while conservatives began to react to what they saw as encroachments on their way of life and way of doing business. Special interest groups appeared, challenging perceived injustices, but sometimes showed their true faces very quickly. When the American Liberty League was formed to oppose the New Deal, a quick check of its genealogy revealed that its powerful forces had combined to repeal not only the New Deal but also Prohibition, that old Progressive favorite. It was successful in the latter, but not the former. In addition to transparency in financial affairs, a new transparency was becoming evident in public affairs as well. More hard questions were being asked about special interest groups and their effect upon society and the average citizen.

As society became more attentive to problems within its economic institutions, the role of the Wild Jackasses began to diminish. Those who retained their seats in Congress after the early 1930s usually aligned with the New Deal, which was more in keeping with their Progressive principles than the Republican party. Others faded from view, their legacy to be determined at some later date. By the late 1930s, the term Wild Jackass had been relegated to the historical dustbin and many of the senators forgotten. Some of the ideas they favored did live on, however, becoming institutionalized in concepts that became part of new law that would live for decades until the deregulatory trend of the 1990s.

When banking and securities dealings were formally separated, new regulatory authority was needed to control Wall
Street. In the past, the problem was that banking authorities
had only a tenuous hold over the securities side of banking and
were ineffective in the face of an aggressive bank that wanted
to expanded further into stocks and bonds. The activities of
National City Company and the Chase National Bank and its
subsidiaries proved that Wall Street practices evaded the Fed
and state banking authorities. Once the securities dealers realized that they were basically independent agents, abuses began
to mount, as the Pecora committee amply demonstrated. The
only problem was that the abuses were recognized after the fact
and a regulator was needed with a new, more stringent set of rules
to help prevent fraud and abuse. The Fed was not in the position to assume regulation of Wall Street and the FTC, the regulator of the Securities Act of 1933, was not dedicated to handling
securities problems.

Politically, the continual stream of revelations from the committee proved embarrassing to the Republicans, who had little
to cheer about. As a counterpunch, an anonymous pamphlet
appeared on Wall Street, sold in a local bookstore and entitled
Frankie in Wonderland, parodying FDR and his reformers. The
dedication read, "To the American eagle, that noble bird, before
it was painted blue and turned into a Soviet duck." The eagle was
a symbol of the National Recovery Administration and was used
extensively in its advertising and on the decals that merchants
used to place in their store windows. The pamphlet, a parody of
Lewis Carroll's *Alice in Wonderland,* was intended to provide some
light relief to the embattled Republicans on Wall Street. Coming
in the midst of the hearings and reform legislation, it proved
about as clever as inviting Smith Brookhart to a dinner serving
booze in the 1920s.

Tightening the Screws on the Exchanges

By early 1934, it was clear that more regulation was on the way
and that it would involve regulation of the stock exchanges

themselves. The main issue at the time was the matter of floor traders on the exchanges acting in a dual capacity, that is, being able to trade for themselves and accepting client orders at the same time. Richard Whitney tried to preempt any strong legislative reaction by suggesting that the NYSE and members of committee meet in conference to iron out any differences before Congress acted. But the Pecora/Fletcher committee rejected the idea, sensing that closed-door conferences with Wall Street would run counter to its mission. Whitney then startled Washington by proposing a new regulatory authority to control the stock exchanges, taking any potential authority away from the FTC. He feared that the FTC would become too powerful in regulating business. His proposed regulator would have representatives from both Wall Street and the Fed, in addition to government officials. While he ruminated, Congress was waiting for an indication from the administration as to the direction of the legislation. In February, a separate group on the Fletcher committee, under the direction of Couzens, was working out its own details in collaboration with Pecora, but it was clear that substantial changes were in the cards for Wall Street. It became clear soon thereafter that the administration wanted to proceed quickly with reform, leaving the opinions of the NYSE and other exchanges out of any consideration. While the FTC initially appeared to remain as some sort of regulator, it was evident that the administration and the Fletcher committee wanted to create a new body to oversee the exchanges. That was envisioned because the administration wanted to license the exchanges so that their activities could be closely monitored. Investment bankers were not included, only those who actually dealt in securities in the organized secondary markets. The bill was introduced in both houses and became known as the Fletcher-Rayburn bill. The member of the House supporting it was Sam Rayburn, a Democrat from Texas, who was a lawyer first elected to the House in 1913. Pecora noted that the NYSE had already brought a barrage of its own public relations to bear against legislation and stated that he looked forward to taking Whitney's testimony about the new bill. "I will have an opportunity to test propaganda with facts when Mr. Whitney appears before the committee," he stated, recognizing that the issue was even hotter than all of the 1933 legislation.[3]

Pecora was referring to a campaign mounted by the NYSE to avoid regulation. A $2 million campaign fund was reportedly used by the exchange to further its agenda, while the committee only had the power of the press to further its own. All of the exchanges began releasing information stating that regulation would only hurt their businesses, nipping any economic recovery in the bud. The Wall Street drive had strong undertones, suggesting a sinister, communist influence on the New Deal. A magazine sympathetic to the New Deal, edited by Raymond Moley and published by Vincent Astor, called the propaganda campaign "Wall Street's Raid on the New Deal." It called incidents of letter-writing campaigns and half-truths used to discredit the bill as an affront to capitalism. Roosevelt had already commented, "A more definite and highly organized drive is being made against effective legislation (for Federal supervision of stock exchanges) than against any similar recommendation made by me." Shades of the American Liberty League, to be formed later in the year, were beginning to develop. The magazine went on to criticize Richard Whitney's comment about capitalism being based upon stock market speculation. It concluded by ridiculing his suggestion. "Thus is developed one of the most extraordinary theories of human progress that has ever been enunciated," it stated. "Perhaps the slogan of this new drive on the New Deal might be borrowed from this suggestion: Prosperity Through Gambling."[4]

As far as the Street was concerned, any regulation was bad for business. The Fletcher-Rayburn bill had the potential to destroy its business, the heart of capitalism. "But whose businesses?" Duncan Fletcher shot back, "Only that of brokers who have lined their pockets by disregarding the interests of their customers."[5] The Floridian maintained a tight grip on his committee against the Wall Street onslaught. It was he who turned the committee's direction toward the money being spent by the investment banking industry to fight reform. A prominent Southern liberal noted with some satisfaction: "Senator Fletcher reminds one of some gray-moss-covered rock that stands the wear of ages in the way he resisted Wall Street attack...history will show only the final result. It will not record, perhaps, the way Mr. Fletcher kept the stock market inquiry going when powerful influences sought to stop it."[6]

The pools operating on the floors of the exchanges continued unabated, and the dual capacity system seemed to have serious flaws. Fletcher also noted that a pool was currently operating in Libby-Owens-Ford stock, conducted by Kuhn Loeb & Co. and having several well-known participants, including Walter Chrysler and Joseph P. Kennedy, the well-known trader who had successfully withdrawn from the market prior to the Crash. Traders were acting with impunity, apparently under the assumption that their activities were outside the law. The committee's intelligence on the exchange floor was improving substantially, and the information would not work to the benefit of the NYSE.

Other than pools, the main thrust of the new bill was almost all of the stock exchange practices that had been previously revealed. Also under examination was margin trading, the practice of buying stock with borrowed money. The Fletcher-Rayburn bill wanted to impose standard margin requirements on traders. During the period leading to the Crash, margins were sometimes as low as 10 percent. Most investors were not aware that when a stock declined, they had to post additional margin or their positions would be liquidated, only adding to further selling. Large, professional traders, on the other hand, used the low requirements to trade stocks quickly for a profit. A uniform requirement would reduce wild speculation, referred to as "gambling" by the committee. Wall Street protested strongly against the proposal, claiming that it would injure those investors who held stocks on margin that had declined substantially since 1929. It was also one of the first times the investment community had invoked long-term investors in its own defense. A group of 18 securities dealers protested the proposal, claiming that it would reduce their ability to conduct brokerage successfully. But the handwriting was already on the wall. A uniform federal margin requirement would be included in the bill.

When Whitney appeared before the committee in March, he told senators that the impending bill was a form of nationalization of the stock exchanges. If the bill increased the listing requirements of the NYSE, as Wall Street feared, then government would intrude too far into traditional business territory. He also likened the proposed securities exchange act to the Volstead Act. "You can't stop a man from taking a drink by passing a law prohibiting it," he asserted, adding that, "Any attempt to regulate by statute and in minute detail the operation of the security markets is just as impossible an accomplishment."[7] Smith Brookhart was already gone from the Senate, but the remark was a subtle swat at the spirit of reform that prompted the hearings two years before.

Whitney, like many conservatives on Wall Street, saw the bill as an attempt to implement social theories that were inimical to the free enterprise system. He and other critics of the bill cited the harm to shareholders if the bill was to pass in a harsh form. The "theories" he had in mind were not specified, but a book by Adolph Berle, published two years before in 1932 and cowritten with Gardiner Means, clearly was on his mind. In *The Modern Corporation and Private Property*, they argued that modern society was severely affected by the trend toward bigness in American business. As companies grew larger through merger and acquisition, shareholder power was substantially weakened to the point where only the large shareholders had any significant voice in corporate affairs, while the small shareholder was becoming disenfranchised. Management at large American corporations did not think themselves accountable to shareholders. In fact, the authors went so far as to conclude that "there exists a centripetal attraction which draws wealth together into aggregations of constantly increasing size, at the same time throwing control into the hands of fewer and fewer men."[8] In other words, the oligarchical nature of finance had been extended to big business as well. They described its effect as the "concentration of financial power."

This was a particularly sensitive criticism of the American power elite, especially as European fascism was on the rise. Big business, as personified by Richard Whitney, did not take criticism lightly, but it was clear that it was on the defensive because much of the analysis became widely disseminated. And part of the book also criticized some businesses in a manner that supported the populist positions of the Wild Jackasses. The authors were heavily critical of the spread of chain stores, noting that many consumer items, ranging from electricity consumption to drugs and cigars, were dominated by large chains that had invaded the average household. The assumption that the new consumer society produced any tangible benefits for the average citizen, who also may have owned a few shares in a company, was mostly a myth as old inequalities were being perpetuated through a new economic hierarchy dominated by the big, wealthy, and powerful.

After the Pecora hearings began, the book seemed to be proved correct by the sunlight cast into the large business enterprises, especially the utilities companies. Although Berle and Means used the Pujo hearings for much of their historical material, their critique rang as true as it would have 20 years before. Testimony revealed that many of the giant utilities holding companies were actually controlled by a small handful of men, although they had thousands of shareholders on their rolls. The Fletcher/Pecora committee concluded in 1934, "By pyramiding corporation upon corporation, promoters with a "shoe-string" investment were enabled to acquire control of the public's money and the industries of the country."[9] The criticism certainly was not new and reflected the impact of Progressive thought since the beginning of the century. Wall Street and the old guard well understood where the theories had originated and had reason to fear them in mid-1934.

Berle, the son of a Congregationalist minister from the Midwest, was a lawyer by training who graduated from Harvard and its law school. After graduating, he worked for Louis Brandeis's law firm in Boston. If much of his language and that of the committee sounded familiar, it was because the crusading lawyer, now sitting on the Supreme Court, had disciples throughout the legal world who shared his passion for subjecting bankers to strict regulation and limiting what he saw as their perfidious influence on business and society. It was Brandeis who kept the pressure on the House of Morgan during the heyday of the Progressives. Along with Sam Untermyer, he provided the collective memory that reformers needed to rein in Wall Street.

Untermyer also testified before the Fletcher/Pecora committee, telling it what he disliked about the proposed securities bill. He had been pursuing regulation for the NYSE for over 25 years and his advice was considered valuable, especially since Brandeis could not testify because of his position on the Supreme Court. For the old guard and Wall Street, he was part of the ideological problem that they had successfully fought for decades. Now, the tables had turned. Richard Whitney's criticism was rejected by Pecora in simple terms. After hearing Whitney's criticism for the second time in a month he declared, "Of course, if all of Mr. Whitney's objections were met, there would be no bill at all . . . this bill does not seek to enact the social philosophy of any special group. It seeks rather to make certain that the wildcat speculation which was fostered and encouraged by the New York Stock Exchange prior to 1929 . . . will not again afflict our people and imperil their prosperity."[10]

It was becoming clear that the Wall Street response was to favor diffuse regulation, aiming to keep the FTC out of any stock exchange business for fear of its potential centralized power. But a new body would have to be created to regulate the exchanges. Even Whitney favored it. The only questions were when it would be created and how much power it would have. But one thing was clear: The new bill would have teeth. The Securities Act passed the previous year was considered somewhat lukewarm, but Pecora promised the new law would be airtight.

Father Charles Coughlin, the "Radio Priest," was also a strong supporter of the proposed law. In his syndicated radio address on April 8, he stated that the bill was an attempt to clean out "the Augean stables of Wall Street." Mincing few words, he continued that Wall Street had reversed the traditional baseball rule to "four strikes and three balls, and plays with a cock-eyed umpire." Wall Street had become accustomed to attacks from him, although dismissing his sentiments out of hand was a mistake. One Midwest newspaper named him as the most popular radio personality in the country, followed by Huey Long. That he was no friend of Wall Street would have been an understatement. A year later, he broke with the New Deal for abandoning principles he held dear. When he did, he took time to denounce presidential adviser Bernard Baruch as "the acting president of the United States, the uncrowned prince of Wall Street." Sounding a warning to the Street and the New Deal, he trumpeted, "Let the unjust aggressors, who for generations have mismanaged the economic affairs of our nation, assume entire responsibility for their tory stubbornness."[11]

Reform was given a strong technical boost by a study that appeared under the auspices of the Twentieth Century Fund, a think tank closely aligned with the principles of the New Deal. The fund was founded in 1911 by Edward A. Filene, a Boston retailer who also founded the famous department store named after him. He was a staunch Progressive and friend of Louis Brandeis. Presiding over the think tank until 1937, Filene molded it into an activist institution, dedicated to changing public policy whenever possible. The study, *Stock Market Control*, advocated legislation to supplement the Securities Act of 1933 and went further in analyzing and making recommendations about many stock exchange practices. It tackled all of the relevant issues discussed by the committee, including pools, investment banking practices, short selling, margin, and the dissemination of sensitive financial news. Some of its recommendations made traders angry. After discussing the specialist system employed by the exchanges, it concluded, "We believe that the services we look for from a specialist can be more efficiently performed, and at a lower cost, under a different system."[12] It proposed that the dual capacity system embodied in the specialists be changed so that they act as either broker or principal, but not both. The study delved into each stock exchange practice, examined it, and made recommendations for change, regardless of how unpopular they might be. While many of the recommendations went unheeded, others were not strong enough and the new securities act would be more firm on many practices such as margin and short selling. The importance of the study also demonstrated that research help enlisted to further reform or the status quo would be used more widely in the future.

Creation of the SEC

The Fed and the Treasury entered the deliberations over the Fletcher-Rayburn bill. The Fed wanted authority to set the margin rate because it was the body responsible for monitoring banking and credit. Once the two entered the discussions, the bill underwent some major revisions. What emerged was a comprehensive law that subjected the stock exchanges to the first meaningful regulation in their existence. The Securities Exchange Act required the exchanges to register with a federal government agency, but not the FTC. It created the new Securities and Exchange Commission (SEC), a body that would assume responsibility for the 1933 act from the FTC and regulate the secondary markets as well. Many stock exchange abuses were reformed. New rules for short selling, floor trading, and reporting were introduced, and the matter of margin balances was given to the Fed, who now had the authority to set the margin requirement. Roosevelt signed the law on June 7 and the new SEC was to begin operation on July 1. Pecora proudly displayed the signing pen given to him by the president as a souvenir, stating that, "I shall treasure this pen as the pen that made effective one of the most constructive pieces of legislation ever enacted. And I really mean that."[13] Even before the ink was dry, positioning for seats on the new commission had already begun.

The five commissioners named by Roosevelt included Pecora, Joseph P. Kennedy, James Landis, George Mathews, and Robert Healey. The latter three were all associated with the FTC.

Kennedy was a surprise choice and was also named chairman, to the annoyance of Pecora, who had lobbied intensively for the job. Particularly irritating was the fact that Kennedy had been rumored to be a member of pools operating that past spring, much to the annoyance of the Fletcher committee. Pecora reportedly was the fifth man chosen and was never in contention for the top job. Despite all of his hard work for the previous year and a half, he had been passed over twice for plum jobs. Nevertheless, he accepted the appointment despite the fact that he had indicated only a few weeks before that he would only serve if he were named chairman.

Choosing Kennedy was a calculated risk for the president. Presidential adviser Raymond Moley considered the former market wizard "the best bet for chairman because of executive ability, knowledge of habits and customs of business to be regulated, and ability to moderate different points of view on the Commission."[14] In addition, Kennedy had supported Roosevelt's election bid substantially, and the support required a major appointment in return. Kennedy had always expressed a desire for public service, especially after he made his fortune on Wall Street, and being financially independent was a strong quality for the new SEC chairman. He also launched a campaign similar to that of Pecora, stating that he would not take a position on the SEC unless he were made chairman. Not all of FDR's advisers thought it was a good idea, however. The irascible Harold Ickes, FDR's first secretary of the interior, kept a secret diary for years while he served in government. Ickes was a former Republican progressive who easily could have worn the mantle of Wild Jackass save for the fact that he did not serve in the Senate. He was a supporter of Theodore Roosevelt's Bull Moose movement and began supporting Democrats against Herbert Hoover in 1928. Franklin Roosevelt offered him the job after the election, telling him, "You and I have been speaking the same language for the past twenty years." The day before announcing Kennedy's appointment, Ickes wrote in his journal, "The President has great confidence in him because he has made his pile, has invested all his money in Government securities, and knows all the tricks of the trade." But he was not convinced. "Apparently, he is going on the assumption that Kennedy would now like to make a name for himself for the sake of his family, but I have never known many of these cases to work out as expected."[15] Luckily for the development of the SEC, Ickes' assessment proved incorrect.

Kennedy described the goals and methods of the SEC as constructive rather than destructive. Wall Street feared that someone with more reforming zeal, such as one of Brandeis's apostles, could permanently damage its ability to raise and trade capital issues. Addressing Richard Whitney's concerns, Kennedy said that the "work of the Securities and Exchange Commission does not mean that the commission proposes to carry out intensive propaganda regarding its activities. Its task is essentially technical—a job that must be done in a businesslike way." Restoring confidence in business was the primary goal. The issue facing the country was clear: "We see at the present time only a little stream of capital issue where before there was a floodtide. We see vast credit reserves left untouched except for the drafts made upon them by city, state and federal demands." Then, addressing Wall Street directly, he continued, "No honest man—no decent institution which seeks to render service, instead of merely achieving profit—need fear the regulations that have been set up."[16]

The investment community reacted strongly to the SEC and the new legislation. One prominent, widely read periodical claimed that the regulations had destroyed speculation, a quality that had made America great. "The reality is that there can be no economic progress in this country as long as the spirit of speculation is dead," it stated authoritatively. "What we need is more speculation."[17] Stock exchange speculation was the subject, the same type that Richard Whitney had often defended. But with the new Securities Act ruling the markets, new issues of stocks and bonds were being segregated into their own primary market that would be separate from the exchanges, also separating the capital-raising process from speculators. The same Wall

Street defense would become well used in the decades ahead, especially when new regulations threatened the status quo.

Aside from specific criticisms, there was also the matter of the New Deal crowding out the capital markets with government agencies. A particularly sore point on Wall Street was the Reconstruction Finance Corporation (RFC), the agency instituted by Congress while Hoover was still president. The RFC became a huge agency designed to loan money to companies in need, avoiding Wall Street and the banks in the process. Over the course of its lifetime, it loaned $50 billion to American businesses of all sorts, from banks to manufacturers, and was criticized constantly for its intrusion into business life. It was not until the late 1940s that Wall Street investment banks were able to slip out from under its heavy weight and begin underwriting corporate issues again. The RFC was the rallying point for those who abhorred federal intervention in the credit markets.

The first months of the SEC's existence were devoted to putting mechanisms in place so that the agency would have Wall Street's respect. In early October, Kennedy and his fellow commissioners visited the NYSE, hosted by Richard Whitney. The market was not particularly active, and they visited on an especially dull day when turnover amounted to only half a million shares. Kennedy revealed that the commission was particularly interested in short selling but was trying to keep an open mind about it and other NYSE practices. Several members did keep a close eye on how the specialists operated, however. They also visited the New York Curb Exchange in their two-day visit but did not examine the workings of the over-the-counter (unlisted) market because it was not a full-fledged stock exchange. They also visited the Produce Exchange since it avidly had been trading shares for several years and proudly advertised the fact.

Despite all the legislation passed, the first two years of the New Deal were not all clear sailing for the Roosevelt administration. In May 1935, a major roadblock was encountered when the NIRA was declared unconstitutional by the Supreme Court. A New York company, the Schecter Poultry Corporation, had challenged the constitutionality of the law after being found in violation of labor laws. It argued that congressional authority had been transferred by the act to the executive branch. The court agreed unanimously and struck down the law. The New Deal was disheartened because even its ideological icon Louis Brandeis was opposed to the law and was one of the nine votes against. After the decision, he told a New Deal lawyer, "This is the end of this business of centralization, and I want you to go back and tell the President that we're not going to let this government centralize everything. It's come to an end."[18] The decision also put many of the new agencies created by Congress in the last two years under a cloud, including the SEC.

The Liberty League

Political opposition to the New Deal also was mounting, especially from Wall Street and big business. Within a year, the apparatus of the Association Against the Prohibition Amendment would transform itself into the American Liberty League, in an attempt to oppose the New Deal and FDR, whom many of its members considered a "traitor to his class." The league was founded in summer of 1934 by John Raskob and Jouett Shouse. Raskob was a former General Motors executive, Morgan ally, and chairman of the Democratic National Committee (DNC). Shouse succeeded him at the DNC. Shouse personally visited the White House and informed FDR of the formation of the group, which also included former Democratic presidential candidates Al Smith and John W. Davis, who as Jack Morgan's lawyer accompanied him to the Pecora hearings. Other founding members included many members of the Du Pont family and Alfred Sloan of General Motors. The league was definitely cut from the same cloth as its predecessor organizations. Like the Navy League and the AAPA before it, it was intended to represent the interests of big business. Although FDR initially welcomed the formation of the league, in deference to Raskob and Shouse, who earlier had been among his supporters, the league often was ignored by the administration. Six months after being founded, the University of Virginia arranged a debate between New Dealers and supporters of the league but could not enlist any administration officials to actually attend. Most claimed they were too busy for a debate. The administration realized that debating the league was a tacit form of acknowledging it. The league was not in a position to do more than mount public relations campaigns against the Democrats since it possessed no real power.

The league was not a political party but more of a pressure group that liked to give large dinner parties. Its main business was to organize a pamphlet campaign against the New Deal, and several books also appeared, antagonistic to FDR, all intended to show the administration as left-leaning and inimical to the free enterprise system. Its best-known function was a huge dinner party given in 1936 at the Mayflower Hotel in Washington, attended by almost 2,000. In front of a veritable Who's Who of American business, Al Smith rose to give a speech denouncing the New Deal. If anyone was unsure of the league's political posture, it became clear when Smith thundered, "There can be only one capital, Washington or Moscow. There can be only the clear, pure fresh air of free America, or the foul breath of communistic Russia."[19] Likening the administration to Stalin may have won points from archconservatives, but the speech made Smith, the former governor of New York and the manager of Raskob's Empire State Building, infamous in liberal quarters. After the speech, a reader wrote the *Sheboygan Press*, stating, "President Roosevelt is trying to save the U.S. for the American people and the Liberty League is trying to save it for themselves."[20] Then he continued to list financial details about the Du Ponts and General Motors, and the amounts spent by the league in its anti–New Deal activities. People from many walks of life recognized that the league, as Herbert Hoover said, represented the "Wall Street model of human liberty" and eschewed affiliation with it in any way. The league still espoused the concept of trickle-down economics that was well used in the 1920s by Republicans who explained economics in a curiously oligarchic fashion. In order for economic stimulants to work, they had to be applied to the top—to the "top" people so evident in the language of the decade. The league was the living embodiment of the idea and was not popular as a result.

The Liberty League was also rumored to be involved in mustering armed opposition to the New Deal. Some of its senior executives were said to be soliciting support from the American Legion and the Veterans of Foreign Wars for an armed force to overthrow FDR. The rumors were never adequately substantiated although they were well known by many in Washington. The link between the league and the Legion became fodder for those who saw a conspiracy against the veterans' bonus, which still was a burning issue in Washington. Despite its star-studded membership, the league achieved little in its short history. It almost completely disappeared after the 1936 elections when it became clear that the New Deal was immensely more popular than Wall Street and big business.

Fixing the Fed

The failure of the Fed in 1929 to prevent the market bubble from exploding had not been forgotten. The actions of the New York Fed that added more money to the banking system as the Federal Reserve Board in Washington tried to raise interest rates was a sore point among supporters of the central bank. The compromises that led to the Fed's creation 20 years before had become glaring examples of structural weaknesses that needed to be fixed if the Fed was to become a true central bank rather than just a group of 12 regional banks that could act separately in some cases. Unlike in McFadden's heyday, the bank needed to be fixed rather than attacked if it was to serve its intended purpose.

The drive to fix the Fed began indirectly in early 1934 when FDR appointed Marriner S. Eccles, a Utah businessman, to be special assistant to treasury secretary Henry Morgenthau. Born in Logan, Utah, Eccles was the oldest of nine children. After attending Brigham Young College, he became familiar with investments and established an investment company that acquired many of his father's successful business enterprises. In 1924, he and his brother joined with a prominent banking family in Utah to form the Eccles-Browning Affiliated Banks, which rapidly began to expand by acquiring banks in Utah and Wyoming. In 1928, he and several partners organized the First Security Corporation, a holding company, that managed the banks that had been acquired. The company was one of the first multibank holding companies in the United States. By the early 1930s he was one of the West's best-known businessmen and was 43 years old when tapped to become Morgenthau's assistant.

Eccles was a nominal Republican, but his ideas did not endear him to his party. Upon being named to the post, he revealed that he favored a special tax on the wealthy to help spread the wealth during the Depression, an idea that did not sit well with his party's hierarchy. He favored tapping the rich through a higher tax rate and a stiff inheritance tax. Despite his own wealth, he saw the nation's problem as a decline in spending. Believing that the rich were hoarding their wealth in the face of a national catastrophe, he stated, "We need no further capital accumulation for the present," although he acknowledged that "this may frighten people who possess wealth."[21] He was correct because Huey Long's similar campaign had many in Washington worried about an outburst of violent populism.

Even more frightening to Eccles's opponents was his nomination by FDR to be head of the Federal Reserve in the fall of 1934. When he was nominated, he remarked on his transformation from a progressive Republican to a New Dealer: "Previous to the last national election, I had always supported the Republican national ticket but was not satisfied with their policies, which were not sufficiently liberal and progressive to meet changed conditions. Mr. Roosevelt's idea of what to do appealed to me and since then I have been a strong supporter of Mr. Roosevelt."[22] Insiders claimed that it was actually his ties to Morgenthau that got him the job—ties that he began to sever shortly after being confirmed.

Expounding on a similar theme, Father Charles Coughlin offered his own plan for reforming the Fed in 1934 in another radio address. He called for abandoning the Fed and establishing a new central bank with a branch in every major city, to be owned by the people through congressional control. Claiming that he still believed in the salvation of Wall Street, he claimed that the Fletcher-Rayburn bill was only half effective and needed to be stronger to return the central banking institution to its rightful place as an institution of the people. The ideas sounded like a combination of those of Huey Long and Louis McFadden, with a sprinkle of biblical metaphor added for radio audiences. The proposal would have proven the death knell for an independent central bank of any sort.

The priest's ideas, while explosive, would prove to be ephemeral, according to one well-known Catholic editor. George Shuster claimed that a hold over 30 million radio listeners was difficult to maintain over the long term, especially since Coughlin's ideas smacked of Nazism. He stated: "It has not escaped the notice of observers that the general contour of his doctrine is oddly similar to that of Nazi socialism. The Nazis too advocated a central national bank, the abolition of interest on money, government control of labor, a better return for the farmers, and the superiority of human rights to property rights."[23] Shuster noted that the priest had risen from obscurity 10 years before to become the number one menace to the New Deal. Coughlin's career had strong similarities to that of McFadden. As it turned out, the prediction proved correct—within a few years Coughlin's popularity began to recede.

Eccles was the author of a reform banking act that became known as the Eccles Act. Throughout the summer of 1935, many amendments were made to it, and several riders were attached that favored the investment banking industry. The bill that passed Congress was a compromise with Eccles's original ideas but provided a sound act in the opinion of even its detractors, like Carter Glass, who believed the Fed was not broken and did not need fixing. The law signed by FDR in August created the

Fed open market committee that would decide on its operations in the Treasury market and provided for salaried members of the board, appointed by the president. The open market committee decided on appropriate actions in the market on behalf of the entire board and then ordered the New York Fed to carry them out. Individual banks were no longer permitted to act on their own, as New York did in 1929.

One of the proposed amendments to the act made by Carter Glass and the Senate Banking Subcommittee would have allowed banks to underwrite corporate securities again. It was attached to the bill but removed at the eleventh hour and left out of the final version. Even the main trade associations representing banks and investment bankers were startled by the inclusion of the section, since Glass and his subcommittee seemed to be advocating the undoing of his own Banking Act a year earlier. The proposed amendment would have allowed banks to underwrite but not retail new securities issues up to 20 percent of an issue's size.

Winthrop Aldrich, a staunch supporter of financial reform, did not favor passing the Eccles Act, testifying before Glass made his amendment. In his opinion, the enlargement of Fed powers was not "liberalizing the Federal Reserve system. It is making it over into an instrument of despotic authority." He went further in attacking, among other things, the proposal that the Fed system alone have the power to order open market operations as a "proposed concentration of power," mischievously using the same term used by Berle and Means to describe the centralization of American industry in their book.[24] The banking proposal clearly had assumed political dimensions, as did all proposals regarding the Fed over the years. The creation of the open market committee and consolidation of operations angered many bankers, who could have lived with the Fed in its original form before the Eccles Act. Now, they were dealing with a reserve bank that was closer to living up to its description as a central bank.

The act that finally passed was declared a success. The American Bankers' Association endorsed it, and market analyst Roger Babson gave it a resounding vote of confidence in his weekly newsletter. "This new act centralizes the control of credit in the entire nation in a board of seven members," he declared, adding that "this board will be politically appointed but bankers now believe there may be no political interference with its policies."[25] As he signed the act, FDR noted that perhaps Carter Glass was the only person fully familiar with its details, but it was Duncan Fletcher who helped push it through successfully. Fletcher's role in helping pave the way for the Eccles Act was recognized by Roosevelt. A grateful president remarked to him, "Take care of yourself—you know how greatly I count on you," an especially timely warning since Huey Long had been assassinated in Louisiana only two weeks before.[26]

Shortly after the Eccles Act was signed, the House of Morgan complied with the Glass-Steagall Act by splitting its investment banking operations from the commercial banking side of the bank. Three partners and other employees from J.P. Morgan & Co. resigned and formed the new firm of Morgan Stanley. J.P. Morgan & Co. and its Philadelphia affiliate Drexel & Co. remained as private bankers. Technically, the split occurred in June 1934, but the bank waited another year to form Morgan Stanley. The bank's partners decided to wait in order to see if the Glass amendment would succeed. "I think they are waiting ... to see if the underwriting amendment in the banking bill will pass," Charles Mitchell told one of his partners at Blyth & Co., the securities firm he joined after leaving National City.[27] But when FDR heard of the amendment, he quashed it, leaving Glass-Steagall intact for the rest of the century. As a result, Morgan Stanley picked up the underwriting business from the bank and, along with many other securities divestitures, helped create the modern American investment banking business.

Of all the members of the Senate Committee on Banking, Glass was perhaps the most friendly to the House of Morgan and investment banking in general. His proposed amendment came as something of a shock, however, despite his reservations about parts of the original act he proposed with Henry Steagall. But the two differed on the Glass amendment. Ray Tucker reported in his weekly syndicated column from Washington about a clever technique used to divert the 75-year-old Glass's attention by Henry Steagall. Steagall introduced some mischievous and outlandish proposals of his own to the Eccles Act to purposely divert Glass, known for his even-handed approach to legislation. When Glass heard that his amendment would not be included in the final version of the Eccles Act, he told Steagall, "It's your crazy ideas on banking that are responsible for my arthritis."[28] Unlike many of the other committee members, Glass was business-minded and realized that the trickle of new capital issues coming to market in 1934 would not help the unemployment situation. Many bankers, including the House of Morgan, had since adopted the position that the Securities Act placed too much of a burden on underwriters and that the Glass-Steagall divorce only helped underline their marginal capitalizations. The fate of investment banking for the rest of the century depended on the success of the amendment, but when it failed, banking was destined to have two sides—commercial banking and investment banking—although in the American lexicon only the former would be considered banking in the strict sense of the word.

Reining in Utilities

Congress was passing legislation in the early days of the New Deal, attempting to correct past injustices and repair structural deficiencies in the financial system. The four major securities and banking acts had already proved their reforming zeal beyond a doubt. However, there was one more area of intense interest to lawmakers, also dominated by investment bankers, which had received wide press coverage but otherwise had been left untouched. That shortcoming was corrected in 1935 when Congress turned its attention to public utilities.

Congress began forming a committee to investigate the utilities industry in the late summer of 1934. The Pecora/Fletcher committee was finished, having made its final report. Pecora was the first choice of legislators in both parties to be counsel for the

new committee. But the former counsel was already busy with
SEC work and did not entertain the idea of doing more inves-
tigative work. The utilities industry presented reformers with a
gigantic task because problems in the industry had been the subject of intense debate for years. The creation of the Tennessee
Valley Authority (TVA) a year before did not end the debate,
which still raged after the collapse of the Insull empire. Utilities
embodied all the evils of corporate America—holding companies, stock dilution, and investment banker dominance.

While hearings were conducted, legislation was being written in both houses. Early in 1935, different bills were introduced
in Congress to tackle the utilities. Legislators primarily were interested in two distinct problems. The first concerned the matter of
varying rates. Electricity and gas were sold at greatly differing
prices around the country, and the higher rates were seen as
a hindrance to economic development. The second problem was
pyramiding through use of holding companies. The modern version of the old trust was used to hold stock of other companies
and enjoy a tax break in the process. Operating companies could
pay a dividend to the parent holding company, which could avoid
paying tax on it and effectively deprive the Treasury of potential
tax dollars, while benefiting the small number of executives who
controlled the holding companies. Insull's empire collapsed
because of the heavy borrowing used to keep his companies
afloat, but the companies that survived the Crash and early Depression years were enjoying the tax benefits while still controlling vast amounts of the country's electricity grid. One of them,
the United Corporation, was controlled by Morgan interests, so
naturally it attracted attention.

Separate utilities bills were introduced by Sam Rayburn and
Burton Wheeler, but they soon joined forces to sponsor what
would become known as the Wheeler-Rayburn bill. The proposals came at the end of a Federal Trade Commission study on utilities that was not complimentary to the industry. One problem
many of the large holding companies faced was manipulation of
the stock of their operating companies. The FTC disclosed that

both the Insull companies and the United Corporation had purchased stock in the marketplace in the late 1920s and early 1930s, with the intent of running up the prices in order to sell new stock at inflated prices. It charged that the stock of the Insull companies had been avidly purchased by Halsey Stuart & Co., Insull's main Chicago-based investment banker, in much the same way that Albert Wiggin had speculated in the price of Chase National stock. Many of the stocks in question doubled in value, as investors took their lead from the bankers and bid up prices. Morgan employed a small Wall Street investment bank specializing in utilities, Bonbright & Co., to affect the price of several of the United Corporation's operating companies. As a result, some of the Rayburn bill's proposals came dangerously close to mandating that some of the holding companies be disbanded because of past abuse.

The industry took almost no time in defending itself. The *Philadelphia Inquirer* said the bill was calculated "to establish a Federal bureaucratic dictatorship for operating as well as holding companies in the public utility field...it is a bald attempt, taking advantage of a period in which every radical proposal obtains support from one group or other, to place an iron collar around the neck of legitimate business."[29]

Opposition formed immediately from investors in utilities stocks and bonds, as well as the utilities companies. A utilities industry group said that the legislation was "based on the assumption that public utility holding companies perform no useful economic function, that they are not only unnecessary but actively pernicious and solely evil and that they must not be permitted to live."[30] Although the language appeared a bit florid for corporate America, the utilities executives who signed the statement were reacting to what was becoming known as the "death sentence" provision in the Wheeler-Rayburn proposals.

The death sentence was included several times in various drafts of the law and deleted each time, but it was included in the final bill that was signed by FDR in August 1935, at the same time the Eccles Act was passed. Roosevelt characterized it as the "biggest" bill he ever signed because it affected one of the largest American industries. The bill had two parts that infuriated the industry. First, it required all utilities holding companies to register with the SEC. Secondly, and even more infuriating, it imposed a death sentence upon some of the giant systems by limiting those holding companies that survived to one operating system only. The days of large holding companies whose activities spanned state, and sometimes international, borders were over. The new formula was simple—one holding company, one operating system. Investment bankers' hold over a vital part of the American infrastructure was finished. Any new securities issued by the companies had to be vetted by the SEC. The stranglehold was broken.

The Public Utility Holding Company Act of 1935 was the most radical of the regulatory laws passed by Congress during the first two years of the New Deal. The service provided by utilities was in the public realm, and there were few ways the giant companies could escape meaningful regulation. Throughout the hearings and the press commentary that accompanied the debate, there were many references to "propaganda" spread by the utilities in an attempt to influence elections and public debate. Harry Truman later remembered in his *Memoirs* the propaganda spread by the power companies from their information headquarters in the Mayflower Hotel in Washington, the same locale used by the Liberty League when Al Smith gave his inflammatory speech.

A good deal of publicity also involved Samuel Insull, who used funds from his companies to make political donations and help fund school textbooks that were favorable to the free enterprise system. During World War I, he also directed Britain's propaganda efforts in the United States, seeking to enlist support for U.S. government assistance. Being a native Briton, Insull was a natural for the job, although his detractors never let the public forget that a massive power system was controlled by a foreigner (even though Insull had been in the United States for decades and probably was more knowledgeable than anyone about the industry, having first been introduced to it by Thomas Edison, his original employer).

Wall Street and Morgan forces did not take the utilities act lying down. A court challenge was mounted, and an army of corporate forces aligned themselves against it. The utilities also began a massive letter-writing campaign aimed at legislators condemning the act, reminiscent of Liberty League tactics against other New Deal programs. The United Corporation, represented by John W. Davis, began proceedings to challenge the constitutionality of the Public Utility Holding Company Act of 1935 and the right of the SEC to force it to register. A Baltimore dentist holding $2,500 in utility bonds was the front man in the suit, represented by Davis. The lawyer later admitted that he had never met his client before walking into the court to try the case. Although the suit was well publicized, it did not succeed, and the SEC emerged victorious as the overseer of utilities holding companies. The Morgan companies had been dealt a severe blow, from which they never fully recovered.

Kennedy resigned from the SEC in September 1935 after the Public Utility Holding Company Act was passed. When he first accepted the appointment, he stated that he would only serve for one year, although he prolonged his stay a little longer until the NIRA situation was settled. The new law substantially added to the commission's responsibilities, and it was not immediately clear whether a new appointment would give the utilities some breathing room or force them to comply with the new law soon. Kennedy was succeeded by James Landis, no friend of Wall Street, reviving worries that the SEC would prove hostile to the Street after all.

New Names, Old Ideas

Three of the Wild Jackasses died in 1936, marking the end of an era in twentieth-century politics. Duncan Fletcher died in June of a heart attack at age 77. Louis McFadden was in New York City in late September, visiting with his wife and son, when he was taken ill at his hotel. He died shortly thereafter at a local hospital at age 60. Two weeks later, James Couzens also died. After complaining of a bad back, he kept a date with Franklin Roosevelt for dinner aboard the presidential train. After dining, he departed and checked into a hospital, where he was diagnosed with a kidney ailment. He died a week later, three weeks after the death of Louis McFadden. The latter two deaths contributed to the folklore of many conspiracy theorists, who suspected plots by bankers had killed the Progressives in order to gain revenge for the past, even though Fletcher and Couzens were in their seventies at their deaths.

Smith Brookhart tried to persuade the administration that he should be appointed to a government job at least twice in 1936. After leaving the Senate, his personal financial situation deteriorated and he needed a job. He first pursued an appointment with the Interstate Commerce Commission. When no action was taken, he turned his attention to the SEC. Roosevelt asked a colleague to speak to William O. Douglas, Landis's successor at the SEC, about the prospect, but no answer was received. After trying once again, Brookhart blamed Iowa's sitting senators for dragging their feet on the issue but again failed to be noticed.[31] The former Iowa senator's bid for reentry into public life failed. Professional rabble-rousers were not as valued by the administration as those reform-minded individuals who also had other visible means of support, in most cases substantially so.

Although many of the Wild Jackasses had joined the New Deal or returned home from Washington, one last attempt at reform legislation was sponsored by someone who easily would have been included in their number had he been elected earlier. During the mid-1930s, Wright Patman, a Democratic representative from Texas, became the favorite bête noir of the Congress in the absence of McFadden. Born in 1893 to poor Texas tenant farmers, Patman put himself through law school at night while working as a janitor. He was first elected to the House of Representatives in 1928 after serving in the Texas legislature and embracing the anti–chain store movement. His interpretation was that the stores represented a Wall Street invasion of local business and should be curtailed to protect the small merchant. Being an avid believer in the power of radio, he often took to the airwaves to score points against his opponents.

One of Patman's first crusades in Congress was on behalf of World War I veterans who had not received bonuses promised them. Herbert Hoover flatly refused to pay the bonuses demanded by veteran's organizations, prompting the first Bonus March on Washington, which resulted in injury and death. The issue was still burning during the New Deal. Roosevelt also indicated that he would not authorize payment of the bonuses since technically they were not due until the 1940s. Patman introduced a bill in Congress to get the bonuses paid, but it was defeated. After the defeat, he placed the blame squarely on the American Legion and Wall Street. The legion "rendered lip service for the veterans and some effective head work and foot work for big bankers and big interests in this country," he asserted, noting that the antibonus forces carried cash to the legion convention in Chicago and that it "was used to buy the influence of certain leaders in the American Legion to get a so-called 'anti-inflation' resolution . . . having for its purpose protection of Wall Street's and international bankers' interests."[32] He was noting the purported link between the American Liberty League and the legion that bred the unproven conspiracy to overthrow FDR. Listeners readily recognized his rhetoric since it was similar to that employed by Father Coughlin and Louis McFadden.

The Bonus March on Washington proved to be the incident that displayed the polarization that had developed in the United States during the early 1930s. The veterans' bonus was passed by Congress in 1924 and the actual payment was to be made in 1945, suggesting that each veteran would receive about $1,000 for time served. Patman played spoiler by introducing his bill in 1929 and asking for immediate payment. The bill did not garner much support in Congress, but the veterans began agitating for it, especially in 1930 as the Depression began to cause increased unemployment. Father Coughlin adopted the cause, among others, and Patman introduced another bill in 1931. When Hoover vetoed it, a grassroots movement began in 1932 among veterans, leading to the march on Washington in the summer. Veterans from around the country joined the march, often commandeering railroad cars for transportation. When they reached Washington, they erected large squatters' camps around the city. But the march was in vain because another Patman bill was defeated in the Senate. After the vote, Hiram Johnson lamented, "This marks a new era in the life of our nation. The time may come when this folderol—these trappings of government—will disappear, when fat old men like you and me will be lined up against a stone wall."[33] Although the firing squads never materialized, the images of the marchers being dispersed by troops led by General Douglas MacArthur, claiming to be subduing a revolution, proved as disturbing as the causes of the march itself. Herbert Hoover claimed that challenge to the government had been subdued, but his critics pointed out that American troops had been used against former veterans on domestic soil.

At the end of 1932, the Associated Press reported that its editors ranked the Bonus March as the second most newsworthy event of the year after the Lindbergh kidnapping. The death of Swedish financier Ivar Kreuger after his empire collapsed ranked third. In a short statement, the agency said, "The bonus march on Washington assumed world notice when blood was shed in a clash between the BEP [Bonus Expeditionary Force as it was known] and the police when the army was called out to evict the demonstrators."[34] Its editors clearly thought the kidnapping and stories about Kreuger, as well as the resignation of Mayor Jimmy Walker of New York, had more human interest material than the march. But the issue refused to die.

Ironically, the Bonus March was viewed by many as an incipient revolution and was roundly condemned on both sides of the political spectrum. Within a few short months, it evolved from a spontaneous idea to an organized march that spanned the entire country. The frightening part to many people was the fact that it seemed to fulfill Marx's idea of a spontaneous revolution against capitalist masters by the oppressed workingman. Violent incidents occurred as the march made its way across the country, only adding to the public outcry. After the marchers had been disbanded by the army and retreated to Johnstown, Pennsylvania, a remarkable spectrum of newspapers condemned it. It was one of the first times that papers in the East and Midwest agreed on something. Papers ranging from the *New York Times* to the *Cleveland Plain Dealer* and *Kansas City Star* were all unanimous in condemning the violence used by the marchers. The kindest remark came from the *New York Daily News*, which while still critical, remarked, "The government cannot surrender to these men. But neither can it afford to go one inch beyond the absolute minimum of violence that may be necessary to keep them on their side of the line."[35] Americans were fighting Americans on domestic soil. Even some Marine Corps units sent to quell the disturbance refused to take up any sort of arms against fellow citizens.

In 1936, a bonus bill introduced again by Patman finally passed Congress, and Roosevelt's veto was overridden, much to the joy of the thousands of veterans who had been eagerly anticipating it for several years. The $2.2 billion package affected over 3.5 million veterans and amounted to about $715 each, providing some comfort from those suffering unemployment and near poverty. At the time, the package was thought to be inflationary by its critics, although some supporters interpreted it as a stimulant, especially since unemployment insurance was not yet effective. It also marked a victory for Patman's populism and ensured that future legislation introduced by him would be noticed. Of his many committee assignments in Congress, he also sat on the House Banking and Currency Committee.

Like McFadden before him, Patman became the thorn in the side of many colleagues. He opposed the first Glass-Steagall Act in 1932 and so infuriated Henry Steagall that the Alabama congressman actually ran toward him in the House chamber, ready to begin a fistfight before being restrained. He also was one of the eight congressmen who voted against tabling McFadden's impeachment resolution against Hoover, earning him derisive laughter from the other members of the House. Even when he did not earn the ridicule of his colleagues, his best efforts were still derided. The method by which the veterans were paid their bonuses was by vouchers that could be redeemed for cash. The vouchers were known as "Patman notes." Duncan Fletcher once remarked that they were not worth their face value when compared with other more "serious" forms of currency.

Break the Chains

Despite other crusades, Patman's main preoccupation was the spread of chain stores. By the 1930s, their spread was being attributed to all sorts of perfidious plots by Jews and Wall Street to control the country. When Goldman Sachs brought a new issue of Sears, Roebuck stock to the market years before, populists had the link they needed to show the collusion between these forces of evil since Sears was run at the time by Julius Rosenwald. The issue began to rise to the surface in the 1920s and continued well into the 1930s, when McFadden and Patman took to the radio to denounce the spread of the stores as un-American. They also blamed European political instability on the rise of chain stores on the continent and included the Jews in their attacks because many of the chains were Jewish-owned.

Patman had an enormous impact upon antitrust legislation through his desire to control the chain stores. In 1936, he introduced a piece of antitrust legislation that became known as the Robinson-Patman Act. Its cosponsor was Senator Joseph T. Robinson, Democrat of Arkansas. It was prompted by the same FTC study that led to the passing of the utilities act the year before. The only effective way to curtail the chains was to ensure that they did not engage in price discrimination. The law proscribed charging different prices in different locations for the same goods. Its goal was uniform prices that would protect the small consumer from big business. Chains were to come under close scrutiny as a result. The law was a clear attempt to protect small storeowners from the expanding chains, whose purchasing power at the wholesale level could indeed lead to lower prices charged to consumers.

Unfortunately for big business, the anti–chain store forces won a victory with the McFadden Act and the anti–chain store law, as it became known, only added to more distress. The Robinson-Patman Act was an odd law, especially in a period when inflation had been the excuse for opposing veterans' bonuses. If the chains could have lowered prices, then the argument against the act would have been fortified; however, in a period of political hyperbole the local argument won over economics. Economies of scale were not an important political argument in the 1930s. Local control and anti–Wall Street sentiment won the day.

Patman's earlier attempt to introduce impeachment proceedings against former treasury secretary Andrew Mellon came full circle in 1936. When Patman introduced the impeachment resolution, he cost his hometown of Texarkana dearly because it was also the home of Mellon's Gulf Oil Company. Infuriated, Mellon moved the operations to Port Arthur, Texas. Later in 1936, he funded a Baptist minister to run for Patman's seat. Drew Pearson, who reported the incidents in his syndicated column "The Washington Merry-Go-Round," concluded that "friends of the ex-Secretary of the Treasury say that he never forgets."[36] Despite the well-funded opposition, Patman retained his seat successfully until 1976, long after the legislative battles of the 1930s had been fought. The memories forged in battles between the New Deal reformers and Wall Street would leave an indelible impression that would endure for 50 years.

A similar sort of argument to the one employed in the 1920s also was used to attack the Fed once again. Patman locked horns with Marriner Eccles when the Fed governor appeared before the House Banking and Currency Committee in February 1937. After Eccles testified about interest rates, Patman then asked Eccles if the Fed was trying to bring about national branch banking in the country. Eccles, somewhat surprised by the question, replied that the topic had never arisen. While favoring some type of branching, Eccles admitted that the topic was not high on his list at the time. But Patman was not dissuaded. He feared that large banks were holding and then selling off large amounts of government securities while not making enough loans to small business.

Although Eccles was nonplussed about Patman's nonsequitor, the congressman revealed more about his intentions a month later. Still bathing in the light of his victory on behalf of veterans, he announced in Congress a bill intended to nationalize all of the twelve Federal Reserve banks. The banks' stock was owned by the various commercial banks in their districts, and he wanted the Treasury to purchase the stock. His reasoning was familiar. "A few big banks have too much control of the monetary system of this country," he asserted, introducing his measure.[37] Fearful of the eventual spread of the big banks and a reassertion of the money trust, he felt the only manner in which to control banks was to nationalize the Fed. In the process, his ideas began to sound very much like those of the radio priest.

The radical idea did not find much support, even in the American heartland. The *Helena Daily Independent* commented: "Everyone supposed that the central bank idea had been pretty well licked with the political subsidence of Father Coughlin... this newspaper doubts that there is anything to be gained by further meddling with the banking system at this time."[38] Those who favored an independent Fed were forced to acknowledge that ownership by commercial banks was better than control by the Treasury. On the other hand, those who distrusted the money trust were forced to admit it required government control, at a time when government regulation and control were rampant. As a result, the Fed remained as the Eccles Act mandated despite the populist outcries.

Patman continued pressing for actions on the chains even after the Robinson-Patman Act was passed. He told a group of retail druggists in 1937 that it was time for a clear-cut issue to be presented to the American people. "Shall a corporation be permitted to engage in retail business in more than one state?" he asked. He continued, "It is my opinion that the American people are ready to encourage local business—locally owned and locally operated—as against absentee ownership or control."[39] Populist politics played well among constituents, but the movement was swimming against the tide. The chains had already made great inroads in retailing and were not about to be stopped. Charles Merrill, the founder of Merrill Lynch, had temporarily retired from the securities business several years before to devote himself to his Safeway chain of grocery stores.

Despite the seriousness of the times, a secret club within the House of Representatives still found the time to induct Franklin Roosevelt into its inner circle. The Demagogues Club had a history of inducting into its ranks members of the House who best personified the name of the group. It was formed in 1934 to include all members of the House who were known for telling "tall tales." In the summer of 1937, they met at a private club outside Washington. They were led by a Supreme Shouter as well as other members simply called Shouters and Persuaders. They proceeded to induct FDR, who was more than happy to have their support rather than incur their wrath. At his induction, the roll call was taken, vocally of course. When his name was called, Wright Patman, designated as a Loud Shouter, bellowed, "I move that he be admitted to the club." The next Shouter added that he wished to amend Patman's motion and admit the president as a life member. There were no dissenters. The president may have been reviled by the Liberty League but his star was still high among those in his own party, even among those most likely to cause trouble on occasion.

Creating the NASD

After enduring so much New Deal legislation, Wall Street began to realize that it had to organize in order to withstand the onslaught of regulations and face the brave new world designed by regulators. New issues and the stock markets had already been curbed, but there was still one part of the market left unregulated. Not all stock trading was confined to the exchanges. The over-the-counter-market (OTC) was left untouched by the 1934 legislation because it was not a stock exchange. It was instead a market conducted by dealers over the telephone and telegraph for issues not listed on an exchange. By definition, it was a potential source of problems in the new regulatory atmosphere.

Since the NIRA encouraged trade group associations, the Investment Bankers' Conference organized itself as a competitor of the older Investment Bankers' Association. Wall Street realized that the New Deal had become a formidable challenge, and no individual firm or small group of firms could face it alone. At the same time, pressure mounted in Congress to pass legislation to control the OTC market. In 1937, a law was passed mandating that securities firms organize themselves more formally. Introduced by Senator Francis T. Maloney, a Democrat from Connecticut, the act was an amendment to the Securities Act of 1934, allowing securities dealers to form national groups to better regulate themselves and arrange codes of conduct and trading. A year and a half later, the securities trade organizations agreed to become the National Association of Securities Dealers (NASD) under the Maloney Act. Its members included almost all dealers in the country. The creation of the organization was extremely important to the development of the markets because as a group the NASD represented a true national marketing network of dealers.

While discussions continued about how to form the group that would eventually become the NASD, another scandal broke on Wall Street that marked the passing of the old guard. In 1938, the firm of Richard Whitney & Co. failed. The NYSE immediately suspended it and began an investigation into its affairs. It was the first suspension of a major brokerage since the SEC was formed almost four years before. Several inquiries were begun, and it was discovered that Whitney had embezzled funds under his management. The five-time NYSE president admitted his guilt and claimed that he acted alone, without the knowledge of his partners or brother George Whitney, a partner at J.P. Morgan

& Co. The authorities acted quickly, and he was indicted and found guilty within a month. At his sentencing, he appeared without family members in court for support, asking his brother and family to let him take the blame standing alone. He was given a prison term of 5 to 10 years for securities theft and served his sentence in Sing Sing, the only president of the NYSE to serve a prison term.

At the end of the 1930s, the moneyed class had been defeated across a broad front. The American public was convinced that businessmen and Wall Street financiers were nothing more than gangsters in expensive suits, intent on robbing the workingman at every turn. In 1936, 65 percent of the population had family incomes of less than $3,000. The same year, Ferdinand Lundberg, a reporter for the *New York Herald Tribune*, wrote a book about America's 60 richest families. Using tax documents and estimates from the 1920s, he reported the listed assets of the super rich, including Rockefeller, Ford, the Morgans, and a long list of other Wall Street people and businessmen. John D. Rockefeller topped the list at an estimated $1 billion, but some of the lesser-known Wall Street figures also had amassed considerable fortunes. The list included bankers and brokers, ranging from the Stillmans of National City Bank to Otto Kahn of Kuhn Loeb and Bernard Baruch, who had an aggregate $2 billion among them. Incomes of several million dollars per year were not uncommon. The theme of the book was adopted by Harold Ickes in the 1938 campaign and mentioned by him in a speech. Sales of the book began to increase dramatically as a result, and it reached the bestseller lists. It was just the sort of book that made the Progressives smile, for it seemed to prove what they had been discussing for years. America had been robbed and now there was proof, of sorts. But war clouds in Europe would prevent any further action against Wall Street and big business. The country's attention was beginning to be diverted after almost a decade of putting Wall Street in the spotlight.

Although the SEC was firmly in place by the outbreak of World War II, its procedures were still being slowly developed.

The agency would evolve slowly, having to deal with myriad issues that arose as Wall Street activity began to increase after the sharp decrease in the early 1930s. Securities houses often developed new practices and techniques quickly, leaving the SEC playing catch-up with the whirlwind of events occurring in corporate America. But the 1940s proved to be a continuation of the 1930s for the securities business. During World War II, the RFC remained firmly in place as the nation's premier financier of businesses, and securities dealers and underwriters played second fiddle to the agency. Only in the 1950s did the economy rebound and the investment outlook improve. With the recovery, it became apparent that the victories won by reformers in the 1930s were substantial and that Washington had effectively shackled Wall Street. The question that remained was simple: How long could reformers keep the financial sector at bay? Wall Street rarely accepted defeat unless it was in its own best interests. But as the postwar years would show, the commercial banks emerged in the late 1940s as the most aggressive financial institutions, seeking to extend their reach despite the laws of the 1930s.

CHAPTER 4

THREE DECADES
OF SLOW CHANGE

It is certainly well that Wall Street now professes repentance. But it would be most unwise, nevertheless, to underestimate the strength of hostile elements.

Ferdinand Pecora

I n the 1930s, reformers had a common cause that united them in their assault on Wall Street and the banking community. Financiers remained disconsolate after the New Deal ended, convinced that the American way of doing business had been dealt a severe blow. If they were to claw back any territory lost after the Crash, the bankers and investment bankers would need a common cause. Admittedly, that would be difficult because the New Deal and subsequent Roosevelt administrations had been so effective in keeping the wolf from the door, whether it came in the form of the Axis powers, gangsters, or Wall Street. Tampering with New Deal reforms would have to wait for a future time when they faded from memory. It became a long wait.

While Wall Street was chastened, the banks were not in the mood for restraint. Although Marriner Eccles was best known for the law that bears his name, he was also symbolic of a trend sweeping through western states in the 1930s and 1940s. Using holding companies as their acquisition vehicles, banks began buying other banks in an attempt to extend their reach into other states. They were not violating the McFadden Act since they were not opening new branches, but they were extending their reach through acquisition and merger. Eccles's own banking company became one of the larger operating in the West, but it was still dwarfed by a purpose-built holding company conceived by A.P. Giannini at the Bank of America, which quickly became known as the "little reserve bank in the West." Needless to say, the Federal Reserve was not amused.

Both sides in the continuing financial battle maintained familiar positions. Bankers and securities dealers claimed that government had no business dictating rules to the markets. Regulators continued to maintain that Wall Street was responsible for the Crash and the Depression and that excesses could never be allowed again. Neither side was fully correct, but public opinion still sided with Washington. The financial services industry learned a valuable lesson from the 1930s fiasco. Public opinion had to be swayed to again support finance. Without it, a long tradition and profitable businesses were destined to remain moribund. In the postwar environment, Wall Street was relatively content. The New Deal helped create a new oligopoly among the top investment banks and securities houses that the banks could not threaten. Less would be heard from the Street than from the banks over the next 50 years. The banks would prove to be a much more formidable foe than many regulators and legislators ever expected.

During the late 1940s and early 1950s, the economy began switching back to normal production and private civilian financing. Interest rates had been controlled by the Fed until the Korean War was finished and were now free to find their own levels again, signaling a return to normalcy for the markets. The market for new issues revived for both stocks and bonds, although the 1950s were known as the decade of new issues of all sorts, dominated by those in defense-related industries. But hangovers from the past still lingered. Wall Street never expected that memories were as long as they proved to be. The Crash and Depression were still vivid memories for many. Ironically, the public appeared to have a shorter memory than regulators, who pursued the Street and the banks throughout the 1950s. The only element missing was the passion of the New Deal. Times had improved, and it was now more difficult to make a case for more controls.

SEC Dilemma

Wall Street securities houses had just been through a long ordeal as the Korean War ended. After being sued by the Justice Department in 1947, the upper echelon of securities firms had just finished an arduous case that lasted for several years. After the war, the government filed suit against 17 investment banks, alleging a monopoly in the way they did business in the past. The case, the *United States v. Henry Morgan et al.*, alleged that Morgan Stanley and others had monopolized the investment banking business by forming syndicates to underwrite securities that excluded many other capable firms. According to the suit, the problem dated back as far as World War I, when some war bonds were underwritten by the old money trust, and continued into the 1930s. Memories indeed seemed to be long, but many of the original bankers and legislators were still alive and active in New York and Washington. After several years of exhaustive testimony, much of it contradictory, the presiding judge, Harold Medina, threw the case out for lack of supporting evidence. Investment banking had been in the docket but now was free to pursue new business in the 1950s, as the demand for new capital increased dramatically after the Korean War. A major cloud had finally been lifted from the corner of Broad and Wall Streets.

One of the first issues to confront Wall Street in better days occurred in the early 1950s. Underwriting was increasing at a brisk pace. Many initial public offerings (IPOs) came to market, demonstrating the new confidence in the markets. Then, ironically, the SEC began to raise questions about its own powers in overseeing new stock issuance. According to the Securities Act

of 1933, new issues had to undergo a cooling-off period between
the time that a new issue was registered and when it was first eli-
gible to be sold. The only advertising that could be done on
behalf of the new issue was the prospectus accompanying it. The
prospectus was a "facts only" brochure accompanying each new
issue, full of financial details that had to adhere to the full disclosure provisions of the Securities Act. The prospectus allowed
investors to determine the merits of an issue. The SEC could not
comment; its only task was to require full disclosure. The actual
quality of an issue was a matter left to the private ratings agencies, which could only comment upon application by the issuer
of the securities.

At the same time, many securities houses were adding to their
research staffs, producing research materials commenting on
the quality of many companies. Much of the research was timed
to coincide with the new issues. The question the SEC was raising was extremely important. Should it be the overseer of this
research as well? Was the research used to entice investors to buy
the issues? Although it did not state it publicly, the implication
was clear: The research may have been tainted rather than objective. Although the agency could not comment on the quality of
the investment reports, it could prohibit them from appearing
or it could prohibit firms that produced them from participating
in any subsequent underwritings for the company involved.

Until 1953, the SEC held that new securities could not be
offered to the investing public until the agency released them
for sale. Then the SEC changed tack and allowed companies and
underwriters to prepare preliminary prospectuses that contained
information about the company during the offering period. But
the larger question remained. Securities houses regularly produced research to inform investors about a company's financial
strengths and weaknesses. If it was produced around the time of
a new issue, was it violating the law? The SEC held that "arous-
ing public interest in the issuer or in the securities of an issuer
raises a serious question whether the publicity is not in fact part

of the selling effort."[1] Initially, the matter sounded like hair splitting, but it became one of Wall Street's most enduring, and unanswered, questions.

Several underwriters gave up participation in large new issues in the early and mid-1950s because of this potential conflict of interest. At first glance, the issue sounded like quibbling, but it masked a much larger problem for Wall Street. Since 1934, when the modern investment banking community was created by the Glass-Steagall divorce, the major underwriters were all partnerships, not connected to commercial banks with access to larger sources of funds. Their capital that could be committed to a new underwriting was somewhat limited and could only be offset by syndicating an issue among many investment banks. Underwriters were already leery of the Securities Act of 1933 because of potential problems with due diligence and did not need any more headaches. Producing research and then joining a syndicate for the same company shortly thereafter seemed like a natural way to sell the new securities, but if the SEC objected then some underwriters naturally demurred. The net effect was to remove some underwriters from the potential lists, a prospect that boded ill for the capital-raising process in general.

One striking incident of the vagueness of the procedures came during the initial public offering for Ford stock in 1956. Since being founded, the company had been a family-run organization with a private capital structure. Then, in a stunning turn of events, it put its stock up for sale, and Goldman Sachs, led by Sidney Weinberg, managed the underwriting. Henry Ford's grandson Henry II ran the company at the time, and was extremely friendly with Weinberg, a relationship that his grandfather probably would not have cultivated because of Weinberg's religion. The issue was for $650 million, and the syndicate underwriting it totaled over 700 underwriters, illustrating the reluctance of some firms to overcommit to an issue. A year later, a new SEC chairman, Edward Gadsby, criticized the Street for publicizing the deal outside SEC guidelines. The underwriters responded that they had informed the SEC of all details, as

Wall Street Wrecking Crew *Today* April 21, 1934.

Bonus Marchers, 1932.

Jack Morgan & Duncan Fletcher, 1933.

Nary a Drop of Wet Legislation, by Morris.

How About a Little Action, Mr. Constable?

Helena Daily Independent, August 1933.

Charles Mitchell and Entourage, 1933.

John Marrinan, investigator for the Pecora committee,
and Peter Norbeck, 1933.

Richard Whitney, 1933.

Carter Glass & Ferdinand Pecora, 1933.

The New Deal, by Talburt, *Pittsburgh Press*, 1933.

FDR as a Happy Warrior, Cecil Orr, *Glasgow Herald*, 1934.

Republican Insurgents, by Berryman, 1932.

Al Smith Giving Liberty League Speech, 1936.

William Borah, 1936.

Walter Winchell & Senator Homer Capehart, 1955.

FDR Signing the Eccles Act, 1935.

Original SEC Members; from left (seated) Ferdinand Pecora, Joseph P. Kennedy, James Landis (Standing) George Mathews, Robert Healy.

THE MAN'S AT THE WOLF'S DOOR, FOR A CHANGE

FDR at the Wolf's Door.

Business Conditions, 1937.

Alan Greenspan at Work, Oliphant © 1996 Universal Press Syndicate.

12/10/96

required. Since the criticism came after the fact, it did not help put the SEC in a good light. The implication on the other side was striking. Would Ford have been denied fresh capital because the SEC could not make its own language and procedures clear?

The SEC concern appeared genuine in light of its own strict interpretation of its powers under the 1933 act but would be difficult to enforce at a time when the markets were heating up. Investors were returning to the stock market, and stock hucksterism again was on the rise. Radio personality Walter Winchell gave tips on his radio program gleaned from news reports. Bucket-shop operations and boiler rooms were opening around the country, selling "hot" stocks to the public for the first time since the 1920s. The SEC staff was small, and even modest increases in its budget for new hiring would not have been sufficient to keep it abreast of the markets. The commission quickly was faced with a choice. Adopt rules that were practical in the face of the market resurgence or be accused of hindering growth in the economy. This was an about-face from the position it found itself in during the Depression.

This seemed like a natural debate between Wall Street and the SEC, but it was remarkable for the amount of time that had lapsed since the Securities Act was passed. In the 1950s, the markets and the economy were off and running, and the debate seemed like one that should have been settled years before. The fact that it was not was not so much a testament to the strength of the SEC's authority as it was to the relative lack of activity on Wall Street since the 1930s. Now, regulators would find themselves confronted with something not seen in 25 years—a bull market.

A serious problem facing the investment banking underwriters was the size of the new issues of securities coming to market. They became larger with each passing decade and required more capital on the books of their underwriters as a result. Since the securities houses were all partnerships in the 1950s and 1960s, this left the partners with the increasingly daunting task of having to leave more capital with their firms rather than compensate themselves or their employees. This made them move into the future cautiously, a distinct benefit for the SEC and cautious investors. Losing one's personal fortune was a strong motivation, and many Wall Street partners were conservative, trying to preserve their firms' capital. Once the securities houses went public beginning in the 1970s, the complexion of Wall Street would start to change, and cautious attitudes would be cast aside in favor of more aggressive business practices on a street already known for aggressive practices.

Skirting Antitrust Laws

Regulators were still active during the postwar years. Wall Street was not entirely subdued, but events of the magnitude of the 1920s and early 1930s were not repeated. Banking was still a problem in the eyes of the regulators because commercial banks were constantly testing the waters to find weaknesses in the McFadden Act. The American experience with regulation was still new and had not been tested during a bull market.

The prohibition against branching across state lines seemed impractical, given the new migration toward the suburbs that began in the 1950s, which put severe pressure on state as well as federal banking laws. Prohibitions against branch banking seemed out of date since the country was growing at a rapid pace and the trend toward the suburbs was proceeding full steam. The chain stores had successfully opened nationwide operations, but banks were still confined to their home states. The old fears of Wright Patman and Louis McFadden seemed unfounded. In the 1950s, the spread of Sears and other national retailers proved that when consumers were faced with hometown merchants charging more than national chains, the hometown merchants' parking lots soon emptied in favor of those offering better choice and lower prices.

Many companies devised a new method of avoiding expansion and being charged with antitrust violations. The Clayton Act, passed in 1914 to bolster the Sherman Antitrust Act, made it illegal for one company to hold stock in another if the result was to lessen competition in the marketplace. But the language of the law also was notable for omitting the term "assets," so many acquisition-minded companies would purchase the assets of another without actually buying stock. The technique worked in banking as well. Many small banks were not public at the time, so a larger bank could simply purchase their assets, avoiding the letter of the law. The loophole was well recognized and in 1950 Emanuel Celler, Democratic congressman from New York, and Senator Estes Kefauver, Democrat of Arkansas, proposed an amendment to the Clayton Act that included the term "assets." As a result, the loophole many banks had used for expansion was now closed, and more vigorous antitrust actions began to contain them, along with dozens of other companies trying to consolidate their activities.

Celler began his congressional career in 1924 when he was first sent to Washington from his working class district in Brooklyn. Kefauver also began his career as a congressman in 1939 before being elected to the senate. He later gained fame as the head of the Kefauver Committee investigating organized crime in interstate commerce. The two carried the spirit of reform from the New Deal. Celler especially was familiar with much of the legislation passed during the 1930s, having been a supporter of the death sentence provision of the Public Utility Holding Company Act (PUHCA), as was Wright Patman, still sitting in the House and as vocal as ever.

Avoiding the pitfalls of the McFadden Act, banks had been aggressively expanding in the postwar period. The most aggressive banking company was the Bank of America (BOA), based in San Francisco. It successfully used a holding company, the Transamerica Corporation, to expand beyond its home state of California by purchasing other financial companies, avoiding the branching issue. Founded at the turn of the century by A.P. Giannini, the BOA was highly successful in developing consumer banking and became a giant in its home state before expanding.

It was never part of the money trust, but it was a feared part of a money monopoly, the 1950s' term used to describe the power accumulated through bank expansion. The term "money trust" was aging and was rarely used, but monopoly was in vogue, because Transamerica was the country's largest institution with more than $7 billion in deposits.

After the war ended, the smaller banks protested the growth of large financial service institutions, and Transamerica was first on their list of behemoths. A holding company act had been introduced in Congress in the late 1940s, supported by many smaller banker associations because their constituents were beginning to fear for their independence. Transamerica held an interest in 47 financial service companies and banks in five western states and was the largest stockholder in Bank of America. The company began its growth in 1938 when it actually began shedding BOA stock, continuing to do so well into the late 1940s. However, the divestment was not enough to placate regulators. While the growth was seen in the East as a creeping monopoly, it was viewed somewhat differently in the West. When Transamerica bought a Reno bank in 1934, the lieutenant governor of Nevada stated, "The resources of Nevada have not been impaired. Recently, the state has been undercapitalized. The coming of Transamerica should and does meet with the approval of our business people."[2] States with an abundance of space needed more capital and often had to rely on the help of outsiders.

Nevertheless, the complaints continued. Finally, in 1952, the Federal Reserve Board voted to force Transamerica to divest itself of its sprawling empire. Fed Chairman William McChesney Martin, previously a successor to Richard Whitney as president of the NYSE, announced that the company was in violation of the Clayton Act. The 1914 law was passed in the wake of the Pujo hearings, which prohibited one company from owning stock in another. It was an antitrust law, designed to reduce cross-company ownership and interlocking directorships, which the Pujo hearings and the subsequent Pecora hearings had been so successful at highlighting. Despite the Clayton, McFadden, and Glass-Steagall Acts, banks still devised ways to spread their tentacles. In the early 1950s, regulators did not accept that interpretation of the laws should be relaxed so that the banks could expand along with the economy. As a result, the company was ordered to offer a divestment plan that began six months later. The board vote was extremely close, however, and one of its members, Oliver Powell, dissented from the majority. He claimed that the majority view "fails to recognize that a certain amount of monopoly is inherent in banking."[3] The remark was to prove prescient in more ways than one. The divestiture took time, however, and eventually collided with congressional action in 1956.

Transamerica was not alone in expanding but was probably the most egregious example of bank growth. Both National City and Chase also had been aggressively expanding in response to the postwar economy. The big New York banks had a natural excuse for pushing the limits of regulators' patience with their expansion plans since they had been limited by the Glass-Steagall Act and state banking laws also shackled their expansion. They needed to expand within the confines of their immediate surroundings. In 1954 Chemical Bank merged with the Corn Exchange Bank. Then National City bought the First National Bank to become First National City. The largest merger of the period came when Chase National merged with the Bank of Manhattan Company to become the Chase Manhattan Bank. In all cases, the mergers were between intercity rivals, avoiding the pitfalls of interstate mergers. New York banking laws, confining banks to their home counties, were not breached, so it appeared that the banks were on solid ground with their expansion. Clearly, no laws had been broken by merging with another bank literally across the street.

But in a classic case of "damned if you do and damned if you don't" critics charged that the mergers were reducing competition by reducing the number of banks in existence, especially if they were retail banks dealing directly with the public. By merging closer to home, within the confines of the McFadden Act, banks were still endangering the public, which had less of a choice in banking services as a result. The problem with the expansion was that banks were not allowed to own stock in other companies. The prohibition predated the Clayton Act, and was found in the 1864 National Banking Act, but applied to national banks only. The Clayton Act merely extended that prohibition to companies in general. How the acquiring bank structured its deal became important. If it was a bank acting as a bank, then it would be in violation of the act if it had a national charter. But if state banks did the same, a storm would erupt because they could do something national banks could not, reopening the old McFadden issue from the 1920s. Clearly, the way around the problem was to use holding companies. Transamerica did it successfully by being organized specifically to buy the Bank of America. National City was particularly aggressive in New York, using its holding company to expand into the suburbs, something forbidden by state law at the time. Emanuel Celler told New York legislators to stop National City's expansion, which was "abhorrent in itself and could start a chain reaction by giant financial institutions in this city that might ultimately wreck the entire banking structure of this state."[4] The idea that "big was bad" still rang clearly in some quarters in Washington. It was clear from the regulators' point of view that the way to control the spread of banks was to restrict the use of holding companies. The purpose-designed shell companies had not been popular since the 1930s and would prove no more popular in the 1950s.

More Power for the Fed

Finally, in 1956, after years of battling Transamerica, Congress passed the Bank Holding Company Act. The law empowered the Fed to be the regulator of bank holding companies. In order to prohibit the spread of banks into areas outside banking, it forbid the holding companies' owning shares in companies other than banks. In any case, the Fed had the power to quash any acquisition. Holding companies attempting to own banks outside their home states were subject to the state laws where they wanted to acquire another bank. In most cases, the provision stopped interstate banking in its tracks because most states did not permit out-of-state banks in their territory. In a sense, both the death sentence provision of the PUHCA and the McFadden Act had been followed closely, if not to the letter. The Fed was the natural regulator for bank holding companies. The Fed's power in this respect eventually would prove the undoing of the Glass-Steagall Act when the tide shifted away from regulation to deregulation several decades later.

Within a decade, the Bank Holding Company Act required some tuning up. Congress responded by passing two amendments. The first came in 1966. It gave the Fed the ability to review and approve acquisitions of bank holding companies with an eye toward determining whether they might reduce competition in the process. However, Congress did not make the law applicable to one-bank holding companies. As a result, many banks transformed themselves into one-bank holding companies very quickly to avoid the Fed. Spotting the loophole, Congress acted again in 1970 to place single-bank holding companies under the Fed's authority. Shades of the old death sentence provision of the PUHCA resurfaced after decades.

The Supreme Court also provided some relief for the opponents of bank expansion. In a decision delivered in December 1966, the court ruled that national banks were bound by state laws concerning bank expansion. National banks could expand in those states where local laws permitted state banks to branch. Only about a dozen states actually permitted this, many in places where national banks were not interested. There was to be no distinction between banks for these purposes. Citing the older existing bank laws, the court concluded that national and state banks had been placed on the same plane in the past and that it was not going to upset the applecart.[5] The McFadden Act had been questionable in the 1920s because of its anti–chain store nature, and now had been engraved in stone for several more decades by the court. The message was clear. The court was not comfortable with rewriting law. That was a job for Congress.

Testing Glass–Steagall

The McFadden Act and the Glass-Steagall Act conveniently were put in the same category by those who wanted to adopt branch banking nationwide. They were simply classified as Depression-era laws that were becoming increasingly irrelevant in a booming economy. But old laws could not be cast as the enemy. Banks would need a new rallying cry if they were to have a chance of rolling back some of the old legislation. Being isolated from the banks, Wall Street was happy to continue its merry ways with no thought of rolling back Glass-Steagall. Any movement for change would have to come from the banks themselves.

Past experience taught that a battle needed an opposing enemy. Economics would not be in the frontline in this argument; it would be the cavalry used to charge once the battle lines had been established. Everyone appreciated that larger institutions were preferable in some businesses to small ones. Large banks could employ economies of scale that smaller ones could not achieve. The wider their base of operations, the more insulated they would also be against the inevitable economic downturn. Big banks were better for the economy. Not everyone agreed, but the argument was compelling. But economic arguments alone seldom won a public debate.

Since the Civil War, investment banks and private banks had been blamed for most of the economic turbulence surrounding the stock exchanges and the various panics that periodically developed. Commercial banks only entered the picture during and after World War I as they crept into the securities business, first by underwriting and selling bonds. Despite the fiascos of the

National City Bank and Chase National during the 1920s and early 1930s, their record was relatively spotless compared with that of Wall Street, whose record of shenanigans ran much deeper in public opinion. But after World War II, it was the commercial banks that became more aggressive, realizing that if the Glass-Steagall Act did not exist they would have clear sailing in the securities business, because the investment houses were relatively small when compared to the bigger banks. Accustomed to their relatively safe position, the securities houses remained placid, choosing to perform their duties within the cartel-like atmosphere created by Glass-Steagall. Banks, on the other hand, became much more aggressive, testing the boundaries of the banking and antitrust laws at every turn.

The postwar years also marked a gradual change in the way economic analysis would be used in future debates about the value of regulatory legislation. Although the economy was booming in the 1950s and 1960s, it became more clear over time that very little was known about some basic economic statistics in the 1920s and 1930s. The issue was not one of hindsight. Government bureaus and cabinet departments kept many statistics, but they shed little light on the actual workings of the economy. In 1920, a private research organization called the National Bureau of Economic Research was founded to apply more rigorous analysis to economic data than had been done in the past. A year later, Herbert Hoover, then secretary of commerce, asked it to conduct "a careful investigation into the cyclical fluctuations in unemployment" and investigate "the merits and defects of various remedies proposed."[6] The recession of 1921 created a sharp increase in unemployment, and Hoover wanted more information that would help formulate government policy. Much of the research group's early work was done at the behest of the Republicans in power, who realized how little was known about the country's wealth and productive capabilities. As a result, it became associated with the party although its intent was always to remain above the fray.

The unemployment question was not settled by the 1921 inquiry. Ten years later, the level of unemployment was still something of a guessing game. And despite all of the propaganda disseminated on Wall Street's behalf during the Pecora/Fletcher hearings and against the Fletcher-Rayburn Act, government spending was miniscule in 1929 as compared with later years. After the Crash, it was measured at only 3 percent of the gross domestic product compared with 20 percent in the 1990s. Popular accounts of the Crash and the hardship it created also were somewhat overdone, since the actual number of investors losing money was much smaller than suggested by popular writers of the day, such as Frederick Lewis Allen.[7] The whole period relied upon anecdotal evidence more than succeeding generations. When subsequent generations realized this, revisionist evidence began to appear, challenging many of the landmark events of the Progressive era.

New analyses of some standard progressive chestnuts demonstrated that all was not what it originally appeared. In 1958, a study appeared asserting that the breakup of the Standard Oil Company in 1911 after a Supreme Court ruling was not justified on the basis of predatory pricing. The study showed that although the company may have been a monopolist at the time, it was not guilty of the practice of lowering its prices to drive competitors out. In short, it was important to get the charges correct rather than simply believe that a monopoly was guilty of standard monopolistic practices. This was the approach of what became known as the Chicago School of antitrust economics. It based its analyses on economics rather than the legal, political, and common law tradition used by the dominant school of antitrust economics known as the Harvard School. What success the Progressive movement achieved in the past was based on the Harvard model, with Louis Brandeis in the forefront. It already was recognized that the antitrust laws sometimes needed a de facto suspension in the face of severe economic difficulties. This occurred during World Wars I and II. During the 1930s, the very formation of the Investment Bankers Conference and dozens of other similar trade organizations was a clear indication that the

New Deal welcomed temporary economic alliances that ordinarily were not tolerated.

1929 Redux?

Although most of the attention was focused on the banks in the 1950s, the securities business did not escape the notice of reformers and critics. Wall Street was still viewed with suspicion every time the stock market moved sharply, either up or down. The problem was a double-edged sword for the Street. When the market went down, speculation was to blame. When it rose, the question was why?

The latter state of affairs began occurring in the mid-1950s when the market began to rise for what observers claimed were specious reasons. By early 1955, the stock market was in a strong bull phase that had lasted almost a year and a half. The Senate Banking and Currency Committee, now headed by Senator J. William Fulbright, a Democrat from Arkansas, decided to begin an investigation into the rise. Fulbright said he preferred to call it a "study" rather than an "investigation." The market rally was not accompanied by improved economic conditions at many of the companies whose stocks were rising sharply. That fact alone bothered the committee because it was reminiscent of 1929. Credit market conditions were also vaguely similar, and even the thought of an unsustainable bubble worried many lawmakers. The new consumer society that reemerged after the war still made many uncomfortable because it appeared to be a repetition of the 1920s. Some newspapers noted that credit among consumers was a potential problem because almost 80 percent of home purchases required mortgages. In the past, many homebuyers actually saved the bulk of the money for a purchase before buying a home. A marked change in the consumer society was occurring in the United States, and it was not recognized immediately by all commentators.

Political explanations were also offered. One Midwest newspaper claimed that the market boom began despite the 1953–1954 recession because Democrats did not show strength in the 1954 elections and the public assumed that the policies of the Eisenhower administration would continue. "The American people have confidence in the Eisenhower administration," it stated. "They believe the President's sound, common sense policies are good for business."[8] As a result, Wall Street braced itself for the first congressional investigation of its actions since the 1930s. The securities business was not happy with the prospect, but the *New York Times* summed up the situation when it commented that Fulbright "and his committee have a responsibility to try to come up with an answer. We have an idea that we speak for a substantial majority of Americans when we say we completely agree."[9] Wall Street executives and traders packed their overnight bags for a trip to Washington. As in the past, they were accompanied by an army of lawyers.

The Fulbright committee conducted its investigation in what had become a traditional style. It invited market operators, analysts, and corporate executives to comment on the market's rise. Naturally, it heard a wide range of opinion. The chief executive officer of Sears, Roebuck confessed that his company pension fund had $30 million in liquid funds but was unsure whether it should buy stocks. Others claimed that the market was about to cause a spike in inflation after several years of less than 1.5 percent gains in the consumer price index. The president of the NYSE wanted to see the margin rate on stock purchases kept at its current 60 percent, while Marriner Eccles testified that it should be raised to 70 percent. The more testimony that was heard, the greater was the range of opinion. But one clear fact emerged from the committee deliberations. None of its members were well versed in the ways of the NYSE and the markets. In fact, they were mainly ignorant of many basic market techniques.

One of the first to notice the problem and comment was market analyst Roger Babson. In his syndicated column, he noted that the committee was trying to make a comparison between the Dow Jones Industrial Average in 1955 and the Dow in 1929. Committee members were trying to compare the calculations scrawled on the back of envelopes. Only 17 of the Dow 30 industrial stocks in 1929 remained in the index in 1955. He also pointed out that they did not know how to adjust stock prices for dividends paid or for stock splits. After not being able to make their crude numbers check, he noted that committee members concluded that they "smelled some monkey business by Wall Street," when a hasty conclusion was not warranted. They also displayed total ignorance of the specialist system of making markets on the stock exchange floors, leading them to draw conclusions that were not relevant. Rather than constantly question Wall Street motives, Babson wrote "The real question is one of educating buyers and sellers of stock."[10] The education was as important for legislators as it was for investors. The criticisms made about the Fulbright committee members' ignorance of the market were similar to those made about the members of the Pecora committee and the original SEC.

Fulbright blamed the rise in prices on what he called excessive speculation but clarified the point. He believed that speculation was being encouraged rather than dissuaded. He told the Economic Club of New York that "tipsters, flamboyant advertising...increases in the amount of credit...the tendency to resent and resist all warnings of caution and the introduction in the market of a rash of new issues such as penny uranium stocks" all contributed to the market's unexpected rise.[11]

The term "tipster" was an old Wall Street term, referring to those individuals who sold what appeared to be "inside information" to unsuspecting investors in the 1920s. The term was still used, and one particular radio personality had already been suspected of possessing private information. Fulbright also sparred frequently with one of the other committee members, Senator Homer Capehart, a Republican from Indiana, over whether speculation or outright rigging was responsible for the market's rise.

Mass Media

Market information broadcast by Walter Winchell over the radio came under scrutiny by the Fulbright committee. When Winchell began reporting on market movements and individual stocks in

1953, he was already widely respected as a commentator on American life. Many listeners and readers immediately interpreted his comments as "hot tips." Naturally, his ability to move stock prices quickly came to the attention of the committee, which challenged his veracity. One of his defenders was Edward T. McCormick, president of the American Stock Exchange, where many of the commentator's stocks were listed. McCormick defended Winchell's comments as essentially accurate, noting that many of his tips did not necessarily work in small investors' favor. Yet they did cause a rush of orders to flood his exchange from time to time. Then at one point in the proceedings, he made a comment ripe with history and politics. He insisted that the market was not too high and that the country had entered a "new era" of economic growth. Fulbright immediately snapped, "Isn't that statement reminiscent of anything?," referring to the 1920s when the term "new era" was constantly used before the Crash to describe the lofty market averages and the new consumer society. McCormick responded, "I feel that our understanding of the economy is growing, that our studies are bearing fruit." But Fulbright would not abandon his point. "Is this because we have returned to the same party in the White House that we had in the Twenties?" he asked rhetorically. McCormick grinned. He responded by saying, "I'm a lifelong Democrat from Arizona. I was appointed to the Securities and Exchange Commission by President Truman."[12]

After McCormick testified, Walter Winchell issued a statement brushing aside McCormick's comments, claiming that it was "somewhat novel to hear a stock exchange president complaining of a rush of orders; it seems only yesterday that Wall Street was complaining bitterly that FDR had undermined the confidence of the country in the financial world." He concluded with an allusion to the radio spoof "War of the Worlds," adding, "Mr. Orson Welles once told the American public a fairy tale and caused a lot of excitement. I told the same people the truth and nobody has yet challenged the veracity of what I reported."[13] Winchell was never accused of divulging inside information although many of his recommendations proved uncannily correct. The issue was raised, however, and would never fully recede again. Divulging information not fully available to the public would be frowned upon in the future, and broadcasters were well aware of the fact.

The current resident of the White House was well aware of the political nature of the Fulbright committee. Dwight Eisenhower told a news conference that he had no opinion on the effects of the Fulbright committee hearings. But he did mention that anyone conducting investigations into the economy should do so with great care so that no damage would be done. The remark was a reference to the fact that the market had dropped during the committee hearings. The postwar economy showed great signs of strength, and the entire discussion seemed a bit out of proportion since the United States was the undisputed world economic power. The hangover from the Depression proved to be a long one, however, and the effects of the Pecora hearings and the regulatory legislation of the past remained vivid. A financial editor from Philadelphia summed up the situation when he told the committee, "One of the country's hidden safeguards throughout the post-war period has been the vivid remembrance of the two depressions—the decline in commodity and stock prices after World War I and the great depression after the 1929 crash. This fear has served the country well."[14]

The Fulbright committee concluded that the market was weak despite the rises in many stocks, but it had little impact on the securities markets. Wall Street remained very political about the committee. There were no harsh condemnations or strident complaints even though it was clear that most brokers and investment bankers thought that the committee was very ignorant of finance in general. The major accomplishment of the committee was to demonstrate to Wall Street that regulators were still watching two decades after the boisterous 1930s. But a problem always surfaced after investigations that produced little tangible results: Further investigations would not be quick in coming unless a major scandal erupted. Fulbright was crying wolf with his "study" of the markets. Further cries of wolf would be taken less seriously as a result, although questions about the role of specialists on the exchanges would be addressed again since it was one of the few issues raised that would endure.

The committee prompted other investigations in the following years. The American Stock Exchange faced a major upheaval when McCormick resigned as president in 1961. The SEC had expelled two of the exchange's members previously for willful securities violations and then began a full-fledged investigation. The exchange began its own internal investigation led by Gus Levy of Goldman Sachs, leading to McCormick's eventual resignation. McCormick was only the third paid president of the exchange, which had changed its name to the American Stock Exchange in 1953. Previously, it was known as the New York Curb Exchange, the name used for the market that did not move indoors to facilities on Trinity Place in New York until the early 1920s. During the 1950s and 1960s, the Amex had been a hub of activity, and many of its newly listed stocks were among Wall Street's brightest stars. The exchange was organized in similar fashion to the NYSE, and any criticism of it was criticism of the Street in general.

Street Transformations

During the 1960s Wall Street was expanding at a rapid pace. The bull market created new opportunities for securities firms to add more brokers and traders to their ranks as stock exchange volume increased. More retail customers were attracted to the markets, and the decade became known as the "go-go years." Wall Street had been democratized more than at any time since the 1920s, and the new social and demographic trend extended into the ranks of the Street itself, not just its investors. There was a radical transformation in the manner in which the securities industry did business.

Although the top investment banks still dominated Wall Street legend and tradition, new entrants were making themselves felt in ways that would revolutionize finance within 10 years. Merrill Lynch, E.F. Hutton, and Dean Witter were among the top wire house brokers, but they were still considered plebian by the Wall Street elite since their strengths were retail brokerage and trading. In order to gain stature on the Street, a securities firm had to demonstrate prowess in underwriting and arranging mergers and acquisitions, specialties that separated the men from the boys and established a narrow pecking order. Many of the older investment banks were still plying their trade much as they had decades before. Morgan Stanley did not have an institutional sales force until the late 1960s, preferring to give the dirty job of selling new securities to others. Salomon Brothers and Goldman Sachs, on the other hand, recognized the need for trading facilities far in excess of what had been developed in the past. Wall Street was becoming transaction-oriented, and corporate clients wanted more than just underwriting and merger advice from their investment bankers. The older firms were slow in providing these new services, leaving the door open for others not traditionally included in the elite.

Some scandals of the decade gave a vivid portrait of how Wall Street had changed. In the early 1960s, a major scandal erupted when Ira Haupt & Co. failed. The medium-size broker loaned margin money to a commodity futures speculator named Tino De Angelis, who had been defrauding the American Express Company and many other brokers and banks for several years. The firm had to close its doors as a result of its dealings with a former Bronx butcher with no visible means of support or background as a trader. Many other firms, including American Express, also lost several hundred million dollars, and the NYSE had to wind down the affairs of Haupt. Although Wall Street always had dubious characters operating on its margins, the affair was the closest a clear outsider had come to the very heart of Wall Street itself.

While the smoke was clearing on the De Angelis affair, better known as the "salad oil swindle," the specialists on the NYSE came under fire for their performance on the day President Kennedy was assassinated in 1963. Violent price swings and some

serious distortions were experienced in many NYSE-traded stocks
after the news of the assassination broke on the floor of the
exchange. Critics quickly charged the specialists with abandoning their duty of trying to maintain orderly markets in the face
of adversity. The NYSE naturally came to their defense, but history was working against them. Almost two years before, similar
charges had been leveled against the traders during a market
drop that critics maintained could have been better handled. In
this case, the criticism did not come from politicians but from
money managers and bankers. Trading patterns suggested that
specialists were selling when the public was buying, helping to
depress prices and leading to suggestions that the market was
rigged in favor of professionals. But the NYSE attributed the
problem to increased volume on the exchange. Keith Funston,
president of the NYSE, commented, "In the face of the highest
volume in more than three decades, exchange specialists exceeded their recent performance records for stabilizing transac-
tions and maintaining price continuity."[15] The specialist system
dated back to the exchange's first days as an organized market
and was vigorously defended as fair and honest.

Some stocks had their trading closed on the day of the assassination, while others remained open for trading and suffered
serious price losses as a result. Floor traders also came under fire
for speculating that day by selling short, adding to the market's
woes. The SEC was conducting one of what would become many
studies of trading on the NYSE and had already recommended
that specialists have their capital requirements increased. Specialists and member firms were asked to respond to pointed
questions about how they operated when maintaining markets
in response to complaints about prices, coming mostly from the
investment community. A particularly telling statistic in 1963 was
that specialists needed to hold on their books only 400 shares of
a stock in which they maintained a market, a relatively small
amount for some frequently traded stocks given the volume of
trading that could occur on heavy trading days. The affair led to

an increase in capital requirements, although it was not the last time that specialists would come under fire.

During the 1960s, several of the quickly rising firms were also developing exotic specialties. Arbitrage became a popular and profitable form of trading at Goldman Sachs and Salomon Brothers, while Merrill Lynch continued to add all sorts of brokerage and investment banking activities in an attempt to become a financial department store without banking facilities. In the early 1970s, the listed options markets opened in Chicago, and many of the securities houses added options trading to their activities. In most cases, the expansion of securities firms' activities meant adding facilities that were within the realm of their defined businesses. At the same time, many banks were slowly attempting to encroach on the securities business by slowly whittling away at activities that fell within the gray area of the Glass-Steagall Act.

Beginning in the mid-1950s, banks began agitating for the power to underwrite municipal bonds. They already had the ability to underwrite general obligation bonds, based upon a community's taxing power, but were forbidden by Glass-Steagall from underwriting municipal revenue bonds, which were not supported by taxing power.[16] As early as 1955, Senator John Bricker of Ohio had introduced a bill that would have amended commercial banks' ability to underwrite revenue bonds. The Investment Bankers' Association immediately began querying its members about the prospect, while smaller municipal dealers complained about competition from banks in general. Underwriting general obligation bonds was not that profitable an enterprise since it was governed by state laws requiring competitive bid underwriting. In the 1950s and 1960s, the market exploded for revenue bonds of all types, ranging from college dormitory issues to those of major highway authorities. The area was growing rapidly and presented banks with new opportunities.

What enticed commercial banks was the fact that revenue bonds did not have to undergo competitive bidding because they were not supported by taxes. In that respect, revenue bonds were the same type of product as a corporate bond as far as an investment bank was concerned. Most investment banks made the bulk of their underwriting revenues through negotiated underwriting with companies issuing stocks and bonds because the fees were higher on corporate issues. State laws mandated that underwriting fees for general obligations be put up for bid and given to the best bidder, meaning that fees were smaller as a result. But the revenue bonds were openly embraced by investment banks as profitable. Commercial banks saw an opportunity and began lobbying for permission to underwrite. The other intention was less clear but would have long-term results if they were successful. Clearly, the commercial banks were attempting to chip away at the armor of Glass-Steagall by testing the waters in a relatively obscure corner of the marketplace that interested only bankers. Other similar tests would follow.

Mounting an assault on the Glass-Steagall Act was not an enviable task. Although it separated the two sides of banking, the law also established deposit insurance and allowed the Fed to establish maximum savings deposit rates (Regulation Q). Attacking parts of the act while keeping others inviolate proved to be difficult since it would require fracturing part of what had become known over the years as the "safety net" erected during the Depression. The safety net was a patchwork of New Deal laws designed to protect savers, investors, the unemployed, and others from the arbitrary actions of big business and reestablish some order to what was a polarized society in the 1930s. Those parts of the safety net were accepted parts of the American economic landscape—the Securities Act of 1933, the Banking Act of 1933, the Securities Exchange Act of 1934, the Public Utility Holding Company Act of 1935, the Eccles Act of 1935, the Social Security Act, several housing and agricultural acts, and a host of other acts creating temporary "alphabet agencies" to produce work projects and other public spending endeavors. The McFadden Act was not included in the list although it was considered useful in restraining interstate bank branching.

Throughout the pre-World War II years, many of the arguments in favor of the safety net and other social legislation were mainly political and social in nature. Laws were judged by their ability to protect the public rather than their potential economic outcomes. Economic analysis was used but usually played second fiddle to the social and historical because it was considered somewhat speculative. The safety net argument was a protective concept. If it safeguarded investors, savers, and workingmen from big business, it could do little harm since big business always showed a remarkable ability to adapt. Protecting those less able to adapt was more important. After World War II, economic analysis began to appear more frequently but was confined mostly to academe. It had already been seen that when it was used by banks, arguing for greater efficiency in the 1950s, it fell mostly on deaf ears. If it were to make any inroads against New Deal banking and securities laws, it would have to be accompanied by a strong political ideology. Economics and politics would prove to be a powerful combination. Economics by itself was argued by only a few within cloistered confines.

After Dwight Eisenhower left office in 1962, the political side of the equation was put on hold as Democrats assumed the White House. After Richard Nixon later assumed the presidency, his administration became so plagued by scandal that dismantling of the New Deal laws was unthinkable. If the Glass-Steagall Act were to be dismantled successfully, it would require a joint effort by Congress, regulators, the White House, and Wall Street acting in unison. Those days had not been seen since the 1920s and were still distrusted by some Democrats in the 1960s and 1970s, although the old reformers were dying out. In the interim, the best the banks could do was chip away at the Wall Street investment banking industry, hoping to accrue its old powers slowly, biding time for better days ahead.

The core of Wall Street was not in danger from the banking industry. Banks could not underwrite corporate securities, and mergers and acquisitions deals were beyond the reach of most because of they required knowledge of corporate finance and financial structure only found on Wall Street. Other areas were more enticing, however. Making Wall Street even more tempting for the banks was the fact that the wire houses began an expansion in the 1960s that made brokerages akin to banks, since they were attempting to reach a wide client base. Brokerage offices were appearing around the country as the bull market of the 1960s fueled a drive to reach as many retail investors as possible. Merrill Lynch opened an office in Grand Central Station in New York City so that clients could stop by and check prices before using the trains. Brokerage offices were becoming crowded with a walk-in crowd who regularly stopped by to read the ticker tape. Interest in securities was at an all-time high, and the banks eyed the brokers enviously, realizing the potential for expansion.

Brokerage became the apple of the banks' collective eye. Glass-Steagall prohibited underwriting and trading of corporate securities, activities that required banks to own the actual securities if only for a short period of time. Brokerage, on the other hand, was not prohibited because it only involved bringing together buyers and sellers, not taking actual positions in securities. Commission banking of this sort was materially different than fee banking, in which a bank acts as principal to a transaction. As far as the banks were concerned, owning a brokerage subsidiary was an excellent way to extend their reach toward, if not into, Wall Street.

Bulled Over

During the 1960s, the role of the SEC faded into the background as the bull market raced ahead. As during all strong markets, the regulator's role was pushed into the background. The SEC also lacked a clear economic theory under which it could operate, finding itself squeezed between the Justice Department's antitrust division and the Federal Trade Commission. The SEC had no economics staff for a 20-year period, from the early 1950s to the end of the Johnson administration in the late 1960s.[17] As a result, enforcement lagged, and Wall

Street began to operate in an environment where the SEC was not feared as it was in the 1930s. The "cop on the corner" concept had been replaced by former corporate attorneys at the SEC who did not see themselves as enforcement officers, but merely as traffic cops giving directions when asked. The precedent being established was risky for investors, as it proved to be in future bull markets when the commission also was overshadowed by rising market indices.

A less than effective SEC did not intimidate anyone. Richard Nixon called the SEC bureaucratic and legalistic during his 1968 campaign for president, in one example of politics intruding again on Wall Street. His remarks infuriated former SEC chairman William Cary, who responded by saying, "Securities regulation in the United States is considered the best in the world and is being copied abroad in an effort to develop enough confidence in the people to invest in new enterprises. To suggest that it should be curbed endangers the very mass capitalism this country has so proudly achieved."[18] Despite its poor funding, the agency still was highly effective in registering new issues and keeping abreast of the markets as best it could, despite some politicians. By the late 1960s, the tide was changing, however. The SEC was now considered too detail-minded for the markets, a position that was unthinkable 30 years before.

Before the banks could become involved in brokerage, a new scandal erupted on Wall Street, quickly demonstrating that brokerage too had its risks. Beginning in 1969, trading volume had reached historic highs and many brokerage firms could not keep pace with the volume of orders generated by customers. The NYSE called for a halt in trading so that the backrooms, or back offices, could catch up with the paperwork. The respite helped some firms, but several experienced serious difficulties. The fallout from the scandal had strong repercussions in the investment community and in Washington.

Many firms could not confirm trades made by customers. Many trades were booked incorrectly or customers had securities stolen from their accounts. Several member firms were forced to close their doors as a result. The NYSE helped arrange bailouts wherever possible, but several firms needed a white knight to save their customers. Goodbody & Co., a medium-size broker founded by Charles Dow earlier in the century, failed in 1970 and was absorbed by Merrill Lynch. The firms that failed were part of what would become a larger consolidation trend over the next decade as smaller brokerages were absorbed by larger ones with more capital and stronger management. But the crisis in confidence among investors had to be solved in Washington because Wall Street again proved it was inept at helping anyone but itself out of its own mess.

In response to the crisis, Congress extended the safety net a bit further by creating the Securities Investors Protection Corporation (SIPC) in 1970, an insurance fund that guaranteed securities and cash in a brokerage account against fraud or theft. Similar to the FDIC, the fund was established to convince investors that it was safe to leave money and securities with brokers, helping to stem the tide of cash transfers away from the Street. When it became clear that SIPC would pass Congress, Wall Street appeared contrite for yet another crisis in confidence. Don Regan, president of Merrill Lynch, recalled that as the bill moved toward final passage, the governors of the New York Stock Exchange sent a telegram to Senator Jacob Javits of New York, stating, "We assure you and your colleagues of our cooperation in a spirit of constructive reform." He also noted that "nothing less than that assurance would satisfy the industry's critics, who had seen too little evidence of such a spirit earlier."[19] Without the SIPC guarantee, the flood of money into the markets would have stopped, and the great democratization of Wall Street that occurred 15 years later would have been seriously postponed.

The crisis had several other effects that were equally long-lasting. The days of the small, marginally capitalized partnership were over in favor of larger firms with wide customer bases. The new firms had more capital on their balance sheets than their older counterparts, and the demand for increased capital was

pressing. Donaldson, Lufkin, & Jenrette had already gone public, followed shortly by Merrill Lynch, which became the first
member firm to be listed on the NYSE. Also in 1970, another
established broker badly affected by the crisis, Hayden Stone &
Co., was purchased by a smaller firm run by Sanford Weill. It
was the first acquisition for the man who would become known
as the greatest dealmaker since Pierpont Morgan. The misfortunes of some would become a bonanza for others seeking to
establish themselves as major operators on Wall Street.

Citibank, Again

While Wall Street was undergoing consolidation, the banks con-
tinually tested the waters of change. Under increasing pressure to
expand and find new profitable lines of business, some of the
larger institutions began to develop products that would test
the Fed's determination to remain an effective regulator. One
of the most aggressive was First National City. The bank had
already developed the first negotiable certificate of deposit in
1961 in order to improve its funding. While appearing on the surface to be just another boring bank product, the negotiable CD
broke new ground by allowing its institutional buyers to sell it
before it matured if cash was needed, having repercussions for
the Fed and Regulation Q. And by being large-denomination
deposits, these CDs had relatively low reserve requirements as
compared to smaller ones. The Fed looked favorably upon the
product, not realizing that financial innovation of this seemingly
harmless sort would challenge its own powers within 15 years.

In 1973, a Ralph Nader task force published a study of
First National City, exposing the bank's foibles. In the true progressive sense, the study outlined many practices the bank used
to circumvent existing regulations. One concerned the negotiable CD and the use of offshore branches in what was known as
the eurodollar market. After the new CDs were accepted as a
legitimate part of the money market, interest rates began to rise

and National City tried to convince the Fed to raise the Regulation Q ceilings so that it could continue to attract deposits. When the Fed refused, the bank then turned to accepting deposits off-shore, which did not require reserve requirements. The money was then loaned back into the United States, completely circumventing the Fed's control. Nader's group was not exposing anything that the banking community did not already know, but revelations of that sort surprised outsiders and showed how the Fed and other regulators often played catch-up with the banks rather than leading them. For his part, Walter Wriston told his employees to ignore Nader's researchers as they interviewed dozens of National City employees.[20]

Building upon this success with more products, First National City, renamed Citibank in 1976, would emerge as the dominant and most aggressive bank of the postwar period. As banks began testing the waters to determine whether they could enter any part of the securities business, Citibank found several areas worth exploring that set off howls of protest from Wall Street. In the early 1970s, municipal revenue bonds were still an issue on Wall Street, and Citibank established a presence in municipal bonds; however, when the bank began offering investment advice to investors, Wall Street sensed real danger. Banks wanted to offer brokerage and investment services and buy seats on the NYSE. The Glass-Steagall Act had always been revered on Wall Street because it protected the investment banks from their larger brethren. The more the act was questioned, the more loopholes it appeared to have. The banks were intent on exploring all of them.

Wall Street was still dominated by strong personalities in the 1960s and 1970s, but no one assumed the dominant position that the Morgans, Richard Whitney, and Otto Kahn had in the years before the Crash. Bankers did distinguish themselves, however, and became dominant spokesmen for the financial services industry. Charles Mitchell had been a key figure after assuming the helm at National City in the 1920s. In the late 1960s, Walter Wriston assumed the helm at Citibank. Wriston was responsible for many of Citibank's innovations and ruled the bank until 1984.

New Securities Law

The Wall Street crisis of the early 1970s convinced many that stronger regulation was needed. As market activity expanded over the years, the primary form of regulation of the exchanges and the OTC market was self-regulation. The responsibility for monitoring trader and broker activities lay with the exchanges in the first instance. The concept was not new. All of the stock exchanges were technically self-governing; the concept was part of many of their original articles of incorporation. The SEC and NASD were ultimately responsible for activities in the markets, but could never be expected to keep a firm hand on the pulse of the day-to-day workings of any market. They were too small and did not have the budget for such activities. Both houses of Congress decided to investigate the matter to see whether a new layer of regulation was feasible.

The House of Representatives chose William Cary, a former SEC chairman under President Kennedy, to study the matter. A Columbia professor at the time, Cary believed that a regulator capable of overseeing both the stock exchanges and the NASD was needed to eliminate problems between the markets. Many stocks listed on an exchange were traded in the "third market," in brokers' offices away from the exchanges. This was another term for "block trading," where dealers crossed orders between buyers and sellers without using the specialist. Technically, the trading was done OTC style, and the jurisdictional problems it could create were evident. As a result, Cary proposed that the markets be combined into a single marketplace where the new regulator would be able to oversee all activities from a broad vantage point.[21]

Cary's view on the role of specialists was not popular on Wall Street. Arguing that the existence of the third market demonstrated that specialists were in danger of becoming anachronisms, Cary suggested that they be reorganized to report to the new regulator. Even more radical was the idea that specialists receive their financing from the regulator. The suggestion was a curious blend of the old and the new. No one suggested that the specialist system be abandoned. Being familiar with Wall Street, Cary argued that the system be kept while adding a new layer of regulation. The new body would report to the SEC, effectively coming between it and the markets directly. The idea was tantalizing but doomed from the start. Adding layers of regulation was something that Wall Street always resisted and in the early 1970s, the idea would not find much support in the securities industry. However, the NYSE board underwent reorganization at the time, being reduced from 33 members to 20: 10 to be chosen from the industry and 10 from the public.

The suggestion, along with dozens of others, was incorporated into a new federal securities law passed in 1975. The Securities Acts Amendments provided much needed regulations on the markets in the wake of the crises of the past six years. The bill was sponsored by two Democrats—Senator Harrison Williams of New Jersey and Representative John Moss of California. The SEC was charged with developing a national market system for securities. This required developing what became known as the "consolidated tape," a composite ticker tape that reported trades from all the stock markets in linear fashion as they were executed. Williams claimed, "The securities industry in the past has tended to look to regulation and restraint rather than to competition to govern the operation of the markets."[22] The idea was that the composite tape would eliminate price discrepancies in the market, forcing a greater level of competition between the exchanges and the NASD than had existed in the past.

The new law also eliminated fixed stock commissions and gave the SEC regulatory power over the municipal bond market. In response to the back office crisis of previous years, it also brought the clearing agents, depositories, and others involved in clearance under the SEC. The law was necessary to clean up Wall Street practices. The Street's reputation would be helped as well because the scandals and crises were tarnishing its image again. But no one could accuse Congress of attempting to put a damper on the bull market, because the stock markets had become very choppy since the late 1960s. The sharp rise in the price of oil in 1972–1973 and a rise in inflation had dampened investor enthusiasm, although the exchanges were still recording strong volume at the time.

Banks began offering brokerage services in the 1970s, charging rates far below what traditional brokers offered. The critical date for Wall Street was May 1, 1975, dubbed "May Day" by the securities business, when fixed commissions were abolished. Many institutional investors had threatened to buy their own seats on the NYSE if commissions were not lowered. James Needham of the NYSE had already gone on record as saying that negotiated commissions would wreck the exchange, and some securities firms executives claimed that they would leave the exchange if they were instituted. The NYSE finally succumbed, agreeing to release its stranglehold on rates. Negotiated commissions would be introduced. One result of the law was the creation of what became known as the discount broker. Over the next decade, many brokers would open their doors for business, charging less for trades than the traditional wire houses. And the banks also entered the fray. Chemical Bank quickly introduced cheaper commission rates that benefited larger retail investors, who could save substantially on large-size trades.

The Conglomerate Elite

During the post–World War II period, a new elite merged in corporate America. A powerful merger and acquisition trend developing in the late 1950s and 1960s had produced a phalanx of new corporate leaders driven to create large corporations through acquisition. The companies they created were unlike any seen before. Through the intricacies of the holding company, these companies absorbed others of all types, shapes, and colors. A new word had to be used to describe them—conglomerates.

In the immediate postwar years, acquisitions-minded businessmen recognized the loophole in the Clayton Act and used newly constructed holding companies to acquire the assets of others. When the Kefauver-Celler law was passed, the loophole disappeared. The idea of acquiring others certainly remained. In order to avoid the appearance of pursuing acquisitions for the sake of eliminating competition, the conglomerators began buying stables of disparate companies, without any apparent regard for the hodgepodge they were creating. They ranged from the small to behemoths. The best known in the 1960s were the ITT Corporation, LTV, Litton Industries, and Transamerica.

In the early days of the conglomerate era, a word of caution was uttered by economist Alan Greenspan. Writing in *Barron's*, he warned about pursuing large companies through antitrust simply because they were large. In an article entitled "Bad History, Worse Economics Spawned Anti-Trust," Greenspan wrote, "Whatever damage the antitrust laws may have done, whichever distortions of the structure of the nation's capital may have been thrown in the way of business organizations, these are less disastrous than the fact that the effective purpose, the hidden intent, and the actual practice of anti-trust laws in the United States have resulted in the condemnation of the productive and efficient members of our society because they are productive and efficient."[23] In this view, a correct understanding of the past would naturally have led to a society free of some of the restraints that had been placed upon it since the 1930s. Views of that nature made Greenspan a natural ally of business and the Republicans.

The conglomerates came under fire from the Nixon administration. Ordinarily, big business and Republicans were considered good friends, but the antitrust division of the Justice Department was aggressive in pursuing the massive companies. But the real story lay below the surface. The Nixon administration pursued the nouveau riche conglomerates at the behest of its friends in traditional corporate America, many of which were afraid that they might become the next target of an ambitious conglomerator.

The conglomerates were considered interlopers into corporate America, not welcome by the old guard. Each company was different, and comparisons between them were difficult. Several like LTV and Litton were heavily involved in manufacturing as defense contractors, while others like Transamerica considered themselves service companies since they were involved in real estate and financial services. Attempting to put pressure on them, the administration reverted to language from the past.

Attorney General John Mitchell became the point man in the Nixon administration's drive against conglomerates. Head of the Antitrust Division of the Justice Department Richard McLaren was also very visible and vocal about his intention to pursue conglomerates. He favored new legislation that would curb conglomerates, including a death sentence provision. "I fear that people take what we are doing as over-regulating, as being anti-free enterprise. I take the position that protecting competition is pro-enterprise."[24] But it was Mitchell who laid out the administration strategy. Nixon was on the record as not being fond of McLaren, and the job of being antitrust spokesman fell to Mitchell. In the process, he used some terms familiar in the 1930s. He announced that any corporation from the top 200 in the country attempting to merge with another from the same group would be blocked in court, to avoid what he called "super-concentrations" of economic power. He was clearly basing his position on the assumption that big was still considered bad, and that very big was very bad. Earlier, the administration had commissioned a study done at the University of Chicago questioning whether conglomerates could be attacked using current antitrust laws. The authors concluded that a vigorous pursuit of the large corporations was not defensible based on present knowledge of how the conglomerates worked. More economic data was needed before any strategy could be adopted. The administration ignored the report and proceeded on its own.

Barron's reprinted Greenspan's comments of 1962 seven years later in order to lambaste the Nixon administration for its anti-conglomerate stance. The newspaper was not alone in opposing the anticonglomerate drive. Labor and the traditional *Fortune* 200 had much to lose through conglomerate mergers and took stands against the movement. The tide had definitely changed since the 1930s and 1940s. Prosperity could be found in many sectors of the economy, and the consumer society, truncated by the Depression and war years, was no longer in any doubt. Legislating in times of hardship was easier than doing so during more prosperous times. Now, rigorous enforcement of antibusiness laws was seen as a threat to prosperity. The Nixon administration discovered the cold, hard facts when the press began questioning its stance. The public found other topics to busy itself with, and the anticonglomerate trend began to dissipate.

Before it did, Congress held hearings on the conglomerates. Emanuel Celler, almost 80 years old and chairman of the House Judiciary Committee, called hearings to take testimony on the threats the large holding companies posed to competition and the public. The hearings began in summer 1969 and invited conglomerators and their investment bankers to testify. The hearings revealed very little about the inner workings of conglomerates that was not already known. The best known of the corporate heads testified about the behavior of their companies and often clashed with Celler and other committee members about their practices, but never admitted wrongdoing. Harold Geneen, the CEO of ITT Corporation, was especially difficult to interrogate since he would not accept any interpretations of conglomerates that differed from his own. He maintained that the organizations were well-oiled machines that bought other, smaller prosperous companies in solid industries in order to add to shareholder value. Big was not bad in this view; in fact it produced economies that were unattainable in smaller, less efficient companies. While not everyone agreed, the conglomerates were not as hated as bankers during the early 1930s and as a result, any chance for anticonglomerate legislation or death sentences against them never materialized.

Events intervened in the early 1970s to take some of the edge off the anticonglomerate campaign. The Wall Street clearing crisis occurred, and the stock market began a decline that helped sink many outrageously high conglomerate share prices. Within several years, ITT, once one of the largest predators among the conglomerates, would find itself the target of many corporate raiders who wanted to dismantle parts of the company for its assets, thought to be worth more separately than as part of the holding company. The conglomerate idea lived on in more successful companies like General Electric and United Technologies, but reformers were never able to conclude their campaign with legislation designed to prevent conglomerate acquisitions.

On the Quiet

While bankers and securities dealers were preoccupied with volatile markets and rising interest rates in the late 1970s, deregulation still was being attempted in small ways. In 1977, Merrill Lynch announced that it was offering checking facilities on its brokerage accounts to accommodate customers. This was a service normally provided by banks and certainly a new twist for brokerages. The novelty in the service was that it could be used to borrow against securities accounts, effectively margining securities for cash. Regulators quickly put the service under a microscope. Two years later, Shearson Hayden Stone continued its expansion into other financial services when its chairman, Sanford Weill, announced an agreement to take over a California mortgage broker. Although not forbidden by law, it showed that brokers wanted to find other profitable lines of business quickly, before they were absorbed by the larger banks. Shearson also became the first Wall Street firm to ever borrow on the bond market, marketing $35 million of debentures to investors. Eight years before it had been the third brokerage house to go public.

The investment banks constantly reiterated the theme that the financial services sector needed to be divided to provide the best services to customers. A senior Merrill Lynch official asked, "Is it sound public policy to allow these institutions [banks] to grow even larger and more powerful?...Merrill Lynch is by far the largest broker-dealer in the securities industry. But in terms of total assets at year end 1977, it would only be the twenty-third largest commercial bank in the country, First Boston would rank thirty-eight, Paine Webber would rank only ninety-seventh...I believe that there is sufficient competition among those now providing services the banks are seeking to expand into so that the consumers of these services are being well served."[25]

In other words, "big was bad" in the financial services industry as it was in government, in the opinion of securities houses. Naturally, that meant only if banks were involved. The cleverness of the mostly self-serving arguments would make the task of deregulation all the harder in the years ahead. For the next decade, Wall Street would be pitted against the banks, protecting its oligopolistic hold on the issuance of securities and related services.

The 1970s were billed as an innovative decade for the financial services industry but would pale when compared with the two decades to follow. Attempts to innovate while enduring scandal and government-imposed regulations were nothing new, but inflation during the decade proved to be the most significant financial news. International events began developing that produced serious shocks to the American financial system. The precipitous rise in the price of oil in 1973, accompanied by rising interest rates, brought unexpected pressure to bear upon banks and Wall Street. No one would have imagined that these pressures would produce cracks in the Glass-Steagall Act and create the threat of secession from the Fed by many banks unhappy about the way they were treated by the central bank. By the mid-1970s it was clear that the good old days of bull markets and double-digit growth in company earnings were certainly finished. For the next 15 years, the travails of the 1960s would seem like halcyon days, because the financial system was about to face its most serious threat since the 1930s.

CHAPTER 5

THE REAGAN YEARS

"Whether you think its good or bad, we've changed the environment."

Walter Wriston, Citibank

Wall Street had always been ruled by a small clique of influential investment bankers intent on preserving the status quo. Throughout most of the postwar period, they were content to use the franchise presented to them by the 1930s legislation to carve out a lucrative, and insulated, business. During the Reagan presidency, their protected turfs came under pressure from commercial bankers, who were not content with the banking universe framed by the McFadden and Glass-Steagall Acts. Although the old laws were still inviolate in the early 1980s, reformers probed them for weak points through which they could be attacked in the name of banking progress.

When commercial bankers began successfully attacking the barriers separating them from Wall Street, they refashioned the financial services industry in their own image. The old white shoe investment banks began to disappear, giving way to much larger securities firms with far-flung offices and a much greater array of customer services than their predecessors. The old notion of a financial department store was making a genuine comeback after decades and would become a reality. In this new, popular form of Wall Street securities firm it would seem that the idea of

190

oligarchy was anachronistic. On the contrary, the new oligarchy that created these institutions was as powerful as those preceding it.

The new power elite assumed its position by constantly emphasizing the idea of consolidation in a global business environment. The brave new world of finance and business required larger firms with more capital and access to larger customer bases than ever before. Bigger was now considered better and was no longer considered the problem that previous Progressives thought; it was now the solution. The view was not universally accepted, but in the relatively thin air shared by regulators and senior bankers it was accepted doctrine and that was enough to insure its success.

Assaulting the laws regulating banking and Wall Street was put on hold in the late 1970s and early 1980s as more important items dominated the political agenda. Much sympathy had been growing over the years for a repeal of the McFadden and Glass-Steagall Acts. Inflation and high interest rates proved to be major stumbling blocks, however. Reform was difficult when the United States faced a major crisis of confidence in its banking system, caused in part by high oil prices and doubts about national policies in the wake of the Vietnam War. Any deregulation was likely to come in the form of slow erosion of old barriers rather than wholesale changes.

Conservative ideology also was set to make a strong return to American politics. Since the New Deal introduced bigger government, it had been a goal of those believing that "government should be seen but not often heard" to reduce its influence. The role of the individual began to be emphasized again, mostly to appeal to the same voters who a generation before had cast such a cynical eye toward big business and Wall Street. Conservative politicians were aided by a newly rejuvenated group of conservative policy specialists at think tanks aiding Ronald Reagan, who carried the torch of deregulation in the face of stiff opposition from many Democrats. A marked shift had taken place in American political sentiment since the end of World War II.

Prosperity brought with it a desire to scale back the influence of the federal government.

In this new environment, Wall Street securities houses remained very conservative, while the banks became aggressive advocates for change. Banks began pointing to the European model of "universal banking" as their goal of offering all sorts of banking services under one roof. Rather than use the 1920s model, they chose instead to point to the growing internationalism in the markets as an example of how the United States should get in step with the rest of the world. This was a marked change from previous decades, but oddly was a repeat of the 1920s when Republicans were happy to point to international trends as important for American business, especially Wall Street. Even the Crash of 1929 was blamed on international events, partly to deflect criticism over the role of banks and brokers in causing and perpetuating the economic crisis. Now the old model was dusted off in a new setting. Other countries had universal banking. Why should the United States be different?

The two major international competitors of the United States were often cited as examples of having exemplary banking systems, for very different reasons. Germany had universal banking, with investment banking, commercial banking, and investment management under one roof. German banks were often major investors in industrial companies and insurance companies and appeared to show no ill effects. The Japanese banking system was more akin to the United States, for good reason. When the United States occupied Japan after World War II, investment banking and commercial banking were divorced, à la Glass-Steagall, by the American administration overseeing the occupation. Despite the separation, Japanese banks became enormous through their famous *keiretsu* arrangements with other financial service companies and industries, where many companies would share the same bank and even corporate name. Major competitors had more integrated banking systems, and the United States should follow suit, or so went the argument.

Critics maintained that both countries had centralized economic power in their banks, crowding out competition. Monopoly banking had a long, tired history in the United States, and no one wanted to see the financial system revert to a money trust in which a few banks controlled the purse strings. But the arguments for economies of scale and greater international competitiveness became very alluring in a period when American industrial competitiveness was assumed to be falling behind and the country was beginning to run large trade deficits. Before the banking system could be addressed, however, a major problem needed to be corrected because the central banking situation in the United States was far from ideal and in need of repair. Politics would enter the picture and make a difficult situation even more troublesome. The new economic and political ideology of the Republicans under Ronald Reagan collided with those who felt that the New Deal had enshrined certain institutional safeguards that should be maintained.

Who Needs the Fed?

The rise in interest rates occurring in the late 1970s was not entirely unforeseen, but it still shook the foundations of many banks. The Fed had the authority to impose a ceiling on the interest rates paid on deposits through Regulation Q. This protected the Fed member banks from having to pay market rates of interest. This group included all nationally chartered banks, since they were required to join the Fed. It also established a national lid because no other banks were going to violate the ceiling since it protected their cost of funds at the same time. When interest rates rose, the banks were always protected and had no reason to suspect that they would be more vulnerable after the OPEC price rises in 1973. But opportunities were calling during this hike in interest rates. As money market rates exceeded bank deposit rates, a natural question began to be asked—who needs the Fed?

The problem was that the reserves Fed members had to leave with the central bank paid no interest. Banks required to place several billion dollars with the Fed to cover their deposits were losers, not earning a penny of interest. State banks were in a more enviable position. They could deposit their state-required reserves and earn interest. For all banks, large and small, this was a great incentive, especially as interest rates began to rise sharply. Banks already had been shunning the Fed for almost a decade, but when interest rates rose, the incentive was even stronger. The prospect clearly worried Fed Chairman Arthur F. Burns. He told the American Bankers Association in 1973 that since 1960, "about 700 banks have left the system through withdrawal or mergers." During the same period, "just over 100" banks joined the system.[1] This caused a regulatory problem for the Fed since it was difficult to exercise monetary control. The number of banks over which it could exercise authority was dwindling. This was not a pleasant prospect in the world's largest and presumably strongest economy.

The defections were not simply a technical matter. During World War II, 50 percent of banks belonged to the Fed and they held 90 percent of the nation's deposits. By the mid-1970s, the percentage of deposits had fallen to 75 percent, representing about 40 percent of banks in the country. The reasons were abundantly clear. In the 1970s, reserve requirements were between 8 and 17 percent of a bank's deposits. There were no incentives for a bank to join the Fed. More ironic was the fact that the old fissure between national and state banks still had not been mended. As the economy grew and the population increased steadily, the banking system was becoming more fractured. In the later years of Burn's chairmanship, the Fed estimated that over $500 million of interest was being lost per year on those reserves deposited at the Fed. During the 1970s alone, only 600 of the estimated 1,700 banks eligible for Fed membership actually joined.[2]

Adding insult to injury, some banks had been flagrantly flaunting Fed regulations. Smaller state banks in New England began offering interest-bearing checking accounts, or negotiable order of withdrawal accounts, dubbed NOW accounts. Traditionally, checking accounts were not allowed to pay interest, but the concept picked up steam in the early 1970s and was offered even by large

New York City banks by the end of the decade. Burns, while sympathetic to the bank's loss of interest on reserves, wanted to rein in these accounts because they too fell outside Fed regulations. When added to the defection problem, they only underlined the problem the Fed was having keeping abreast of the money supply. But the coup de grâce was another product, which finally forced monetary reform from Congress.

Wall Street responded to the rise in interest rates by developing a new investment product. In the early 1970s, some mutual fund companies began offering money market accounts to the public. The accounts were like any other mutual fund, representing a diversified investment for the small investor. In this case, it was a money market mutual fund offering high interest rates. While the banks were offering rates protected by Regulation Q, the mutual funds offered them at much higher levels. The public responded by pouring several billion dollars into them within the first several years of their existence. Suddenly, the lexicon of investors began to change. Rather than talk about stocks and equity mutual funds, terms like "yield," "coupon rate," and "commercial paper" began to dominate nationally syndicated financial advice columns. Everyone was searching for the highest yield possible from a money market mutual fund.

The banks had no response to the rapidly developing trend. The products they offered were woefully inadequate as interest rates climbed. In early 1975, the funds reached the $2 billion level. Within 4 years, they reached $35 billion, the equivalent of the deposits held by one of the larger banks.[3] Wall Street enjoyed the phenomenon as the banks suffered. New product development had found a winning product despite a spotty stock market and a suffering bond market. Although the new funds were not wildly profitable, the Street still had discovered a way to retain investors' money during bad times. Investors would simply switch from equity investments to the money funds when interest rates rose. The banks were having a totally different problem. They were being deprived of funds necessary for lending. The Fed, for its part, was extremely unhappy with all of the developments because it was losing its grip over the credit system at a time when strong discipline was necessary.

The NOW accounts offered by smaller state banks also amply demonstrated that the Fed was only in charge of the larger federally chartered banks, but had far less control over the small institutions that still made up a large percentage of the country's banks. The smaller banks were offering an account the larger banks could not offer, a situation that would not last long. When some of the large banks began offering the NOW accounts, the Fed was faced with another dilemma. If it penalized them, it faced more defections. By the late 1970s, the Fed was faced with a serious erosion of its power unless Congress intervened.

The Volcker Fed

In 1979, the Fed chairmanship became vacant when William Miller, Arthur Burns' successor, resigned to become Treasury secretary. President Carter appointed veteran New York Fed member Paul Volcker to replace him. Unlike many of his predecessors, Volcker had extensive experience in international monetary affairs and was quick to recognize the problems caused by volatile exchange rates. Since the New York Fed acted as the Treasury's agent in the foreign exchange markets, the choice was a shrewd combination of interest rate and foreign exchange rate management. Volcker was well liked on Wall Street but quickly proved his independence when an announcement concerning a shift in Fed policy was announced in October. He was already on record as favoring a strong monetary policy to combat inflation. Volcker announced that the Fed would begin setting targets for the money supply in an attempt to rein it in, allowing interest rates to rise in the interim. After the announcement was made in early October, the bond and money markets suffered one of the worst days in their history, with interest rate rises eroding prices. The new policy of targeting the expansion of the money supply was a new emphasis for the Fed, and many

Wall Street analysts dubbed the new policy "monetarism." Some classic monetarists like Milton Friedman later disagreed with the name for the policy, but Wall Street labeled Volcker and the Fed "monetarist" nevertheless. Not everyone thought Volcker would stay the course, however. Noting that the new chairman had been present at the dismantling of the Bretton Woods system of fixed exchange rates in 1971–1972, one commentator mused that the new policy would be short-lived. "Long before the flash point is reached," one claimed, "the Fed seems sure to relent. The result will be a fresh round of inflation."[4]

Targeting short-term interest rates, the Fed applied a sharp dose of reality to the markets through open market operations like reverse repurchase agreements, where funds were drained from the banking system. It would be the most dramatic use of the tool since open market operations were established in their current form by the Eccles Act 44 years before. The policy had a rapid effect. The discount rate was already at 12 percent when rates were allowed to rise even further. The markets were sent reeling for the next four years with the strongest dose of monetary policy announced by the Fed in its history. Volcker was purposely vague concerning how high interest rates would be allowed to rise. "The broad thrust is to bring monetary expansion and credit expansion within ranges established by the Federal Reserve a year ago," Volcker stated, describing the new policy.[5] Over the next two years, Treasury bill rates soared into double digits, and the federal funds rate (for bank reserves) rose to over 20 percent at one point. Both the stock and bond markets began a tumble lasting several years.

Wall Street and the banking community understood the reasons for applying a strong dose of monetary policy, although the results were not pretty. Congress had already extended the years to maturity on Treasury bonds from 20 to 30 years, and long bond yields rose to 14 percent within a few years of Volcker's initial announcement. And Volcker was also amenable to liberalizing banking regulations. He was already on record as favoring a liberalization of the rules on interstate banking.

Recognizing that banks showed a "natural disinclination" to competition, he favored reciprocal arrangements among the large states to encourage interstate banking on a regional basis. The McFadden Act was proving a hindrance to effective national banking, but nevertheless was enshrined and proving difficult to dislodge since many smaller banks used it as a shield from larger out-of-state banks.

Shortly after Volcker was named to the Fed chairmanship, the Joint Economic Committee of Congress celebrated the fiftieth anniversary of the Crash of 1929 by conducting hearings. It heard testimony from Alan Greenspan concerning the likelihood of another crash given the economic turbulence of the past several years. Greenspan stated that he thought the prospect unlikely, agreeing with John Kenneth Galbraith's testimony that the Crash had been caused by insane speculation in stocks, something that certainly was not happening in the 1970s, although the Dow had reached 1,000 several times. Greenspan was worried about deficits, however, especially those caused by shocks from the outside. Oil price shocks could create an enormous debt structure that would become difficult to dig out from under. Mounting debt meant even higher interest rates. Greenspan was back in the private forecasting business after having served as President Ford's chairman of the Council of Economic Advisers.

The new emphasis on monetary policy drew criticism from many quarters. Politicians, including Jimmy Carter, were critical because high interest rates did not help their reelection prospects. Bankers and economists claimed that the Fed was not adhering to its own ambitious targets for the money supply while applying a dose of medicine that caused gyrating interest rates. Others saw the new, higher rates as a prescription for high unemployment. But Volcker did not waver. He noted, "I don't like to see big gyrations more than anybody else," but was firm in his resolve to choke inflation through growth in the monetary aggregates. The fight had consequences, however. High interest rates attracted foreign capital and the dollar began to rise quickly on the foreign exchange markets. Unemployment remained high, bringing political criticism from many quarters, some unexpected. Democrats were critical of the emphasis on the money supply, including Senator Ted Kennedy of Massasachusets and Representative Henry Reuss of Wisconsin. Conservative Republicans also criticized Volcker, demanding to know when interest rates were coming down so that the president's programs would have no Fed interference.

The fight on inflation also brought sharp criticism from the corporate sector. Lee Iacocca, chairman of Chrysler, labeled the Fed policy "madness" for causing volatile interest rates. Don Regan, soon to be Ronald Reagan's Treasury secretary, suggested that the policy was sound but that the new administration would find other ways to combat inflation to complement Fed policy. Since Volcker was a Carter appointee, Republicans could not be seen giving unqualified support to a Democratic-supported Fed chairman. The new administration soon adopted an economic policy of its own, which in many ways counteracted the Fed, appearing to be a throwback to the 1920s.

High interest rates did not slow the banks' aggressive moves into financial services. In 1980, banks still had not cracked the ranks of underwriting municipal revenue bonds. They began to make arguments that would be employed later in the broader battle against Glass-Steagall. The president of the American Bankers' Association told his organization that over 70 percent of municipal bonds being issued were revenue bonds and that it was time for banks to enter the ranks of underwriters. If they did so, they would help lower the cost of underwriting by providing competition for the investment banks. Municipalities would then be able to request competitive bids for underwriting to find the cheapest underwriter. C.C. Hope, chairman of First Union National Bank, told a conference of bankers: "Bringing an end to the Glass-Steagall Act provisions which prohibit banks from underwriting revenue bonds has long been a goal for bankers to broaden their investment base while at the same time better serving their communities. Certainly in these days of impatience with high taxes and high inflation we must ask how anyone can rationally oppose any program that could lower some of the cost of government."[6] The argument was a bit disingenuous because the vast majority of municipal issues were small and the savings would have been negligible. But the matter of costs was now entering the argument and was difficult to refute.

The Fed policy also spawned a group of market analysts dubbed "Fed watchers." The Open Market Committee was now more important than ever, and the watchers monitored the Fed's actions closely to determine what its next move might be. Incorrectly guessing about a move in the open market could cost a money market or bond dealer substantial amounts of money, so anticipation became the newest game on Wall Street and in the banking industry. The policy became even more intensely monitored after President Reagan announced tax cuts in 1981. Personal income tax rates were cut twice, but little effect was seen afterward. It appeared that consumers were spending the money, only adding to the inflation problem. Interest in Fed policy and inflation was unprecedented. The Fed had not been the center of public attention since the 1930s.

Investment banks were also busy during the early Volcker years. In 1981, Sears Roebuck announced that it was acquiring Dean Witter & Co. for $600 million. The retailer planned to place brokers in its retail outlets so that shoppers could invest while they shopped. The combination of Sears outlets and Dean Witter branches was inviting. The announcement followed the merger of Bache, a Wall Street wire house, with Prudential Insurance, and Shearson Loeb Rhodes, another wire house, with American Express. The mergers were not in violation of banking or securities laws, but the Sears acquisition was considered the most unusual because it was based upon an assumption that shoppers were also investors. They proved not to be, and 15 years later Sears began shopping for a buyer for Dean Witter, which then merged with Morgan Stanley. The real test in 1981 came when Bank of America announced its intention to buy Charles Schwab, a leading discount broker. In the years since negotiated commissions were implemented, Schwab had become the best known of the discounters. The acquisition did not technically violate Glass-Steagall because Schwab did not underwrite; its functions were solely those of a broker. Nevertheless, it sparked a lawsuit, which eventually made its way to the Supreme Court. Other banks had already tested the waters in this area but not on such a large scale. The deal succeeded but the business plan did not, and Schwab later bought back its share from BOA and became independent again. Not all of the expansion plans were successful, but once the floodgates had been opened more would follow.

Fixing the Fed, Again

Since being founded, the Fed had acquired powers through various laws passed for sound economic or political reasons. Yet the 1970s' experience with defecting banks, high interest rates, and money market funds demonstrated that the central bank did not have total control over the banking system. American politics and federalism were to blame. The idea that banks had to stop their expansion at state lines was arbitrary but was in keeping with the Jeffersonian notion that local control was preferable to federal control. When a truly national system, such as the Federal Reserve, was needed, its structure and powers were often incomplete because some small entity would insist, rightly or wrongly, about protections and safeguards guaranteed by the Constitution. There was nothing new about the argument, but it caused enormous confusion in banking circles.

Fed control came to a boiling point over the matter of reserves. Throughout the years, it could only set reserve requirements for those banks that voluntarily joined its system. The majority of others were controlled by their respective states. High interest rates began to have a deleterious effect on this system, and the Fed was actually losing control rather than gaining it at a time of extreme monetary volatility. Volcker's predecessor at the Fed, William Miller, attempted to resolve the reserve interest problem by proposing that the Fed begin paying interest to banks on their reserve balances. The idea did not sit well with

Representative Henry Reuss, a Democrat from Wisconsin. Reuss was Wright Patman's successor as chairman of the House Banking Committee and a dedicated populist in the Wisconsin tradition of Robert La Follette. When he heard of the proposal, he informed the Fed that if Miller attempted to introduce a resolution to pay interest, he would introduce his own resolution to have him impeached.[7] The populist mantle fitted Reuss well, but his background suggested that he might have been more accommodating than a traditional old school progressive. Born in Wisconsin in 1912, he attended Cornell and graduated from the Harvard Law School. He served in government in a number of capacities before being elected to the House, serving in the Office of Price Administration and as counsel to the Marshall Plan. He entered Congress in 1955 and served as chair of several of its banking and economic committees. He did not stand for reelection in 1982. His threat worked, and the Fed backed away from the idea of paying interest on reserves. The memory of Louis McFadden was not entirely forgotten.

Matters were not helped when rumors circulated that large banks like Citibank would withdraw from the Fed if they could not earn interest on the increasingly large amounts they were required to leave with the central bank. Faced with these potentially explosive issues, Congress responded by passing the Depository Institutions Deregulation and Monetary Control Act in 1980, a highly technical piece of legislation that had two sides. On the one side, it freed banks from interest rate ceilings previously imposed by Regulation Q.[8] On the other, it revamped the Fed's powers to bring it in line with the marketplace. All banking-style institutions now had their reserve requirements set by the Fed so the requirement was now uniform. While not a perfect solution to a tricky problem, the Monetary Control Act did tighten the powers of the Fed at a crucial juncture in its history.

The new law also included a host of other technical provisions that helped the Fed's stature as Volcker was applying a strong dose of monetary authority. Erosion of the Fed's power had potentially serious repercussions since, as agent of the

Treasury in the markets, it conducted auctions of new Treasury securities and also performed foreign exchange market interventions when required. The Monetary Control Act strengthened its scope considerably. For purely public relations purposes, the banks ignored much of the technical monetary control material in the law and concentrated on the deregulation side, something that they could trumpet to their customers. Most proclaimed that they were now free to pay higher interest rates and that customers would be better served. Privately, many groused about the lack of interest on reserves because it amounted to a penalty on Fed member banks, but little could be done to change the decades-old policy. There were still members in Congress like Henry Reuss who believed that the Fed represented big banks and that they should not receive special treatment because of their member status. Progressive political ideas had all but receded from view except in the constituencies of some Midwest politicians who still viewed the Fed as an institution too reliant on the big banks.

Supply Side

While the Volcker Fed fought inflation with monetary policy, the new Reagan administration proved Don Regan correct by implementing it with its own policies. Having an administration do one thing while the Fed was attempting something else was risky because the two sides did not always see eye to eye. The Reagan administration was interested in lowering taxes and providing a stimulus to the economy, objectives that ran counter to an inflation fight at the same time.

In the last year of the Carter administration, the Fed contended with interference in its fight with inflation when the president announced a series of special credit measures that lasted for six months. The measures helped bring interest rates down temporarily but when they were lifted, rates rose quickly again. Carter had been unsuccessful in balancing the budget, an issue in the 1976 election, and began preaching austerity and spending cuts as means of combating inflation and high tax rates. During the 1980 election campaign, Reagan took a completely different tack, preaching tax cuts and low inflation rates while advocating increases in defense spending and limited other spending cuts at the same time. The campaign was the opposite of the Democrats in tone, cheerfully optimistic about the future despite what appeared to be serious contradictions in its economic philosophy. Despite the contradictions, no shortage of Republicans signed on to the new philosophy in hopes of gaining favor at the White House and in Congress. The ideas of John Maynard Keynes were giving way to ideas that had not been tested empirically, although they had been seen in the distant past in a similar, if less sophisticated, form.

The Republicans had strong individuals in place to help win the argument. In the House, the strongest supporter of what became known as Reaganomics was Representative Jack Kemp, a Republican from New York. Joining him were Senator William Roth, Republican from Delaware, and a host of converts from more traditional Republican ranks like former Treasury Secretary William Simon. Alan Greenspan, former chairman of the Council of Economic Advisers under Nixon and Ford, also joined the Reagan side. From academic ranks, Arthur Laffer of the University of Southern California became the guru of the Republicans in the early days, preaching what was known as "supply side" economics.

The thrust of supply side arguments was that tax cuts would provide incentives for individuals and businesses to invest. Shifting emphasis from the consumer side of demand to production, it argued that the net after-tax effect on wages was more important than gross wages. Because of inflation, taxpayers had been experiencing "bracket creep" inflation, meaning that their wages were being subjected to higher taxes as inflation pushed them into higher marginal tax rates. By cutting taxes and putting more money in the hands of investors, the economy would return to a healthy state. But the political side of the argument was equally, if not more, contentious. Supply-siders argued that tax cuts could be accompanied by increases in government spending. Traditionalists argued that tax cuts required cuts in spending as well. The supply side theory sounded too good to be true. If the concept was applied, tax cuts would create more investment and a healthier economy, and would accommodate increases in defense spending. No losses to the government would occur if tax reductions were implemented. Arthur Laffer once demonstrated the relationships on a hastily drawn graph on the back of an envelope. Those who had practiced monetary and fiscal restraint for years became incensed. Was economics that simple?

Clearly not, argued many economists. One nonbeliever was Alice Rivlin, who was leader of the Congressional Budget Office during the 1980 election campaign. She wrote a letter to Republican Senator Orrin Hatch claiming that the concept had little empirical evidence supporting it. "So far the studies have shown that the impacts are very small in the short run," she stated. But those ideas were less controversial than those she had made a year earlier in a memo to Hatch in which she described critics of traditional economic forecasting models as "an extreme right wing claque who should not be given an audience."[9] Although she attempted to distance herself from the remark, it was clear that supply side arguments were being used by conservatives to paint a bright economic future when austerity was currently on the table. Alan Greenspan gave his blessing to supply side methods after the election. When asked if the basic theory of supply side economics was correct, he responded, "In principle, it's an unassailable proposition." He then qualified the remark by adding, "Were investment strictly focused on creating pre-tax profits rather than on after-tax rates of return, production would be specifically enhanced."[10] The emphasis was slightly different, but the endorsement was appreciated. The economy could have its cake and eat it too. Voters responded well to the early Reagan program, but the honeymoon did not last long.

The supply side argument also had extensive help from conservative think tanks supporting Reagan and his ideas. Liberal think tanks like the Twentieth Century Fund and the Brookings Institution aided Democratic administrations over the years on a variety of economic matters. During the Carter administration, the American Enterprise Institute (AEI) arose to take up the challenge of providing economic opposition to the administration. Founded in 1943, the AEI budget had grown 10-fold since 1970, and when the Reagan administration took office, it had a war chest of over $10 million per year. After Carter defeated Gerald Ford, the organization named Ford, along with former Republican officials such as William Simon and Arthur Burns, as fellows along with resident scholars such as Irving Kristol and Herbert Stein. Its economic expertise was considerable since they represented some of the most committed conservatives in their party.

Another conservative think tank working on economic issues was the Heritage Foundation, somewhat more conservative than the AEI. The organization was known for its publicity-minded research and team efforts, which helped to produce the *Mandate for Leadership*, a thousand-page tome presented to Ronald Reagan that covered all aspects of government bureaucracy and policies. It was especially valuable to Reagan when he was first elected because it aided him considerably in the process of nominating new political appointees in Washington, a place with which he was not familiar at the time.[11] In the past, Democrats had been aided immeasurably by reports from research groups such as the Twentieth Century Fund and the Brookings Institution. Now it was the conservative Republican opportunity. As parts of the New Deal came under attack during the Reagan years, it became clear that lessons of the past would be used by the Republicans for their own future agenda. *Mandate for Leadership* became required reading in Washington policy circles because it was viewed as a precursor of the future under Reagan. It was described by a reporter as "a blueprint for grabbing the government by its frayed New Deal lapels and shaking out 48 years of liberal policies."[12] Reagan did not disappoint his followers. At his inauguration, he claimed, "Government is not the solution to our problem. Government is the problem."

The hefty tome covered many aspects of government, from the structure and emphasis of cabinet departments to the administration of federally related agencies. It dealt with the Glass-Steagall Act in a section under the SEC. Acknowledging that the act was passed because of the Depression, it stated the current arguments for banks wanting to underwrite municipal revenue bonds, which had become a persistent issue in the early history of discussing Glass-Steagall. While not specifically calling for a repeal or even an amendment to allow banks to do so, it claimed that if banks were allowed to underwrite revenues, "these competitive advantages...would cause many brokerage firms, particularly small and regional firms to go out of business." Another area of interest, especially in light of the Wall Street scandals of the previous decade, as well as a furor over American companies paying bribes to foreigners in order to do business abroad, it stated that additional bureaucracy was not needed and that the SEC could handle any problems arising concerning corporate accountability. "There's no reason to believe that increased federal intervention in this area would improve corporate America...once begun, there would be no way to stop a burgeoning bureaucracy from multiplying."[13] The tone of the position was descriptive, although it was based upon the assumption that any reader would find the ideas of competition and efficiency commendable while abhorring bureaucracy and intervention at the same time.

Trickle Where?

The great irony in the supply side argument was that the administration seemed to be endorsing a trickle-down, or percolator, theory of economics that had been decried in the 1920s. Republicans had always preached that stimulants should come from the top down in society and that by providing incentives for the wealthy, all would benefit. In the 1920s, that was easier to identify as an elitist concept since the national wealth was skewed in favor of the wealthy. In the 1980s, the wealthy still paid the highest proportion of taxes so any trickle-down theory naturally would appeal to them. One dissenter to the Reagan program was David Stockman, director of the Office of Management and Budget in the Reagan administration. Within a year of the 1980 election, he became disillusioned with the premises upon which the economic policies of the administration were based. In what became an infamous article in the *Atlantic Monthly*, he expressed his dismay that the administration's policies would lead to massive budget deficits rather than a balanced budget by 1984, as claimed. Recognizing the historical problem first hand, he said, "It's kind of hard to sell 'trickle down' so the supply side formula was the only way to get a tax policy that was really 'trickle down.'" More damning still were his comments that "the approach of across-the-board tax cuts was always a Trojan horse to bring down" tax rates for the wealthiest.[14]

Stockman's comments proved shattering on Capitol Hill. Speaker of the House Thomas (Tip) O'Neill, a Democrat, called the comments "devastating admissions." Many Reagan administration officials spoke off the record, claiming that his comments hurt the administration but that he was too valuable to be fired from the economic team. A small California newspaper offered some advice to Stockman via fourteenth-century cleric Thomas à Kempis when it said, "It is easier not to speak a word at all than to speak more words than we should."[15] The major problem that Republicans anticipated was that Stockman's influence on Capitol Hill would be eroded since he clearly believed the policy was erroneous. If the chief spokesman for the policy believed it was ridden with errors, how could it be sold to Congress?

Wall Street's initial reaction to the Reagan program was skeptical. When the Street resisted the premise that budget deficits do not matter, Reagan called Democrat leaders in Congress to the White House to impress upon them the fact that Wall Street's focus was too narrow and that his plan was workable. But interest rates had not yet moved lower and bond prices sank, producing record high interest rates. Wall Street recognized that the policies ran counter to Volcker's inflation fight and that the two could eventually counteract each other. The short-term effects of supply side did not appear as predicted, and the financial markets refused to believe the administration's program was practical.

As a result of administration policies, the two biggest budget items became interest payments on U.S. government debt and defense spending. High interest rates proved a lure for foreign capital, and the dollar soared to record highs in the foreign exchange market. The Fed was partly responsible for the phenomenon by keeping pressure on the money supply and bank reserves, forcing interest rates higher. Its job was made more difficult by administration policies, which appeared to be inflationary. The strong dollar made imports cheaper, and a trade deficit started to mount, only adding to Wall Street fears about the ability of the administration to exercise fiscal caution.

Fears of Deregulation

From the first days of the Reagan presidency, deregulation was on the mind of many Republicans. Although Ronald Reagan professed admiration for Franklin Roosevelt, there were clear signs that part of the regulatory structure erected during the New Deal was coming under attack. Reagan admired FDR for his decision-making ability, especially under severe pressure, but the idea of state influence in business affairs did not work with the conservative Republican philosophy of less government. Talk of deregulating the banks and Wall Street began shortly after he took office but took several more years to get off the ground. Espousing supply side economics gave one indication of the immediate future. It became a convenient method of sidestepping institutions like the Fed and the traditional, regulated banking structure in favor of ideas that were more "market oriented." The only question was whether this market orientation had anything new within it or was just a return to policies of the distant past.

Amid the discussions of deregulation, Wall Street quickly grew fonder of Glass-Steagall than at any time in the past 50 years. Any deregulation apparently would not affect it directly, but it would have a profound impact on the banks since they were the institutions most severely affected by the various 1930s' acts. Wall Street learned to live with the wall of separation because it was insulated from the rest of the financial services sector. Glass-Steagall had created an oligopoly within that part of the financial services industry deemed too risky to be owned by other financial institutions, especially fiduciaries. Wall Street had been insulated for 50 years and had learned to like its independence. Rumblings about deregulation increased its anxiety and threatened its way of doing business.

An early shot was fired in the battle when the administration proposed in 1982 that the law be relaxed to allow banks to underwrite securities. The proposal went to a Senate banking subcommittee, where it naturally met with opposition from Wall Street and approval from the banks. In testimony, a Goldman Sachs partner stated flatly, "Only a truly separate securities affiliate can avoid a repetition of the misfortunes of the 1920s and early 1930s that necessitated the passage of the Glass-Steagall Act." An executive of Morgan Guaranty trust took the opposite position, claiming that the separation gave securities firms a "major competitive advantage" over the banks. After listening to both sides of the argument, Senator Jake Garn, Republican of Utah, remarked, "I wish both sides would stop kidding each other and sort of insulting the intelligence of this committee, everybody can keep trying to protect their own piece of turf and nothing will happen here, I guarantee you; it can go on and on."[16]

The comment proved prescient. The proposal did not materialize, although repeal of Glass-Steagall became a hotly debated topic during the 1980s. The investment banks had good reason to fear the commercial banks. The banks constantly tested the resolve of regulators over Glass-Steagall but not in particularly overt ways. In the 1970s, Bankers Trust had been distributing commercial paper on the part of major corporations. The bank had been criticized for doing so but managed to keep one step ahead of the Fed. This was a particularly sensitive area because Goldman Sachs was considered the leader in distributing dealer-placed commercial paper and had been doing so since the nineteenth century. Finally in 1984, the Fed ruled that Bankers Trust had in fact been underwriting corporate securities through the commercial paper market during the 1970s. The bank responded by saying that it had stopped the practice. The Securities Industry Association sued in federal court for a definition of commercial paper, and the Supreme Court obliged by ruling that the short-term notes were in fact corporate securities. The whole question seemed a bit overdone since the SEC had already defined commercial paper decades before as a corporate debt obligation of less than 270 days from original issue that did not have to register with it unless it was longer than 270 days. But the dispute did show that the banks easily could begin practicing activities in the gray area of the Glass-Steagall Act without much fear of meaningful reprisal.

Another problem getting in the way of investment banking reform was the first savings and loan crisis that occurred in 1981–1982. High interest rates and the appearance of money market funds had taken a severe toll on the S&Ls, many of which were relatively small institutions. By the early 1980s, over $100 billion had found its way into money funds at the expense of banks and S&Ls. They began to lose money at a historic rate, and many were forced to merge with larger institutions or close down. Banking reform became the order of the day, but it was not the sort discussed before. This time it involved the thrifts and the Fed was not involved.

The typical American thrift institution was an anomaly in the 1980s—a limited type of bank with little protection in a deregulated world. It could not compete with money funds, made only mortgages and home-related loans, and offered few other financial services of any type. Since these thrift institutions also were regulated by the Glass-Steagall Act, any expansion of their powers would have to come from Congress. Loosening their requirements would not be as politically sensitive as changing the rules for commercial banks. But typical of all financial deregulation, politics got in the way of effective legislation and sowed the seeds for disaster seven years later. How they were regulated followed a standard pattern, but the liberalization gave a good indication of what could occur in a new deregulated environment.

A new financial services bill was sponsored by Jake Garn and Representative Ferdinand St. Germain, Democrat of Rhode Island. Garn was born in 1932, attended school and college in Utah, and was elected to the Senate in 1974. He was chairman of the influential Banking Committee and served until 1992, when he decided not to stand again. He later was a member of the space shuttle Discovery mission in 1985. Ferdinand St. Germain was born in 1928 and was a lawyer from Rhode Island. Elected as a Democrat to the House in 1960 after serving in the state legislature, he also served as chairman of the Banking, Finance, and Urban Affairs Committee. He was unsuccessful in a reelection bid in 1988 after being tainted with scandal from the S&L crisis that had developed earlier that year.

The Garn-St Germain Act was banking legislation aimed at the S&Ls. It took a commonsense approach to the problem of their small size and allowed them to add more assets to their balance sheets than had been allowed in the past. As a result, they were able to expand into areas such as credit cards and commercial lending that previously had been the preserve of commercial banks. But one measure would not stand the test of time. They also were allowed to add corporate bonds to their list of permissible assets. This was the first time since 1933 that depository institutions were allowed to purchase corporate securities. The reasoning was simple enough: Corporate bonds yielded more than mortgages and had the advantage of being liquid. This exception to the Glass-Steagall Act seemed sensible except for one twist. In the 1980s, corporate bonds also included junk bonds, and the S&Ls actively began buying these low-rated bonds. No one was certain of how these investments would perform if a financial crisis or recession occurred.

When the act was passed in 1982, interest rates were effectively deregulated and banks were free to pay interest at market rates, since Regulation Q had been circumvented and eventually would disappear. It appeared that the thrift industry had been saved from a hostile environment, but what was not clear was that the S&Ls were invaded by an army of junk bond salesmen, mostly from Drexel Burnham Lambert, under the direction of Michael Milken, and sold billions of low-quality bonds with high yields.

Although interest rates were volatile during the early 1980s, they dropped for a short time in 1982, giving the stock market heart. The reduction in the long-term capital gains tax and the accelerated depreciation found in the tax package of the year before helped the market move higher. Not all commentators were willing to credit the Fed with the rise in the market, however. Journalist and commentator Louis Rukeyser thought that he saw the beginnings of a bull market in late 1982, but would not attribute the change in investor sentiment entirely to Volcker's actions. The fundamentals were in place for a strong bull market in the 1980s as some had been hoping. Rukeyer wrote: "The market's rebound appears to have sensible underpinnings. Excesses routinely appear...but if we do not ignore the inflation tiger, as we recover from recession, this market could be the one to tell your grandchildren about."[17] In fact, the stock market began moving up before the war on inflation had been won.

Monetary policy alone did not take all of the Fed's attention in the early and mid-1980s. The structure of the banking system was also of keen interest because reforms were still important. The Monetary Control Act did not solve all of the problems because branch banking was still a burning issue. The McFadden Act had long been interpreted as a pork barrel issue hanging over from days past, although tampering with it would be difficult after almost 60 years. The financial system had become accustomed to having a large number of small and regional banks operating, and restructuring them was not an easy matter. Nevertheless, big was considered better in banking for reasons of safety, so the Fed proceeded with suggestions for dismantling McFadden.

The banks took heart when the Fed began pressing for a relaxation of the act. Paul Volcker called on Congress to pass new legislation revamping the banking system in 1985 in an attempt to dismantle it. Using the regional banking pacts used several years before, he urged Congress to act within three years. At the time, about 14 states had taken his earlier suggestion and signed compacts with each other, allowing banks to branch across their state lines. It was well recognized that the McFadden Act emboldened states to remain insular over the years and that many hid behind it to prevent out-of-state banks from invading their territories. Advocates of interstate banking had always pointed to the Canadian experience during the 1930s to prove that interstate banking worked and was not the potential problem McFadden originally thought. The Canadian banks fared better during the Depression than their American counterparts. For his part, Volcker did not openly advocate interstate branching, partly in order to assuage the smaller banks, which were stiffly opposed to the idea. Merger was a more effective way to foster interstate banking, and he recommended that no banks within the top 25 be allowed to merge. The recommendation was hardly on the fast track, however. Many small banker groups were lukewarm to the idea. The large banks would have to lead.

Pressing for Change

As the old banking regulations were being dismantled slowly, the leader in the battle for change was Citibank. The atmosphere during the first Reagan administration was friendly to deregulation. What Congress could not accomplish legislatively could be accomplished in a de facto manner by the larger financial services companies. Bigness in government was being attacked through the administration's idea of the New Federalism. Reagan proved to be a strong leader in public opinion polls, and he used his popularity to lead a marked shift in American life. The Reagan Revolution was in full swing, dedicated to closing the books on the New Deal. The Urban Institute, a liberal think tank, concluded that Reagan had adopted "the approach of Wilson and Roosevelt in order to pursue the objectives of Coolidge and Harding."[18] In order to reverse the role of government in society, the same sort of strong leadership that ushered it in would be used to return much power to the states.

One of the problems with the new concept of federalism was that success already had been achieved in keeping the large banks out by using state laws and the McFadden Act to block branch banking. The objectives of the smaller state banks had already been met. If the McFadden Act were rolled back, they would be faced with an invasion of larger banks. The philosophy of the New Federalism may have helped states at the expense of Washington, but deregulation at the federal level ironically confronted small banks with an invasion of big banks. The old laws insulated them as Glass-Steagall insulated Wall Street from the big banks. Rolling back Depression-era laws meant bigger banking institutions. The New Federalism seemed to have a built-in contradiction that would affect the entire financial system in the United States.

Throughout the 1970s and 1980s, Citibank had been one of the larger institutions pressing for just that sort of change. Under Walter Wriston, it constantly sought new markets and was prepared to do battle with any of the states that stood in its way. Wriston was born in 1920, and his father was a historian and president of Brown University. He attended Wesleyan and graduate school at Tufts before embarking on a successful career in banking. Unlike many bankers of his generation, he recognized the shifting sands in his industry and the gradual changes taking place despite the regulations. Although many bankers and Wall Streeters scoffed at the Sears incursion into brokerage by acquir-

ing Dean Witter, Wriston noted, "You have to be crazy not to per-
ceive that these people [Sears] have a tremendous franchise on
the American people."[19] Unlike many of his contemporaries,
Wriston recognized the power of marketing in helping to dismantle the barriers to bank expansion. While Sears was not successful with brokerage in the long run, it was much more
successful in fostering the concept of branching to customers,
regardless of where they resided.

In Wriston's last years at the helm of the bank holding company, Citicorp was the largest bank in the world, with over $130
billion in deposits. A firm believer in Charles Mitchell's concept
of the financial department store, he also recognized the vital
role of changing communications in the financial services industry. Banking and financial services were simply a matter of reaching customers with information they could use. The reach had
to be national, not regional. If the banks would not respond to
the challenge of truly national banking, the nonbank financial
companies would. The Fed had already coined a term for financial companies that performed banking services—nonbank
banks. If the banks were not aggressive enough to respond
quickly, the nonbank banks would dominate the business.

If Citibank's official position was to be believed, the bank was
not interested in dismantling Glass-Steagall. A senior executive
of its merchant banking unit in 1979 remarked, "I do not know
a single bank in the United States that has any interest in amend-
ing Glass-Steagall to allow banks to underwrite corporate debt or
equity securities. Nor do I know of any bank currently interested in providing a general brokerage service to the public."
Regarding his own bank, he cited a letter written by Wriston to
former SEC chairman Roderick Hills stating, "Citibank does not
desire to enter the public brokerage business or the business of
underwriting, or dealing in, securities of other corporations in
general competition with the investment banking industry." But
if investment banks thought their turf was safe, he fired a salvo,
warning, "Citibank does, however, feel that the commercial

banking industry can contribute to the efficiency of the capital formation process in the US in a manner consistent with the purposes of the Glass-Steagall Act."[20] The banker went on to say that this could be achieved by providing advisory services to companies and channels to the markets for customers seeking investment opportunities. Citibank could either work through the act, which seemed improbable, or the law was irrelevant to the new environment it was trying to fashion. Experience suggested the latter.

Citicorp's experience in New York convinced it that it had enough clout to break down barriers elsewhere. In the early 1980s, New York State still had usury laws on its books, limiting the amount of interest that lenders could charge customers on loans. The problem with these laws was that the loan rates could actually be lower than the interest rates paid on deposits and CDs in the new deregulated environment. If the situation persisted, banks would lose heavily. Citicorp actively lobbied New York to abolish its usury laws, to no avail. Then it discovered another state that proved more receptive to its plans. Citicorp officials persuaded officials in South Dakota to roll back their usury law in return for a subsidiary to be opened in the state. The potential employment caused South Dakota to proceed quickly and comply with the request. The subsidiary embraced Citicorp's credit card operations, which could charge any interest rate customers would bear without fear of violating usury ceilings. In the wake of the experience, New York also capitulated and removed its own usury laws, proving to critics that big banks had a distinct advantage in using political clout.

Foes of Bigness

One critic of expansive banking was Ralph Nader, who objected to Citicorp's argument that competition would be enhanced by expansion into nonbank activities. Nader claimed that Citicorp "conveniently overlooks two key subsidies which give it preferential access to funds—Federal Government insurance of bank deposits and the implicit United States Government guarantee that giant banks like Citicorp will not be allowed to fail."[21] All banks making the same argument fell into the trap. They were partially insulated from failure by Depression-era laws designed to protect customers. Ironically, the same laws protected the banks against failure at the same time.

Nader had opened the Pandora's box in banking, mentioning a doctrine that was becoming popular in the 1980s called, "too big to fail." The Federal Deposit Insurance Corp. (FDIC) insurance fund was limited, especially when faced with the prospect of guaranteeing a big bank's deposits. The idea suggested that the Fed and other regulators would have to step in and help rescue a bank rather than be a direct guarantor of its deposits. The issue was not merely a moot topic for long. In 1984, the largest banking failure in American history occurred when the Continental Illinois National Bank and Trust failed, leading to the biggest rescue operation ever mounted. The bank had been hobbled with a portfolio of bad loans both domestically and internationally, and depositors began withdrawing their deposits from its eurodollar facilities in London and elsewhere. As a result, the bank was faced with an enormous liquidity crisis and required help, although most of the deposits were institutional and were not insured by the FDIC.

Regulators mounted a rescue, led by the Fed, involving an ad hoc consortium of banks putting up the necessary money to ensure that the bank stayed in business. Continental clearly filled the bill as "too big to fail." Regulators did not have the necessary funds to prop it up, so a group of banks had to be assembled to provide temporary assistance. The bailout was a success, but critics quickly pointed out that the rescue was put together too quickly, without appropriate Congressional hearings. Making matters worse, the FDIC became a major shareholder in the bank by terms of the bailout agreement. Not everyone was happy about the prospect of using federal money to bail out a large bank without proper discussion. Ferdinand St. Germain complained that "it is the simple fact that the full faith and credit of the Federal Government stands behind the insurance funds and behind the FDIC actions—ill-considered or not."[22]

Never far from banking controversy, the comptroller of the currency defended the bailout by suggesting that deregulation was needed if the problem was not to surface again. In a memo written to the administration, the comptroller's office stated that "one of Continental's problems may have been that deregulation hasn't gone far enough." If the bank had been allowed more diverse loans than the oil loans that helped bring it down, it might have been able to survive intact. By implication, those in favor of deregulation were blaming the existing banking laws for the narrowness of many banks' loan portfolios. In addition to domestic oil loans, many banks were also heavily exposed to countries in the developing world. The 1980s was the decade of the third world debt crisis, and many commentators believed that the banks would not have overextended themselves to the developing countries had they more opportunities at home, such as the securities and insurance businesses.

Although those in favor of deregulation saw the Continental Illinois crisis as an opportunity to further their cause, others took the problem as a sign of danger that needed heeding. Although there was no major financial crisis occurring, one syndicated columnist noted that time proved to be too great a healer. "A new generation has no personal experience of the crack-up of the banking system," wrote Anthony Harrigan. "It is very enthusiastic about the idea of the deregulation of all fields of business."[23] Quoting Representative Charles Schumer of New York, he noted that psychology was very important in retaining the integrity of the financial system. Banks were supposed to be low-risk places for the public to deposit funds, not high-risk securities or insurance operations. The idea had merit but was too quickly becoming identified with the 1930s rather than the 1980s.

Securities underwriting was not the only business the banks envied in the 1980s. Insurance was also on their wishlist of potential new businesses. Real estate was another candidate, especially since some of the securities houses had bought real estate brokers. In the Senate, William Proxmire, a Democrat from Wisconsin, was one of the administration's closest allies for bank deregulation. Ironically, he was not in favor of banks entering the life insurance business or real estate. The reason had nothing to do with banking safety or soundness. It was purely a matter of turf. The insurance industry in particular had a very strong lobbying group in Washington and much greater political clout than Wall Street as a result. An official at an insurance trade group summed up the situation well be stating, "The Reagan administration is taking judicial notice of reality, that there are 220,000 [insurance agents], active in every congressional district in America . . . they recognize that their theological drive to deregulate at any cost would hit a brick wall."[24] The drive to deregulate would begin to focus more on the securities industry than any other for political reasons. Insurance agents and real estate agents had more extensive political clout and potential public support than Wall Street, which was still seen as an enclave of the rich and infamous.

Proxmire was not being entirely unfair to Wall Street. In his proposals, banks could own securities firms and securities firms should be allowed to own banks. The theory was simpler than reality, however, since the securities firms could probably afford only smaller banks. Proxmire was usually aligned with Democrats favoring close control of the financial system, but on the issue of Glass-Steagall he favored a revision of existing law. Many banking analysts thought that Proxmire was only in favor of chipping away at Glass-Steagall rather than repealing it. Born in Illinois in 1915, his background was hardly one of a Wisconsin populist. Educated at prep school, Yale, and the Harvard Business School, he moved to Wisconsin, where he unsuccessfully ran for governor several times before being elected to the Senate in 1957. In the 1970s, he became known for exposing government waste during the Cold War, being especially critical of the defense department for spending large sums on simple items such as ashtrays and light bulbs. His criticisms could be found in a book published in 1980 entitled *The Fleecing of America*. In 1986 he became chairman of the Senate Banking Committee.

For the most part, Democrats opposed deregulation on two grounds. First, it was a Reagan policy and could be opposed for that reason alone, although the historical argument still reverberated strongly as well. Some Democrats were willing to overlook those arguments, favoring any legislation that would help the banking industry become more efficient. Within a decade, the New Democrats would begin to join Republicans on the matter of banking deregulation, but in the 1980s the issue was still contentious.

Victory, Almost

Interest rates dipped and then rose again in 1984, causing some of the highest bond and money market yields recorded in the United States. The Treasury borrowed at 14 percent for 30 years, and the bond became the highest-yielding Treasury ever issued. The spike in rates proved to be the last, however, as they began to fall in 1985, vindicating Paul Volcker's strict emphasis on the money supply. The stock market was not poised for a genuine rally until interest rates and inflation came down.

As the inflation war appeared to have been won, Morgan Guaranty Trust produced a publication entitled "Rethinking Glass-Steagall" in 1984. One of its major contributors was Alan Greenspan, a Morgan director. The pamphlet became part of the overall attack on the law and was widely read. Momentum appeared to be gaining strength for a repeal of the law, although the current drive for repeal was over five years old. Then events intervened, and the drive was put on hold again. No one could justify dismantling the law in the face of more shenanigans on

Wall Street and a falling stock market. Events were interceding at a rapid pace to slow reform in the 1980s, making many advocates of deregulation impatient.

The fight against Glass-Steagall was led by Citicorp in the mid-1980s. In 1984, the holding company filed an application with the Fed to operate a securities subsidiary that would underwrite corporate securities. The application had no forewarning, and the Fed reviewed it for almost a month before acknowledging that it would consider it. Citicorp cited Section 20 of the law, claiming that the language of the act allowed banks to underwrite corporate securities if they did so through a separate subsidiary that was not principally engaged in corporate securities underwriting. Most big banks already had those subsidiaries in place. Their principal activity was distribution and trading of Treasury securities and money market instruments, securities not excluded by the 1933 law. The bank claimed that it would limit the revenues from underwriting to only 20 percent of the subsidiary's revenue, thus avoiding the language of the law.

The application took Wall Street and the Fed by surprise. "Never before has anyone seriously questioned the heart and soul of the Glass-Steagall Act, which is underwriting," an SIA executive remarked.[25] No one was certain why the bank filed the application when it did or how it came to choose 20 percent as an operational number. However, it was part of its overall plan to attack regulations and see how the playing field looked after the smoke cleared. The bank remained characteristically quiet on the issue, but the application began a long process in which the percentages would be seen again, leading many to wonder openly who was actually controlling the reins of the banking system, the Fed or the banks themselves.

Part of the bank's motivation came from the defeat two months earlier of a reform bank bill introduced in the Senate by Jake Garn. The bill called for banks to be able to underwrite municipal revenue bonds, commercial paper, and mortgage-backed securities. Garn introduced the bill in part because he and others in favor of at least some form of deregulation were afraid the comptroller of the currency would begin approving dozens of applications from other banks and nonbanks that would allow them to cross over into other areas of banking. But the idea did not fly in the Senate. It was opposed by Democratic Senators Daniel P. Moynihan and Donald Riegle of Michigan, who effectively talked it to death without actually mounting a filibuster. Garn had reason to worry that a regulatory agency might usurp the powers of Congress, but it was not the comptroller that did so.

Reformers thought they had victory in sight when the Federal Reserve Board decided in the spring of 1987 to allow banks to underwrite municipal revenue bonds as well as mortgage-backed securities and commercial paper. The board's decision came quickly after New York State began considering a similar move, which would have wide repercussions because many of the major banks were in the state. The issue also raised an old, haunting question. New York had the authority over the banks applying for the increased power because they were all state-chartered banks. Among them were Chemical, Bankers Trust, and J.P. Morgan & Co. Clearly, the banks decided that it was time to unravel Glass-Steagall and were mounting a united assault. But they were also members of the Fed, although they were not nationally chartered banks. The applications at the state level were sure to reverberate quickly at the central bank. An executive at the New York Bankers Association put it simply when he said, "The whole notion is to put as much pressure on the Congress and the Fed as possible to get Glass-Steagall modified."

The position was wholeheartedly backed by president of the New York Fed Gerald Corrigan. The only reservation he had was that commercial companies should not own banks. The issue of how these securities operations would be constructed was also crucial. The New York bankers favored using "sister companies," affiliates of holding companies separate from the banks. Companies that were affiliates of the banks themselves were too close to the deposits of the commercial banks and also had a history as the sort of institutions most likely to fail, damaging the bank directly, in times of financial crisis. The New York banking department was being prudent, however, and would not consider letting the banks into new lines of business in a large-scale way; the banking department would limit the amount of revenues banks could derive from these activities to 25 percent. Other numbers would be bandied about, but it was obvious that banks were almost in the securities business again.

A hearing was held at the Fed to discuss the applications. The boardroom was filled to capacity as the Fed listened to the traditional arguments by the banks for enhancing their powers. The SIA clearly was in the opposition, so regardless of the decision the Board reached there was bound to be dissension. It was not clear whether Congress would, or could, act in time, so the decision was left to the five Fed Board members. Proxmire had already warned Volcker, "The clear and overriding intent of the Congress in enacting the Glass-Steagall Act was to prohibit banks from underwriting ineligible securities, whether directly or through affiliates. The applications at issue here fly in the face of that congressional intent."[26]

The Fed Board voted on the issue after being pressed by the banks and capitulated. In a 3–2 vote, it granted the applications of Citicorp, Bankers Trust, and J.P. Morgan to underwrite the debt securities. Most of the other major banks waited in the wings. Paul Volcker, an advocate of bank reform, did not vote for the applications, nor did his colleague Wayne Angell. The three members in favor were Manuel Johnson, Martha Seger, and H. Robert Heller. All except Volcker were Reagan appointees. Volcker and Angell demurred because they did not believe that the Fed had the authority to roll back Glass-Steagall—only Congress had that power. The Fed agreed to allow the bank subsidiaries to obtain 5 percent of their revenues from the activities and said it would review the action in a year. Proponents of strong bank regulation were upset, as would be expected. "This is a hole in the dike and it threatens the safety and soundness of our banking system," said Charles Schumer. "It's alarming to believe that the

Fed, usually the great defender of the banking system, is now leading the deregulatory charge."[27] Similar frustration was expressed by the SIA, which filed a suit to overturn the ruling.

Most observers though that victory had been won and that the recommendation made years before by *Mandate for Leadership* would be carried out. Before the champagne corks could start popping in Republican circles, the House intervened, putting an end to the celebration. Supporters of regulation and Paul Volcker decided to stall the changes for a year so that the issue could be studied further. They were not yet willing to give up the fight. Representative Jim Leach, a Republican from Iowa, proved to be the swing vote on the issue and decided to support the stalling tactic as a gesture of support for Volcker. "Let's win one for Paul" became his motto as he voted for the delay. Congress appreciated Volcker's refusal to allow the Fed to make banking policy by itself without going through appropriate legislative channels. The issue died until March 1988.

The Reagan White House threatened a veto but was put in a delicate position. The delay was part of a larger banking bill that also gave immediate aid to the thrifts' insurance fund, which was dangerously low and needed an immediate infusion of cash. Vetoing the package would have resulted in the fund going bankrupt, an untenable position for any administration to take. As a result, the one-year moratorium stood and was not challenged. Then events intervened to put the entire issue under a cloud again.

Crash or Collapse?

The most publicized crisis of the late 1980s was the stock market collapse in October 1987. The 25 percent drop in the market indices was the worst ever recorded, essentially twice that of 1929. In the months prior to the setback, the market had become increasingly jittery over interest rate fears. After having fallen back from their all-time highs, short- and long-term rates were feared to be on the rise again. In 1987, Paul Volcker left the Fed chairmanship and was succeeded by Alan Greenspan. Although Wall Street admired Greenspan, there was some question whether he would be as aggressive as Volcker in combating inflation. He had been known for years as a supporter of Reagan's policies for the economy, as contradictory as they often seemed. At his confirmation hearings in August 1987, he indicated that rates would be allowed to rise if necessary, as a part of the Louvre Agreement on foreign exchange rates. One of his first actions at the Fed was to raise the discount rate. The market became jittery at the prospect, and the stage was set for the market rout two months later. The message was mixed, however. The original interest rate drop benefited the dollar, which fell on the foreign exchange markets, helping a trade balance that had sunk into deficit because of the dollar's precipitous rise.

The dramatic market fall on October 19, dubbed "Black Monday," revealed many other structural weaknesses in the market structure that previously had gone unnoticed. Because of the flaws in the specialist system, a good deal of third market trading was conducted by block traders; many of the trades were in foreign stocks, traded away from their home exchanges like London, in order to avoid local British turnover taxes. When the American markets began to drop, many foreign stocks fell quickly in sympathy with little or no lag time. The market rout became truly international, although there was no specific international economic news to explain it. When the smoke cleared, the British stock market had fallen 26 percent and the German had fallen 22 percent. The real losers were in the developing world. Mexico and Singapore fell about 40 percent, while Australia and Hong Kong fell almost 60 percent. With losses of that magnitude, reformers had little room to call for deregulation, at least for the moment.

The market collapse reflected badly on the Reagan administration, which had painted a rosy picture of the economy ever since it took office seven years before. Paul Volcker had expressed skepticism about many of the administration's policies as his term neared its end, and as nationally syndicated columnist Jack Anderson claimed, "The last laugh in all this, if he were so insensitive to indulge himself, would have to go to [him], who left the Fed post a matter of weeks before the October disaster." Anderson went on to characterize Reagan's public posturing in the aftermath of the collapse as "Coolidge Returns to the White House."[28] Volcker left the Fed post after developing a great mystique. During his tenure, monumental problems had arisen and had been tackled successfully. Yet not everyone was unhappy to see him go. As one Midwestern banker said, "It seems almost natural that the Volcker myth should, like a good soldier, just fade away, making room for fresh initiatives." Those favoring less Fed initiative in dismantling New Deal laws would not be so happy, however. The stockmarket reacted poorly, not having his legend to lean on when it was needed. Everyone who had been preaching prosperity over the previous years was caught off guard. Only a few Wall Street analysts predicted a crash, but in traditional bull market fashion were given little or no credit for anticipating it. As far as Wall Street was concerned, the event was only an interlude.

The collapse prompted a Presidential inquiry, headed by Nicholas Brady. One of its suggestions was the establishment of a market "circuit breaker" which would shut down trading on the NYSE if the percentage drop exceeded certain levels. A curious byproduct of the investigation and subsequent findings was the term "market break." Instead of calling the drop in the indices by a more clear, intelligible term, market break was used. The term last had made its appearance in Republican circles after the 1929 Crash. In 1987, it appeared that the rout was not causing a depression or recession, so the more polite term was used. But the market rout was closer to the classic 1929 Crash than most observers were willing to admit.

In previous crashes and panics, the banking system also felt the strain and banking failures occurred on a fairly large scale. In 1987, Greenspan quickly announced that the Fed would make funds available to the money markets for any banks suffering temporary liquidity problems, a standard comment by the Fed during times of distress. The irony was that the 1987 rout was followed by a crisis not directly connected by commentators to the market drop at the time. The S&L industry again was in the throes of another major crisis that would require a federal bailout. In this case, the crisis was one of Washington's making to a large extent because it was the first sign that deregulation of banking institutions in the early 1980s was not working out as well as planned.

Strains on the Safety Net

When the Garn-St Germain Act allowed thrift institutions to purchase corporate bonds, it opened a Pandora's box of abuses in the junk bond industry that eventually helped destroy many S&Ls. Many thrifts bought low-rated bonds from Drexel Burnham Lambert and the other Wall Street houses specializing in high-yield issues without realizing the risks involved with this kind of debt. After the market rout, the first recession in a decade set in, causing the revenues of many junk bond issuers to fall. By 1990–1991, a record number of corporate bond defaults occurred, almost $20 billion. The thrifts were forced to write off the investments, forcing many to seek merger partners or close their doors. The industry already was ailing before 1987, and the events of October only hastened the demise of many small institutions. The Garn-St. Germain Act was meant to liberalize the thrifts but only helped hasten the demise of many, all in the name of market reform.

Although serious structural problems began to appear in the thrift industry, Wall Street had its own version of the causes of the market rout. In one case, it sought to blame the problems on futures traders who had introduced trading on stock indices. Much of this trading was done at the major futures exchanges in Chicago, rather than in New York. The intercity rivalry surfaced when NYSE officials blamed Chicago, claiming that short selling of the indices caused many stocks to fall. At the time, the idea of using stock index futures in investment strategies was known as "portfolio insurance," and stock traders delighted in blaming the "insurers" for their problems. When the smoke cleared and heated discussion ended, the markets had a few trading safeguards in place but never settled the argument about who was responsible for the collapse. But the precipitous drop in prices convinced critics of deregulation that the markets and the banks should be kept separate. When markets are volatile, people need a safe place to keep their money that is insulated from the vagaries of equities, argued one California newspaper. After the collapse, the *Mountain Democrat* wrote: "Separation and independence of banking and security markets are important checks and balances to keep our economy in equilibrium. If any good can come out of the stock market crash, it would be to heed warning signs and keep banks out of the security underwriting business."[29]

Proponents of deregulation argued that the underwriting business could be integrated and still be safe. But the experience with the sudden collapse was obvious. Many of the new issues in syndication (being underwritten) at the time fell precipitously in value, handing their underwriters sharp losses. This was just the sort of exposure from which critics wanted to insulate the banks. But critics faced a strong adversary in Alan Greenspan, who had already gone on record as favoring expanded powers for the banks and the repeal of Glass-Steagall. The market collapse and the impending thrift crisis ensured that deregulation would have to wait for better days, although they were not far off.

Those favoring the status quo were clearly worried about Greenspan assuming the helm at the Fed. After he was nominated to be Fed chairman, some doubts were expressed about his independence from the Reagan administration. He had already served it in several important posts, mostly advisory capacities, and critics wanted to hear that he would remain above the political fray. The Fed was not a part of the executive branch but a separate, independent entity, and some legislators, notably William Proxmire, wanted to ensure that it remained that way. Greenspan's connection to J.P. Morgan & Co. was also an issue legislators wanted to be clear on. As part of the disclosure process, he was required to fill out a form, submitted to both the White House and Congress, listing any possible conflicts of interest. He stated that he would recuse himself from any decisions made by the Fed involving J.P. Morgan & Co. He had served Morgan Guaranty Trust, and the holding company, for 10 years as a director. "I plan to sever all previous relationships and recuse myself if at any time the interests of past business associates or clients are directly involved," he wrote on the form.[30]

Other parts of his testimony would not necessarily coincide with actions taken shortly after he assumed the chairmanship. After testifying for several hours about his views on many economic and political matters, he was questioned on his view of the antitrust laws. He had already gone on the record as saying that he opposed them but conceded to his questioners, "It's more important that the laws be adhered to rather than my personal [belief] that a law may be right or wrong."[31] How he viewed the relationship between antitrust laws and the banking laws was not clear, however. If the proposition that Glass-Steagall was a very effective antitrust law dressed in banking law language, then New Deal Democrats had much to fear if he was not true to his word.

Greenspan's long-time advocacy for a repeal of Glass-Steagall led then Representative Charles Schumer of New York to make a strong case for keeping Glass-Steagall as it was. Arguing that the reasons for passing the law were still valid, he argued, "If a bank thinks it can make more money as a securities firm, let it become one. Let's not destroy a stable structure that, since the Depression, has provided capital for entrepreneurs, confidence for depositors, and healthy profits for America's financial service companies."[32] Schumer would repeat the argument many times again in defense of Glass-Steagall, especially since the one-year moratorium was to be reviewed the following spring.

The quest for interstate banking and bank brokerage operations got a significant boost in 1987. The Securities Industry Association brought suit to prevent the comptroller of the currency from allowing national banks to operate brokerage operations without regard for the McFadden Act. The comptroller maintained that the McFadden Act applied only to core banking services such as taking deposits and making loans, not to establishing brokerage operations. Five years before, the comptroller approved applications by two banks to provide discount brokerage, and the lawsuits began. When the case reached the Supreme Court, the justices agreed with the comptroller and allowed banks to establish brokerage operations.[33] The SIA received support from the Independent Bankers Association, representing the smaller state-chartered banks.

The two comptrollers who were in office at the beginning and the end of the legal proceedings were both Reagan appointees committed to bank liberalization. C. Todd Conover, who made the original ruling, was previously a management consultant in California specializing in bank issues. His successor, Robert L. Clarke, was a lawyer who worked in banks during his teenage years in New Mexico. After graduating from law school, he established a banking department at his law firm and specialized in banking law until named to the post in 1985. The comptroller's office could be quite active in reform, while at other times going unnoticed except for performing its normal regulatory duties. The Reagan comptrollers were active in striving for reform when the situation merited but often found themselves at odds with the smaller banks and securities and insurance groups, all trying to preserve their own turfs in the face of inexorable bank expansion.

Despite the strides being made at chipping away at the old laws, the Wall Street scandals and the third world banking crisis made progress painfully slow. Reformers were also wary of the S&L crisis since Michael Milken and Drexel Burnham were involved. Clearly, the Garn-St Germain Act had backfired, allowing thrifts to load up on exactly the sort of assets Glass-Steagall originally had tried to prevent. The major question now facing reformers was how to continue the drive for deregulation in the face of these setbacks. The S&L crisis could be explained by showing that S&L managers were naïve and bought inappropriate investments from Drexel Burnham salesmen when they should have known better. Their quest for high yield forced them to overlook many of the bonds' low credit ratings. Recognizing human frailties was not part of the law, however. In order to prevent the problem in the future, it would be necessary to separate securities operations of any sort from the banks or thrifts that owned them. Otherwise, the problem would be repeated in the future even though Glass-Steagall had been successful in preventing the issue from arising for over 50 years.

Small Success

Shortly after Alan Greenspan assumed the helm at the Fed, many reformers thought that the Glass-Steagall and McFadden Acts would be substantially revised or repealed shortly. Pressure had been building for 15 years, and finally victory seemed to be within reach. George Bush succeeded Reagan in the White House, and the administrative structure remained in place to pressure lawmakers and regulators. Only a bull market was needed to complete the picture.

Within weeks of the stock market collapse in 1987, Greenspan conferred with Senator Proxmire and FDIC and Treasury officials in an attempt to share thoughts on bank deregulation. Proxmire was the highest-ranking legislator known to be in favor of modifying the laws, and his advocacy in the Senate was crucial. He was also one of the few Democrats who openly advocated change. But how banks would be allowed to underwrite was an important debating point. The way it could be done was through affiliate companies. A holding company could create a securities affiliate through which it could do securities business. But the ownership of the subsidiary, which needed built-in protections against losses in other subsidiaries or the parent company, called firewalls, was not a simple matter and needed to be fully defined. Greenspan supported a bill before the Senate, dubbed the Proxmire-Garn bill. It was more properly called the Financial Modernization Act of 1987. The name proved long-lasting although it would be more than a decade before it became law.

After considering the options, the Fed came out in favor of a compromise in which smaller banks could establish securities affiliates and still answer only to their primary regulator, the FDIC or the comptroller of the currency. The only stipulation was that the Fed, as regulator of holding companies, would retain tight control of the securities activities at the holding companies within its orbit. The technical side of the argument was much more arcane. It involved having subsidiaries at the major bank holding companies that would legally operate on their own, being considered legally separate entities from the parent. Under this idea, known as the doctrine of "corporate separateness," the parent would not be held liable for the losses at a subsidiary because the subsidiary would be standing alone and the "corporate veil" would not be pierced even if it lost substantially.

A week later, Greenspan testified before a House banking subcommittee. Again advocating a repeal of Glass-Steagall, he said that he wanted banks to engage in a broad variety of underwriting activities. He made clear the idea of separateness. The safeguard was that the activities would be confined to a separate affiliate of a holding company. While momentum was building in some influential circles, it was having the opposite effect in others. Even if Proxmire could convince the Senate of the merits of his proposed bill, sympathy in the House was lacking. The chairman of the House Commerce Committee was dead against repeal of the law. His committee was central to any proposal becoming law, and he vowed to block the attempt. The opposition did not surprise onlookers. John David Dingell Jr. was a Democrat from Michigan, first elected to the House to fill the vacancy caused by the death of his father. The elder Dingell, also a Democrat, first entered the lower chamber in March 1933 as the Democrats seized Congress in the FDR landslide victory. Dingell Sr. was a supporter of the original Glass-Steagall Act as well as other New Deal reforms and passed the baton to his son, who also favored liberal Democratic causes. Dingell Jr.'s position was supported by various lobbies representing the securities, real estate, and insurance industries. A spokesman for the American Bankers' Association succinctly noted the opposition Dingell faced when he said, "The interesting thing is that you have the chairman of the Senate Banking Committee, a Democrat, and all the banking agencies and the administration coming forward with basically the same approach. All this has come since the problems in the stock market and those who have looked at it think it was not a problem that should deter action."[34] The assessment proved correct but was off by a decade.

Greenspan made it clear to Congress that the time was ripe for changes despite the October debacle in the market. Repeal of Glass-Steagall would respond "effectively to the marked changes that have taken place in the financial marketplace here and abroad," he stated, invoking the international side of the argument as further proof.[35] Despite his standing as a private economist before coming to the Fed, not everyone accepted his version of marketplace dynamics. Lines were quickly drawn along industry lines. The insurance companies and securities firms still demurred but were not accompanied by strong consumers' groups, who also saw a danger in adding new services to banks. The consumer groups' argument was that banks were not performing the old services as well as they should and that adding new services like investment banking would only make them more institutional, not retail-oriented. Banks had been practicing "red-lining" when making mortgages in minority neighborhoods for years, effectively denying mortgages to minorities based upon the racial composition of neighborhoods. What good would investment banking services do in underbanked places where even basic services like checking and savings accounts were difficult to find? Unfortunately, the consumer side of the argument would be heard but never heeded. And progress was not quick. Six months later, the Fed chairman was still making the case: "The [Federal Reserve] Board strongly supports this generic authorization of securities powers so overwhelmingly approved by the Senate," he stated concerning the Proxmire-Garn proposal. "I would urge the House in its deliberation in the months ahead to adopt an approach similar to that of the Senate."[36] However, events were about to overcome deregulation yet again.

The unseen side of the argument to allow banks greater powers stemmed from the fact that many of them were losing money because of their involvement with less developed countries. The third world debt crisis had ravaged many banks' income statements and balance sheets during the 1980s. As a result, many were short of capital by the late 1980s, a situation banking regulators in the major industrialized countries took very seriously, especially after the fall of Continental Illinois. After a major debt crisis in Mexico was narrowly avoided, regulators decided to impose uniform requirements on banks in the major industrialized nations.[37] The new requirements they imposed were certainly more rigorous than anything witnessed before but were necessary to ensure that a major bank would not fail again, having a potential domino effect on others around the world.

The new rules had a direct effect upon the number of loans a bank could make. If, on the other hand, banks could find other ways to make money without lending, they would be encouraged to do so. The motivation was fee banking, or paying for services rendered by a bank to an institutional client, rather than relying on interest paid on loans. Investment banking fit the bill for banks extremely well, and as a result the large banks in particular began pressing even harder for liberalization of the rules. When Alan Greenspan assumed the chairmanship of the Fed, they had the ally they needed to proceed.

Ironically, the increase in capital requirements for banks only strengthened the argument of those favoring deregulation. Weak banks would be stronger with a greater array of services, and their stock would appeal to investors. But these arguments were only accepted by bankers, sympathetic regulators, and Fed watchers. The issue was unknown outside of a very small circle. And since the House majority was Democratic, there was little chance that the Proxmire bill would ever pass in its original form. The issue was popular in the Senate but had little chance in the House without the support of Dingell.

Reformers were heartened when the SIA suit was heard in a federal appeals court in February 1988. The court ruled that the Fed was legally correct in its decision to allow the banks to underwrite revenue bonds and commercial paper. Technically, the body engaging in the underwriting had to be a subsidiary of the holding company. When it originally made the ruling, the Fed would only allow the subsidiaries to earn 5 percent of their revenues from underwriting. They could not be "engaged principally" in the underwriting of what the original Glass-Steagall Act considered ineligible securities, namely corporate securities and revenue bonds. Shortly afterward, the SEC also stated that it would support revision of the act since it believed that it would not harm investors. The two events encouraged reformers, and legislation finally materialized.

The Proxmire bill came to a vote in the Senate a few weeks later. The upper chamber passed it by an overwhelming 92–4 vote. But even after the strong statements made by many senators about modernizing the financial system, the House remained less enthusiastic. Dingell and St. Germain pointed to the problems in the banking sector as well as the stock market collapse and wondered why anyone would push for reform until the air cleared. The question was valid. The public was generally unaware of the banking problem, having familiarity only with the stock market collapse. Major reform was being advocated by a small number of legislators and their banker allies in an attempt to roll back a fundamental part of the original New Deal safety net. The term "safety net" was not used in the arguments for fear of making it a wider public issue. The courts had ruled that the

Fed action was legal. But was it appropriate given the gravity of the issue?

The SIA appealed the decision to the Supreme Court but lost again. The justices voted 7–2 to uphold the lower court decision. Those looking for the old safeguards to be preserved were not accommodated. The bankers claimed it was within their power to underwrite a broad range of securities if loopholes could be found in Glass-Steagall. The Fed helped them find those loopholes through its own powers, vested by Congress in the Bank Holding Company Act. Discussions about the safety net and protecting depositors were secondary to the rights of the banks in these cases. A small group had claimed a major victory in overturning a basic law by using its own regulator to make the case. After the decision, Charles Schumer summed up the feelings of members of the House concerning the ruling. "We will rue the day that shortsighted judges and closed-minded ideologues at the regulatory agencies decided that they should rewrite our banking laws," he lamented.

In the face of the Senate bill and the Supreme Court ruling, the House began to have second thoughts about its recalcitrance. The ball was rolling downhill, and attempts to stop it were probably futile. The House fashioned a bill, designed mostly by St. Germain, that would restrict banks from engaging in real estate and insurance while introducing consumer banking benefits at the same time. One of the consumer items was a requirement that banks begin to offer low-cost banking services such as checking accounts and check-cashing facilities to the elderly and the poor. Bankers were not impressed and vigorously opposed the proposals. They were joined by Alan Greenspan, who claimed that the banking system could not afford the costs it would have to assume to provide the consumer services. And in language somewhat stronger than that used by previous Fed chairmen, he made it clear that he wanted change, allowing banks into more lucrative areas without saddling them with the extra costs implied by the consumer measures. "I cannot emphasize too strongly that the banking system is urgently in need of modernizing changes," he told St. Germain. "The future vitality of the banking system depends upon a demonstration that Congress is capable of taking action."[38]

After almost a decade of Republican administrations, full progress had not yet been made in rolling back the Glass-Steagall Act. The way was clear after the Supreme Court ruling, but the House still dragged its feet, refusing to fully comply with the Senate, which was pro-banking and less consumer-oriented than the lower house. Soon it became clear to reformers that they would have to take more action themselves if Congress would not act. Bankers and the Fed began making further plans to dismantle the law, but constantly applied pressure on Congress to act. Another 10 years would be needed to finally claim victory. In the interim, events suggested that it was still possible for a trade group to enforce its will on Congress and then portray it as a victory for all.

CHAPTER 6
DEREGULATION IN THE 1990s

"As America tries to recover from the worst stock market crash in its history, the Federal Reserve Board wants to put banks in the security underwriting business. Is this a joke?"

Mountain Democrat, California

A s the 1980s ended, it was clear that bankers had persuaded regulators that entry into the securities business was in the best interests of banking. The stakes were high. Foreign banks had engaged in the securities business and were posing a real threat to American banking influence outside the United States. According to bankers, the growing internationalization of the marketplace called for the old domestic restrictions to be replaced with a more modern, functional approach. The threats were vastly overstated, however. American banks wanted to be like foreign banks only when it suited their purposes.

The 1990s were characterized by more cant than had been experienced since the 1930s. Bankers evoked images of American banks falling behind the Japanese and the Europeans. Wall Street securities houses began reciting the well-known problems that could occur if banks entered the securities business, as if the issue had ever seriously mattered to them before the banks became more aggressive. Politicians representing various constituency groups pushed their own agendas, most calling for repeal of the

New Deal laws. Some administration officials made arguments for repeal that would be embarrassing if they were not so disingenuous. The 1990s was the decade of deregulation as other industries were freed from decades-old restrictions, but banking and Wall Street would be the last ones affected.

Deregulation was the mantra between 1992 and 1999. Old laws severely curtailing specific industries were replaced with a more lenient, market-oriented approach that catered to the 1990s' feel-good utilitarian philosophy. The utilities and telecommunications industries were deregulated, and the results would begin to be felt by the end of the century. Utilities mergers became common, and phone companies also began to merge, creating new giants to compete in the market that AT&T was forced to abandon in 1984. In the 1980s, the Garn-St Germain Act helped create the S&L crisis. In the 1990s, deregulation in utilities would help create the Enron crisis, and in telecommunications it would help create fraud at WorldCom, the telecommunications giant created only in the early 1980s to fill a void left by the breakup of AT&T. The only question left concerned Wall Street and banking. Would deregulation in the financial services sector lead to problems that could have been prevented by keeping the old safety net regulations in place? What little that had been accomplished already had disastrous consequences.

In the 50 years since World War II, the business and investment climate certainly changed. Gone were the fears of big business. Replacing them were discussions about the merits of giant companies in the global business environment. Mergers and acquisitions were also in vogue, especially since the early 1980s, when a merger boom began, accompanying the bull market in stocks. At the same time, organized labor underwent a serious decline, being heard from far less than in the past about big business issues. Labor traced its decline to the firing of air traffic controllers by Ronald Reagan during his first term. Without the traditional muscular language and threat of industrial action, big business in general experienced little opposition.

Labor problems were not usually experienced in financial services, but consumerism was capable of creating waves for banks and brokers. Mergers between large banks and brokers could be challenged on the grounds that they could negatively affect the level of services offered to customers. As a result, many bank mergers and mergers between securities houses were justified on the basis of costs. Two banks merging could reduce the cost of services to the average consumer, who would clearly benefit in the process. The problem was that none of these claims were validated any more than some of the claims being made for repealing Glass-Steagall. But the consumer defense by the banks did eventually lead to a new interstate banking law replacing the McFadden Act. If big was better, then coast-to-coast banking was the ultimate answer to consumers' desire for better services at a lower price.

The same argument had been used for years against Glass-Steagall. Bankers claimed that they could underwrite for smaller fees than the investment banks. Allowing them to do so officially would lower costs for industry in the process. But Wall Street knew that selling the issues was an entirely different matter, and on that front the banks had no experience at all. Underwriting meant successful placement of securities as well; without it the process was incomplete, and the bankers could not offer any rebuttal in defense.

The Heritage Foundation added another plank to the conservative agenda by advocating repeal of the restrictive banking laws in 1989. In the third of its book-length policy reports for the Republican administration, it advocated repeal of the two favorite bête noires of reformers and added a third. It advocated, "Glass-Steagall should be repealed, as should the 1956 Bank Holding Company Act, which restricts bank activities and ownership, and the 1927 McFadden Act, which restricts interstate banking." It then sounded the battle charge that would reverberate throughout the 1990s and beyond: "Anyone should be able to own a bank, and bank holding companies should be able to own any other type of business, as long as the bank is adequately and separately capitalized."[1]

The original mandate for repealing Glass-Steagall and McFadden suddenly became wider. The only question was whether the regulators would adopt the same view. Clearly, the big banks agreed.

Citicorp Attack

Citicorp remained in the front ranks of the assault on banking and securities regulations. After Alan Greenspan became Fed chairman, the bank continued to push its agenda as aggressively as it had pushed for the dismantling of usury law ceilings earlier in the decade. As far as the bank was concerned, rolling back Glass-Steagall and the McFadden Act were the next natural hurdles to be cleared, and it pursued its objectives relentlessly. Walter Wriston stepped down as CEO in 1984 and was succeeded by John Reed, but the direct attack was led by its vice chairman Hans Angermueller. In the wake of the stock market collapse in 1987 and the S&L crisis, it had to proceed more slowly because Democrats in Congress were very leery of deregulation during a financial crisis.

Standing in Citicorp's way was John Dingell. He and his colleagues were skeptical about the bank's overseas operations during the October 1987 collapse and wanted more facts about their role, if any, in the debacle. Dingell was considered a formidable obstacle to deregulation, and as long as he was in office reform faced an uphill battle. He clearly was not sympathetic to the bank. "They think they can buy anything," said one of his aides, referring to the bank's lobbying efforts. The counsel to his House subcommittee put the congressman's position in clear perspective. "Dingell is very committed to preserving as much of Glass-Steagall as possible," he said. "Citicorp and Continental show why we have a Glass-Steagall to begin with." Although not chairman of the House Banking Committee, he was chairman of the Energy and Commerce Committee, and the issues were considered commercial, therefore falling under his scrutiny.

For its part, Citicorp disagreed. Uninformed legislators were only standing in the way of necessary reform. At a gathering of the American Bankers' Association, one of its executives stated: "Since those who are debating the various crises don't fully comprehend the changes being wrought, any proposed remedies will have only the most fleeting benefits, or none at all, but many of them, and particularly those in Washington, are approaching these problems with the wrong perspective." He probably was not aware of how similar his comments were to those made in the 1930s criticizing the original 1933 legislation.[2] The comments were indicative of Citicorp's method of attacking regulation. They would act first, informing the Fed only after the fact. In Wall Street and banking circles it had always been clear that the regulators often followed the big banks' lead, and Citicorp's strategy in the 1980s was certainly no different.

Continued opposition from prominent Democrats in the House kept any bill from reaching the floor for a vote despite efforts by William Proxmire in the Senate to introduce reform legislation. House speaker Jim Wright and Fernand St. Germain closed the books on any further attempts to pass a bill in 1988, postponing the issue to the following year. The two Houses of Congress were in direct opposition, and a stalemate ensued. As soon as it was clear that no action would be taken, the banks immediately sprang into action. Chase Manhattan, Morgan Guaranty, and Bankers Trust all filed applications to underwrite corporate bonds, while Chase also requested permission to underwrite preferred stock and Morgan requested permission to underwrite common stock as well. The banks realized that Alan Greenspan was inclined to support the applications, and they were betting that the Fed would preempt Congress and give them the green light. The prospect did not appeal to Charles Schumer, who said, "If, in the eyes of Congress, the Fed starts legislating, it will create a counterreaction. The one thing that will unite just about every side of this issue is the idea that the

Fed is taking away our legislative prerogative."[3] Issues were coming to a head after years of wrangling and apparent foot-dragging
by the House. The only question that remained was whether the
Fed would actually preempt Congress and allow banks to circumvent Glass-Steagall.

The answer came in a matter of weeks. In January 1989 the
Fed allowed bank holding companies to underwrite corporate
bonds if it was done through a separate subsidiary company. The
banks argued that for a decade Wall Street firms had offered
money market mutual funds and cash management accounts for
their customers and that they were being held to a different standard when they wanted to offer investment banking services.
The Fed agreed. The decision was one of the most contentious
ever made by the central bank and brought mixed reaction.
Unanticipated support came from Japan, where banks also
thought they had been treated unfairly since the Americans
imposed a wall of separation on their banking industry after
World War II. An official of a large Japanese bank noted, "The
approach could lead to an early amendment to the act [Glass-
Steagall] and this approach could be adopted in Japan as well."[4]
But the House clearly was not amused and called Greenspan to
testify before the Banking Committee.

Greenspan's testimony covered a range of topics, but the
most acrimonious part was reserved for his action on the applications. He bantered with Representatives Mary Rose Oakar, a
Democrat from Ohio, and Barney Frank, a Democrat from
Massachusetts. Greenspan told the panel that the Fed was
required to act on applications with 90 days of being filed. If it
did not, the banks could then conduct underwriting as they saw
fit. But he did not mention that deadlines were often extended,
and that omission brought the wrath of several committee members. Oakar responded first by stating, "You could say no, pending the outcome of legislation." Greenspan replied by saying,
"No we cannot...What I am saying to you...is that we are
required basically to respond to the applications." After noting
that the Fed was well supplied with lawyers to settle issues like

that, she responded, "I think you took advantage at a time when we weren't organized to arbitrarily make that kind of decision. I personally resent it."[5]

The handwriting was on the wall, however. Barney Frank added a note of realism, remarking to Greenspan, "You didn't preempt us, we 'disempted' ourselves... We didn't act for one reason. The people who were in a position of power [in the House] didn't like the way the votes would have come out... now that you've done it, we'll probably pass a bill."[6]

Frank's admission sidestepped an important issue in which it seemed only members of Congress had an interest. The Fed used its powers through the Holding Company Act, granted by Congress, to grant powers to banks that Congress itself was divided over. Administrative fiat won out over legislation, and the implications were clear. Alan Greenspan would be portrayed during the bull market of the mid-1990s as the most powerful man in America and the hero of most on Wall Street and the banking community. He began his ascent to that honorary position in January 1989 with this ruling.

Traditional Wall Street was not singing his praises yet, however. The SIA brought suit to prevent the applications from being approved. It effectively blocked the original grant of underwriting powers in 1987 after the Fed approved revenue bond underwriting, and it was hoping to stall the proceedings again. The latest ruling closely followed the first in dealing with the "engaged principally" part of Section 20 of Glass-Steagall. Bank subsidiaries were allowed to earn no more than 10 percent of their revenues from these new activities, a fairly tight constraint. The decision about underwriting common stock was put on hold for a year. But it was a start. If the percentage could be increased in the future, banks would fully be in the investment banking business, regulations or not. The safety net had developed a major hole, and it was not being addressed directly. True to form, Wall Street would find a way to turn this apparent calamity into some tidy profits.

The Fed thought that firewalls put in place between the holding companies and their subsidiaries would be sufficient to prevent the sort of disaster Glass-Steagall was intended to avert. This sort of thinking put a great reliance on modern risk management techniques, in which quantitative models were used to assess risk and prevent risk from spilling from one bank activity to another. These techniques were unknown in the 1930s and appeared to be another case of time overtaking earlier laws that were considered outdated. That was the brighter side of the story. The darker side suggested that the banking system was in serious trouble, and the best the Fed could do was approve expanded powers in order to give the banks some hope that they could make money in new ways. In either case, it seemed like an enormous concession to the constituents by the regulator, who was supposed to know best, not simply follow Citicorp's lead.

The banking system was not in the best shape at the end of the 1980s. Many banks were scrambling to find new levels of capital mandated by the international agreement at the Bank for International Settlements, and the S&L industry was in shambles. Shortly after George H.W. Bush was elected, Congress began working on a bailout designed to close the least efficient thrifts, while allowing others to merge to become stronger. As part of the package, the Financial Institutions Reconstruction, Recovery, and Enforcement Act (FIRREA) finally passed in 1989. The law created the Resolution Trust Corporation, an agency dedicated to providing the funds for closing failed thrifts and selling their viable assets. After another decade of excesses, brought about in large part by the deregulation of the Garn-St Germain Act seven years before, the new agency sounded suspiciously like the old Reconstruction Finance Corporation, founded in the 1930s to stimulate the economy. Ironically, both were organized during Republican administrations battling the excesses of their own previous policies, which looked remarkably similar on the surface. Unlike Reconstruction Finance, Resolution Trust borrowed the money it needed from the bond market and used it to buy thrift assets. The new agency incurred some notable losses in winding down many large thrift institutions, but eventually proved successful. Many thrift institutions turned in their licenses and became savings banks as a result of the crisis, happy to put some distance between themselves and the disgraced industry.

The role of Michael Milken and Drexel Burnham Lambert in the collapse of the thrift industry was on the mind of Congress as it mulled over the banking problem and the stock market collapse. Dingell indicated that his committee wanted to talk to Milken before he was sentenced for his role in the insider trading scandal that previously brought down Ivan Boesky and Dennis Levine. "I think he might have things we'd be interested in hearing," Dingell remarked. Milken's previous appearance before the same committee was a nonstarter because he invoked his Fifth Amendment rights, refusing to testify. It was clear that the United States was in the midst of a market and banking crisis, but the full extent was not clear. As many junk bonds declined in value in the wake of the market collapse and the recession that followed, the thrift institutions began to fail because of their exposure to the junk bonds allowed by the 1982 deregulation. A small crack in the safety net had been exploited by Wall Street and bankers, and the results had been disastrous. Would the current trend toward full deregulation produce the same or even more catastrophic results? The question was legitimate, but the answer was not forthcoming.

Foreign Competition?

Alan Greenspan continued his own lobbying efforts before Congress, pushing for reform. In the summer of 1989, he invoked internationalism, singling out the House for its failure to approve Senate reforms. "There is no question that we are being significantly suppressed by the Glass-Steagall Act restrictions," he told a Senate banking subcommittee. His comments were echoed by Senator Christopher Dodd, a Democrat from Connecticut and the chairman of the committee, who said that it was, "unacceptable to most Americans that we should end up playing second fiddle in financial services," to other industrialized countries.[7] At the time, Citicorp was the only U.S. banking company ranked in the world's top 10. The argument was persuasive on the surface, but it failed to note that the top 10 list was compiled by listing assets of the banks in U.S. dollars. When the dollar was weak, the foreign banks all were valued higher than the Americans, so the list was not truly indicative of bank strength. But when a case could be made for American banks "falling behind" foreigners, the rhetorical value far exceeded other considerations.

Congress still would not act, not being persuaded by the arguments, and the Fed moved closer to full-service banking by allowing banks to underwrite equities. It approved an application by J.P. Morgan & Co. and took the most significant step yet to tear down the Glass-Steagall wall. Morgan used the foreign competition argument to strengthen its case, knowing full well that Greenspan favored it. The underwriting would have to be done through a separate subsidiary that derived the bulk of its business from trading government securities, as a primary dealer in the eyes of the Fed. Regardless of the structure, the SIA again criticized the arrangement, citing the dangers to the financial system, but the argument was too tendentious to be taken seriously. And the measure had support from some unexpected quarters.

The chairman of the embattled FDIC, William Seidman, commented, "It's appropriate to have commercial banks trading securities as long as they are done by carefully segregated units," supporting the idea that the firewall concept was sound. Others were far more critical. Representative Henry Gonzalez, a Democrat from Texas and chairman of the House Banking Committee, remarked, "It is irresponsible of the Federal Reserve—under any rationale—to willy-nilly add massive new risks to the banking system at a time when the taxpayer-supported insurance fund is strained to the limit," referring to the FDIC.[8] Seidman called for repeal of Glass-Steagall and McFadden and revision of the Bank

Holding Company Act in order to modernize the financial system. Throughout most of the clamoring, Wall Street's voice was muted by the demands for reform.

The *New York Times* joined the chorus by saying that the time was ripe for repeal. It added an interesting interpretation by noting that the Fed's gradual approach "has many advantages. Unlike sweeping legislation, the Fed's experiment is small, carefully controlled and easily monitored. That way the Fed will be able to prove to Congress what works before anyone turns the nation's banking laws upside down."[9] The *Wall Street Journal* also agreed with the granting of additional powers to Morgan, but added a sarcastic note from the head of one large brokerage house. "Banks certainly have an embarrassing record for running the banking business in the 1980s," remarked Benjamin Edwards, the chairman of A.G. Edwards Inc. "I think we do a lousy job in the banking business," he noted, adding, "It would surprise me if the banks do a good job in the securities business."[10] The paper noted that the securities industry had little leverage in the issue. The *Los Angeles Times* noted, "The securities business is no great shakes right now. Underwriting is slow, there is already fierce competition and profit margins are narrowing. The addition of big banks will further crowd an already crowded market." The paper added that the trend was instigated by a familiar banker. "It was a banker who saw this time coming," it remarked. "John Reed, now chairman of Citicorp, and his predecessor, Walter Wriston, started this more than a decade ago."[11] The move toward more aggressive banking had snowballed to the point where the financial department store was no longer just a historical curiosity or a business school model. It was now a fact awaiting final approval from Congress.

Official Congressional action was still years away. By late 1990, George Bush's treasury secretary, Nicholas Brady, conceded that the chances of passing meaningful legislation were no better than even. The thrift crisis was coming into better focus and provided some chilling reminders of the past. Some thrift CEOs had clearly defrauded their institutions or marketed questionable bonds to depositors, masquerading as insured deposits. Like their 1930s predecessors, the bank failures caused by chicanery and theft did not shake the larger institutions in the money centers. The smaller institutions in the west and the southwest especially suffered but did not cause many ripples on Wall Street. The S&L crisis bore many similarities to the 1930s bank failures: They occurred on levels that would not create many waves in Washington or New York unless they were aggregated. When the numbers were added, the problem was of much larger scale than many would have imagined. It was a national crisis occurring mainly on the local level. In that respect it was not unlike the banking crises of the late 1920s and early 1930s.

Farewell to the McFadden Act

The battle among key Democrats in the House, the Fed, and the banking industry showed no signs of abating in the early 1990s. Every time the administration and its allies thought they had enough votes to carry new legislation they were thwarted by House committees dedicated to saving Glass-Steagall. The effect was polarizing and became one of the first examples of political antagonisms that characterized national politics during the decade.

Another attempt at liberalizing bank law was made during the Bush administration but was blocked in the House by Henry Gonzalez and Dingell. Their own proposal made the firewalls too high, in effect dissuading the banks to enter the securities business because the regulations for doing so would have been too rigorous. The discussion on the House floor centered on the 1930s laws, their intent, and the Garn-St Germain Act of 1982. No one wanted to see the same mistakes made again, and the new powers allowed by Dingell and Gonzalez set new, higher barriers. Everyone agreed that legislation was needed, but they disagreed over its language. "This is an historic moment," remarked Representative Edward Markey, a Democrat from Massachusetts. "We don't want to tie the hands of the bankers.

We want to make them competitive. But we don't want to repeat the mistakes of the 1980s."[12] The Garn-St Germain Act was a mistake couched in good intentions, and Congress did not want the same to occur again.

Unlike the New Deal laws, the McFadden Act was always recognized as a piece of pork barrel legislation passed during a frenzied period of American politics. Unfortunately, it played to the basic fears and divisions among bankers themselves and found a unique place in legislative history as a result. The conflict between national banks and state banks over the years was the financial service sector's version of a civil war fought over the issue of banks' rights. As imperfect as McFadden was, it maintained the peace between the two factions until the conflict began to subside. It was never considered a part of the safety net or as a measure protecting bank customers. It simply prevented banks from internecine warfare.

Success would come sooner rather than later. After years of complaints and failed attempts, the McFadden Act finally was reversed in 1994. Congress approved the Riegle-Neal Interstate Banking and Branching Efficiency Act that finally abolished the prohibition against interstate banking. After almost 70 years, the banking system was finally able to integrate geographically. The state banks complained about the law but were placated when they discovered that out-of-state banks would have to buy a bank in their state before they could open any new branches. This allowed many smaller bankers to sell their companies to larger banks at hefty premiums. It seemed that old habits, and complaints, died hard.

The bill was sponsored by Senator Donald Riegle, a Democrat from Michigan, and Representative Richard Neal, a Democrat from Massachusetts. Unlike Glass-Steagall, it had the approval of Congress, the Fed, and the Clinton administration, which had displayed strong support for banking reform. Its passage was certain enough that some banks began announcing interstate mergers in anticipation of the plan before it passed Congress. Since the early 1990s, intrastate mergers had been occurring, with some notable banking names joining forces. Chase Manhattan and Chemical merged in 1995, but after the bill became law, interstate mergers were announced in an attempt to create the nation's first truly interstate bank with coast-to-coast capabilities. The logistics of merging banks could be formidable, and the first successful attempt occurred when NationsBank of North Carolina bought the Bank of America, headquartered in San Francisco. Although not present in every state, the bank would be the first to claim that its reach extended from ocean to ocean

Traditional politics began to play less of an influence in banking and Wall Street in the mid-1990s. The Clinton administration shared its Republican predecessor's desire to revamp the laws in favor of "competition." After Robert Rubin, a former Goldman Sachs partner, became treasury secretary, the administration began its own drive for reform. This placed great pressure on stalwarts in the House who fought for continued regulation, since they were now made to appear contrary to their own party. In early 1995, Rubin advocated repeal of Glass–Steagall and changes to the Bank Holding Company Act so that banks could engage in the insurance business. This was a radical departure for a Democratic administration and one of the most radical calls for action by an administration since the 1930s set the tone for regulation in the first place. If Congress were to act with the administration, every law passed for investor protection as well as that of financial institutions since World War I, when the states passed insurance legislation, would be set back.

Many in the insurance industry, like the investment banking industry, hung anxiously on every word from official Washington. During the 1990s, Conseco, an aggressive insurance company, was acquiring other insurers at a breakneck pace. It was a Wall Street favorite before falling on lean times later in the decade and finally filing for bankruptcy as the new century dawned. Much of its growth was attributable to its chairman Stephen Hilbert, a prime example of the growth-by-acquisition chief executive of the 1980s and 1990s. He told *Institutional Investor*: "I think the insurance industry is going to have a viable role from now on. And I also think that when you take a look at what's going on with Glass-Steagall . . . and all those different regulatory changes that you're going to see that banks really come after the insurance industry. The financial services industry is absolutely changing. And I think we're just in round two of a 15-round bout as far as consolidation goes. Over the next five to ten years, you're going to see an awful lot of action."[13] Clearly, some insurers were beefing up operations through mergers with the hope that they would be acquired by a bank once regulation was swept away.

Alan Greenspan continued applying pressure on Congress at every opportunity to pass the necessary legislation. But the Fed had extended its powers as far as it could by allowing the banks de facto power in securities and other previously forbidden services. The one area left where the Fed had room to maneuver was the percentage of revenues allowed to securities subsidiaries, which they could earn from underwriting. Before long, that would become the next tool to be used from the Fed's arsenal. For its part, Wall Street had become convinced that fighting reform was no longer in its best interests. Two of the largest retail-oriented firms, Bache and Smith Barney, had already been acquired by insurance companies. Bache was bought by Prudential and Smith Barney, part of Primerica, was purchased by Commercial Credit Group, run by Sanford Weill. The trinity of financial services—banking, investment banking, and insurance—had yet to come full circle, and the last leg would prove the most difficult.

When Republicans finally seized control of the House in 1994, John Dingell lost his chairmanship of the Energy and Commerce committee and Republicans assigned banking reform to the Banking Committee, which was in favor of repealing Glass-Steagall. The move appeared to clear the way for hasty reform, but the issue again became stalled. Representative Jim Leach, a Republican from Iowa who chaired the House Banking Committee, introduced a bill in the House allowing bank holding companies to own securities firms and banks but went one step further by making the Fed the regulator of all subsidiaries. The concept was not a far stretch from the Fed's powers found in the Bank Holding Company Act, but was too much of a stretch for Treasury Secretary Robert Rubin. He argued that the measure would give too much power to the Fed at a time when it had been exercising inordinate amounts of de facto influence. Rubin claimed, "History shows that bank failures generally result not from securities-related activities but from deterioration in the quality of banks' traditional assets—loans."[14] The concept was correct, but history was taking a beating since banks had not been in the securities business for the previous 60 years. The issue was becoming political again, but many were glad to hear Rubin's arguments since the Fed under Alan Greenspan was quickly becoming the most talked-about institution in Washington.

Reformers were clearly wringing their hands by late 1995 because it appeared that repeal was not going to pass Congress. A bill introduced by Leach did not materialize, leading the congressman to say, "Logic does not always prevail over the power structure." Repeal had become a hot issue and had great staying power, more than anyone had thought since 1981. Despite the fact that the Fed, the banking industry, the Reagan, Bush, and Clinton administrations, most newly converted Wall Street firms, and many members in Congress wanted repeal, the issue could not be resolved successfully. Then Speaker of the House Newt Gingrich effectively derailed any thought of effective repeal, bowing to the demands of the insurance industry by inserting a clause in pending legislation effectively keeping banks out of the insurance business indefinitely. All of those insurance agents still wielded considerable political clout in Washington because of their sheer numbers. One banker summed up Gingrich's actions by stating blandly, "There are a lot more insurance agents out there than bankers."

Washington discovered just how many there were in the spring of 1995. More than 14,000 agents descended on Washington and began actively lobbying for protection from their members of Congress. It was their version of the Bonus March, and they were more successful because Gingrich eventually succumbed to their pressure. Naturally, bankers' groups opposed the clause, and the Glass-Steagall repeal began to lose momentum. Wall Street dissidents supported the insurance agents, and chances of repeal began to fade quickly. By mid-1996, most hopes of reform had dissipated, but Leach refused to let the issue die. He wrote a letter to Alan Greenspan, asking the Fed to expand the securities operations of bank holding companies from the present 10 percent of subsidiary revenues. Greenspan responded in 1996 by moving the percentage higher, to 25 percent. Moves of this sort kept the issue alive when all other avenues failed. Not everyone was pleased, however.

Extending the allowed percentage from 10 to 25 percent set in motion a number of bank and investment bank mergers. Banks searched for top-notch investment banks they could acquire whose revenues would not put their own operations at risk in the new formula. Deutsche Bank acquired Alex. Brown when it bought Bankers Trust in 1998, and Roberston, Stephens was acquired by the Bank of America. The Deutsche Bank acquisition in particular seemed to be a perfect example of the foreign competition everyone feared, especially when it first acquired Bankers Trust. But less well-known was that any foreign bank operating in the United States was as subject to the Fed as any domestic Fed member, so the threat of foreign competition was vastly overdone in this case. In some cases, Wall Street made healthy profits when the commercial banks opened their checkbooks for the mostly smaller, regional investment banking firms.

In a move highly reminiscent of 1929, Comptroller of the Currency Eugene Ludwig decided in 1996 to allow nationally chartered banks to underwrite corporate securities through subsidiaries. In the absence of any other action, the move was interpreted as another shot at Glass-Steagall by a regulator, although there were restrictions imposed on how much could be underwritten. The measure would not apply to state banks, but the message undeniably was clear: It was time to allow banks into the forbidden zone. But it was becoming apparent that a catalyst would be needed to break the logjam. If events were to play true to form, the catalysts would have to come from Wall Street or the banking industry since Washington appeared to be handcuffed. Representative Marge Roukema, a Republican from New Jersey and member of the Banking Committee, remarked that only Congress had the authority to define which services banks should engage in and what sorts of firewalls should be erected. She was reacting not to Greenspan's various measures but to those of the comptroller. Congress was still hoping that the reform could be achieved by actual legislation rather than a relaxing of the rules by the Fed or the comptroller, but it was quickly losing ground.

New Deal Revisited?

Even casual observers could detect a repetition of 1930s' political language once the Clinton administration took office. The new president described his early months in office as the "first 100 days," in a clear reference to FDR. Was his administration proposing a new deal of its own? Republicans who had been working feverishly for years to roll back New Deal laws sat up and took notice. But the similarities never developed. If anything, the Clinton years looked more like those Republican administrations as far as financial reforms were concerned.

Then, in an even more unusual twist reminiscent of Louis McFadden and Andrew Mellon, similar events and language appeared in late 1995. The Congress, led by Republicans, forced the government to a near default by refusing to increase the debt ceiling, as requested by the Clinton administration. Such requests were routinely granted as the need for borrowing expanded along with the economy. As a result, the government was thrown into temporary crisis with a default on its outstanding debt looming as a real possibility unless the limit was improved. Then, Robert Rubin intervened by borrowing $60 billion from a government trust fund, averting the crisis until a political settlement could be found. The move infuriated some Republicans. Representative Gerald Solomon of New York threatened to impeach Rubin, claiming he exceeded his authority. But the crisis was averted, and Rubin quickly was dubbed the greatest treasury secretary since Alexander Hamilton, an honor previously conferred on Mellon. Rubin's stature grew as the budget deficit began to decline because of increasing federal tax revenues, due to the strong economy and the bull market. Despite the similarities, however, the new administration actually espoused the deregulation mantra of Greenspan and House Republicans and soon advocated a dismantling of New Deal banking laws.

Not all of the significant legislation in the mid-1990s centered on banking. In 1995, Congress passed contentious legislation designed to reduce the number of lawsuits being brought by investors against publicly traded companies. As part of Newt Gingrich's highly publicized Contract with America, the law proposed that the guidelines under which a lawsuit could be brought against a company offering securities to the public be changed. If the investor sues, claiming the company omitted important information in its offering, the company could merely claim that it forgot to include it. Columnist Anthony Lewis, who commented on legal matters and the Supreme Court, put it simply when he said, "An investor who sues for fraud must show that the defendant made a fraudulent statement 'knowingly' or 'recklessly.'" If the company could show that it did not, there was no basis for the lawsuit. He called this an "I forgot" defense, one that was acceptable under the language of the act. "A ludicrous notion?" he asked rhetorically. "Not at all. It will be the law if a bill reaches the floor of the House this week and wins final passage."[15]

The House and the Senate both passed the bill by large majorities, but President Clinton vetoed it under pressure from investor and consumer groups. The veto was overridden, however, handing the president his first such defeat. Part of the general protection afforded by the Securities Act of 1933 had been diluted in the opinion of many observers. Supporters of the bill included the SIA, accounting bodies, and the National Association of Managers. Opponents included the administration, consumer groups, and most trial lawyer associations, who quickly saw their livelihood being threatened. But the issue was divided on party lines. Many notable trial lawyers were Democrats, and the unnecessary litigation filed by many was seen as inefficient and nettlesome. The new Republican majority used the opportunity and bipartisan support to get the law passed but clearly overlooked the "I forgot" defense, which would reappear in various forms at the end of the bull market in the early 2000s.

More securities legislation was passed in 1996 but did not address the deregulation of banks. Congress passed the National Securities Markets Improvement Act, immediately called the most significant overhaul of the industry in years by SEC Chairman Arthur Levitt. The new law was actually a bit of deregulation in its own right because it eliminated state review of mutual fund prospectuses and advertisements. The SEC was given the primary responsibility for supervising mutual fund advisers who managed at least $25 million in assets. An electronic database also was planned so that investors could check for complaints against investment advisers before investing with them. The law was meant to consolidate supervision of mutual funds in the SEC's hands, although it would be used some years later to argue against the ability of state attorneys general, notably Eliot Spitzer of New York, to bring lawsuits against the funds and others who were supposed to be regulated by the SEC.

Growth by Merger

The event that sent bank reform into high gear occurred in 1997. The process had been painfully slow for reformers but progress was being made, and now a Democratic administration had climbed on board the deregulation train. Despite almost 70 years of regulation, it was clear that big business still reigned supreme and managed to determine its own future. The time was ripe for changing things to suit the new mood on Wall Street. If the old laws were not rolled back during the bull market of the 1990s, they would have little chance when it came to an end. And it was also time to reward anyone who aided in the quest to consolidate.

Like many of the notable financial events in Wall Street history, the catalyst for change would be an individual with a decided penchant for changing the status quo in favor of expanding business and profit potential. The story of the dismantling of financial regulations had its origins in the career of Sanford Weill, the chief executive of Travelers Insurance in the mid-1990s.

Weill was born in 1933 and lived with his family of modest means in Brooklyn before attending military school and Cornell. He got his start in 1958 when I.W. "Tubby" Burnham gave him a job at Burnham & Co., a brokerage founded in 1935, during the Depression. Burnham's firm would later give Michael Milken his start on the Street as well. Weill started ambitiously and within several years began his own brokerage, leasing space from Burnham. His early partners included Arthur Levitt, who later would become chairman of the SEC. His small firm grew rapidly. From the beginning, Weill expanded his firm through acquisition. His first opportunity to expand came during the back office crisis that hit Wall Street in the early 1970s.

In 1970, Weill purchased Hayden Stone, a retail broker, adopted its name, and eventually became its CEO three years later. The deal was unusual because Weill's firm was only a fraction of the size of Shearson, but in the gloomy days of the back office crisis in the early 1970s any firm that wanted to save another was welcome to do so. A smaller buyer could succeed where ordinarily the merger would have not been possible. After purchasing another firm in 1974, the name was again changed to Shearson Hayden Stone. Five years later it repeated the pattern by buying the ailing small investment bank Loeb Rhoades & Co., becoming Shearson Loeb Rhoades. After purchasing more than a dozen small and medium-size firms, Weill then sold Shearson to American Express in 1981, staying on as third in line to the chairman.

Despite being named president in 1983, Weill quit American Express in 1985. A year later, he emerged as the CEO of the Commercial Credit Corp., a consumer credit company that financially was on its knees. Most of Wall Street had written him off because of his affiliation with the company, which was not in the forefront of financial services companies. Relegated to apparent obscurity, Weill reemerged by employing a familiar tactic. He began a series of mergers using Commercial Credit as his acquisitions vehicle. In 1988, he acquired another financial services company, Primerica, which owned the old-line securities house Smith Barney. Discarding the Commercial Credit name, the new company became known as Primerica and had over 1,800 offices offering a range of financial services. Within a period of seven years, Weill had made his way back to Wall Street as a dealmaker in his own right. He did not make his reputation by doing deals for others but by arranging them for his own group of companies.

Far from finished, he then purchased Shearson back from American Express. Then, in 1993 he acquired The Travelers Corp. for $4.3 billion. The deal increased Primerica's assets to more than $100 billion. Shearson Smith Barney was the second largest broker in the country, behind only Merrill Lynch. After the acquisition, the company became known as The Travelers and had four major divisions—securities brokerage and underwriting, insurance, consumer lending, and asset management. Two of the previously forbidden types of merger were now in place. The only component lacking for full-service financial department store was banking. Weill then purchased the jewel in his Wall Street crown by acquiring Salomon Brothers in 1997 for a hefty $9 billion. The new securities subsidiary of Travelers became known as Salomon Smith Barney. Smith Barney was an old retail firm tracing its history back to the Civil War period, while Salomon was one of the top institutional houses on Wall Street, especially strong in arbitrage and bonds. Since the 1970s, it successfully had challenged the older investment banks such as Morgan Stanley and Dillon Read and made serious inroads into their traditional strengths—mergers and underwriting. Despite the aggressive purchases, Weill and Travelers were still not in major danger of bumping into Glass-Steagall since the crucial element—commercial banking—was not in the mix.

Following the acquisition of Salomon Brothers, Weill was forced to close the firm's previously successful equities arbitrage unit because of huge losses. Even as Travelers was absorbing Salomon, the company was in the early stages of a deal that would leave Wall Street, regulators, and critics gasping. Weill had been seeking more acquisition targets, banks among them. He then proposed that Travelers and J.P. Morgan & Co. merge, a suggestion that clearly shocked Morgan chairman Sandy Warner. In order to overcome the protests that it was illegal for an insurance company to take over a bank, his lawyers, notably Charles Prince, the company's general counsel, pointed out that a loophole in the Glass-Steagall Act (as he interpreted it) allowed the possibility, provided that the insurance company operations be spun off within two to five years. If that could be achieved, then perhaps Glass-Steagall could be repealed within that time, allowing the deal to stand without a divestiture. Once Weill was convinced that the possibility existed, he called Alan Greenspan to gauge his reaction. As predicted, Greenspan told Weill he was "open to the logic" that Travelers was proposing.[16] The light was green for a financial services company to acquire a bank; for the first time since the Depression.

In addition to Citicorp, J.P. Morgan & Co. also was in the forefront of the assault on the banking law. Being one of the first commercial banks allowed into equity underwriting gave it an edge that it was able to exploit. Morgan's argument was more than curiously historical. It produced a study entitled "Glass-Steagall: Overdue for Repeal." Arguing that the eurobond market, where commercial banks had always been free to underwrite without restriction since it was offshore, was less dominated by an oligopoly of investment banks, and underwritings were spread more evenly among all sorts of banks. The U.S. market, however, was dominated by top-tier investment banks. Between 1990 and 1994, well over 90 percent of debt and equity underwritings in the United States were done by the top 15 firms in the industry.

Morgan argued that these sorts of domination by the top firms were "indicators of a concentration unequaled in all but a few U.S. industries." This was an admission that the bank would never have made in the 1930s when it was fending off Congressional critics. If the wholesale banks were allowed into underwriting on an unrestricted basis, costs would drop as "competition" increased. Oddly, the argument for greater competition was purely oligarchical in nature. Only the top banks were included and Morgan wanted to be one of them.

The point was accepted by bankers from both sides of the industry interested in seeing Glass-Steagall repealed. John Thain, a partner at Goldman Sachs, and Michael Patterson of J.P. Morgan & Co. both made the same point before the House Committee on Banking and Financial Services. Patterson argued forcefully for reforming Glass-Steagall when he said that the very point "was repeated by Treasury Secretary Rubin [formerly a Goldman Sachs partner] in his testimony to this committee a month ago when he said: 'It is difficult to argue that the security underwriting risk of an investment bank is greater than the loan making risk of a commercial bank.' As the business of banking and finance continues to evolve rapidly, and as the financial and risk management needs of clients around the world change and grow, U.S. institutions must have the same flexibility as our global competitors to adapt, to innovate, and to lead."[17] In terms of competition, the world of finance was becoming too small to allow distinctions in the banking business.

The Morgan deal did not proceed for many financial and corporate cultural reasons. Weill was well-known on Wall Street, but the proposal was not one that Morgan would entertain from the nouveau riche since the bank cherished its history and corporate culture. Weill then entered secret discussions with John Reed, the CEO of Citibank, for a potential merger that would make another venerable old bank the target of the largest acquisition to date. Even by Wall Street standards, the idea of an insurance company and an investment bank acquiring one of the largest and best known commercial banks while the old banking laws were still on the books was audacious, to say the least. But Weill knew something that the rest of the Street could only guess at. The Fed was a supporter of the idea and would give him enough room to maneuver without upsetting Congress. The last question was simple. Would Congress finally acquiesce and repeal the parts of Glass-Steagall that were obnoxious to bankers?

The Ultimate Loophole

When Travelers began talks with Citicorp about merging, the same two-year promise was used again. In this case, it was Weill's lawyers giving legal advice to Citicorp, usually in the front ranks of seeking loopholes in the law itself. It was also clear that when the huge deal did pass regulatory muster, Congress would have the incentive it needed to repeal the relevant sections of Glass-Steagall once and for all.

The deal would be proclaimed to be a merger of equals, a term used to politely describe a takeover. Mergers between two equal parties were easier to justify to antitrust regulators in the 1990s political climate. Despite the language, Travelers clearly was the buyer in the deal. Citibank was not in a position to make overtures to an insurance company because of existing legal restraints. Weill was under no such constraints. He was not subject to the Holding Company Act and certainly was not as conservative as Citibank senior management. But the legal situation was still far from settled. As he and Reed worked out the details of the merger, time was of the essence. Would regulators accept the interpretation of the two-year grace period assumed by Travelers' lawyers?

The general consensus at the time was that the merger would not put the bank or the financial system at risk. Accordingly, regulators were sophisticated enough not to allow problems that would undermine its viability to brew at a bank. The *New York Times* opined, "In one stroke, Mr. Reed and Mr. Weill will have temporarily demolished the increasingly unnecessary walls built during the Depression to separate commercial banks from investment banks and insurance companies. . . . A collapse in the company's [Citigroup] securities and insurance operations could drag down the commercial bank. But that will happen only if Federal regulators fall sound asleep."[18] The question naturally turned to the nature of the firewalls between subsidiaries of the bank. Were they strong enough to prevent a fire from sweeping from one subsidiary to other parts of the holding company, threatening the entire structure? Falling asleep was not the problem. Unforeseen consequences would prove disturbing. Long-Term Capital management still loomed on the horizon.

Well aware of the safety problem, the Fed addressed the issue frequently in an attempt to win over undecided lawmakers. Fed Governor Susan Phillips told the Senate, "One important protection is the placement of securities activities in a separate subsidiary of the bank holding company, rather than in the bank itself or a subsidiary of the bank. Because non-bank subsidiaries of a bank holding company operating under Section 20 of the Glass-Steagall Act are affiliates of a bank, they are not under the bank's control, do not have their profits or losses consolidated with the bank's..."[19] The protection needed explaining because critics wanted to know how the subsidiary could stand alone from the bank and still be affiliated with it in any meaningful way that would actually help the banking industry.

While the Fed pondered the problem presented to it, dealmakers suffered some uneasy nights' sleep as opposition formed to the recent House attempt to reform banking law, known as H.R. 10. Opposition to H.R. 10 arose from several quarters, including the Clinton administration. The administration feared that such a huge bank holding company could easily circumvent the objectives of the Community Reinvestment Act (CRA, originally passed in 1977), which required banks to make loans to their neighborhoods as a way of supporting local economies, especially in the inner cities and minority neighborhoods. During the Clinton administration, unlike previous administrations, consumer groups were having some influence. "We are concerned that the bill would diminish the effectiveness of the Community Reinvestment Act," claimed one consumer advocate. "Financial conglomerates envisioned under the bill would shift activities to holding company affiliates, where the CRA does not apply." In this instance, mergers were loudly attacked on a proconsumer basis.

Ralph Nader opposed H.R. 10 and pulled no punches in his critique of the bill. He claimed, "If Congress stampedes this legislation, as the giants in the financial industry demand they do, the day will come when the corruption or speculative risks facilitated by the bill will materialize into gigantic taxpayer obligations to bail out these debacles." [20] Although the comments were taken as rhetorical at the time, several months later the giant hedge fund Long-Term Capital Management failed, requiring a substantial support operation by the Fed that amounted to a temporary bailout.

Consumer groups could complain but could not stop the deregulation movement. Hundreds of community organizations joined forces to plead with members of the House and Senate banking committees to oppose the bill. Then, two other regulators of the banking system also publicly stated that H.R. 10 was not in the public interest. In a letter to Senators Alphonse D'Amato, Republican of New York, and Paul Sarbanes, Democrat of Maryland, Acting Comptroller of the Currency Julie Williams and Director of the Office of Thrift Supervision Ellen Seidman stated that parts of the legislation "would undermine the safety and soundness of the insured institutions regulated by our two agencies," referring mainly to thrift institutions.[21] They also complained that the language of the bill affected their two agencies specifically but did not affect the Fed or the Federal Deposit Insurance Corporation (FDIC). By implication, the complaint suggested that the bill was written for the Fed and the FDIC specifically, leaving them out of the loop. Williams later noted, "We must have legislation that truly advances the needs of consumers and communities...in my judgment, H.R. 10 is not that legislation."[22] But even less influential regulators were left disappointed in the wake of the deregulation fervor.

In the months that followed the Travelers/Citicorp merger, while H.R. 10 was still being debated, vested interest groups continued to do battle. Senator Phil Gramm, a Republican from Texas and primary supporter of the bill, did not see H.R. 10 as a threat to the CRA. He wanted references to the CRA deleted from H.R. 10. He considered the bill so important that the administration would be forced to concede and sign it in its original form, acquiescing to the demands of the banking industry. In 1998, his sole opposition to the bill, originally containing references to the CRA, killed it in the 1998 Congressional session.

Ralph Nader pressed his objections. He complained, "The bills before Congress have been cobbled together from wish lists of the various industry groups and in the process, the rights of consumers have been trampled, or more often, ignored."[23] The complaints continued for another six months. Although deregulation was closer than at any other time since 1933, it still was not coming quickly enough for its advocates. The clock was now ticking on the giant merger.

Securities firms finally changed their tune and actively lobbied for the passage of H.R. 10. Merrill Lynch took the position that it should be allowed to acquire a bank because if the power was not extended to securities firms, they might disappear entirely. "Within a few years there will be a handful of players doing financial services and Merrill Lynch wants to be one of them," stated a Merrill official. "Banks can buy us but we can't buy a bank," added another, noting that the arrangement that Travelers and Weill worked out with the Fed could do securities firms harm since they did not have the same access to the Fed as the banks.

The new, combined bank cum insurance and securities holding company was huge by any standard. The newly created Citigroup had assets in excess of $1.5 trillion, 250,000 employees, and revenues of over $80 billion. The deal also helped bring Weill's personal wealth close to the $1 billion mark.[24] Although the Fed accepted Travelers' time schedule of two years to either repeal legislation or divest, deregulatory legislation was needed if the deal was to stand. The Fed did its part by approving the merger in October 1998, but the ink was not entirely dry. It approved the

deal on the condition that Travelers and Citicorp conform to all
the requirements of the Bank Holding Company Act within two
years of approval. It also stated, "The Board's approval is also subject to the condition that [Citigroup] conform the activities of its
companies to the requirements of the Glass-Steagall Act..."[25]
Only hard lobbying by Citigroup would put the necessary pressure
on Congress to repeal the relevant sections of Glass-Steagall.
Otherwise, divestiture would be on the horizon within a few years,
a prospect unthinkable in Wall Street terms.

Intense lobbying was exactly what followed. While still on
the table, H.R. 10 proved a bonanza for lobbying firms. In 1997,
it was estimated that financial services companies spent over
$177 million on lobbying efforts and $100 million was spent on
Congressional elections in the 1998 campaign, supporting legislators friendly to the bill. It was the largest amount spent by any
sector of the economy to support candidates during that time, giving some indication of its importance to the financial services
industry.[26] Critics remained skeptical, however. Did anyone
understand how this new leviathan would work or manage
its risk?

The Fed naturally threw its weight behind the bill. Alan
Greenspan told the House, "The Board strongly supports the
approach to financial modernization embodied in H.R. 10. We
believe it would improve the efficiency and competitiveness of
the financial services industry and result in more choices and
better service for consumers."[27] The volume had now been
turned up by the central bank on a recalcitrant House. If it were
not for the vast chorus of interest groups pushing for repeal, the
Fed's acceptance of the Citicorp two-year formula would have
given rise to serious criticism had the fact been widely publicized. The fact that everyone appeared to have been on the
same page illustrated that the Fed had turned to consensus politics in this instance, rather than exercising its role as a strong
regulator. From the perspective of the banks, deregulation was
long overdue, and the best that the central bank could do was
agree. This was not out of line with past Fed reactions to crises,

but did illustrate that the Fed itself was acting as nothing more than the holding company of its affiliates, the banks. Apparently, its job was to find a consensus that would appeal to everyone while offending as few as possible. Since most of the critics had no real political muscle to speak of, the process was simple once Congress finally got on board. But consensus was not a substitute for effective regulation. All it meant was that when a crisis occurred, everyone could agree that it was not their fault.

Demise of Glass–Steagall

In the elections of 1998, Senator Alphonse D'Amato, a Republican from New York and strong supporter of H.R. 10, lost his bid for reelection. This was a blow for both his party and reformers since he was chairman of the Senate Banking Committee. The loss left Phil Gramm to fight for reform in the Senate, being the other best-known advocate for repeal. Was it possible that another roadblock had been hit so late in the game?

Not this time. While the Senate was considering H.R. 10, Alan Greenspan again recited the need for the bill to pass. In 1998, he told the Senate Committee on Banking, Housing, and Urban Affairs, "H.R. 10 is a comprehensive approach to the issues of financial modernization, and it is fundamentally a sound bill. No legislation that endeavors to address financial modernization will be considered ideal by all, but time will allow its rough spots to be worked out."[28] How those rough spots would be ironed out had to be taken on faith because time was of the essence.

As the debate neared a close, it was clear that repealing Glass-Steagall was really an antitrust matter, not simply a banking issue. That side of the argument had been kept in the background throughout the years. Fed Governor Laurence Meyer made this clear when he testified before the House. Concerning the Fed's powers, he stated unequivocally, "The Federal Reserve's administration of the antitrust laws in banking has helped to maintain competitive banking markets in the midst of the most significant consolidation of the banking industry in U.S. history. It is the

Board's intention and expectation that this will continue to be the case in the future."[29] Greenspan had already been on record for years before as opposing much of the content of the existing antitrust laws. More recently, he promised the Senate at his confirmation hearings to honor the laws on the books.

In the fall of 1999, H.R. 10 finally passed Congress, and it was clear that the Financial Services Modernization Act (the Gramm-Leach-Bliley Act) was ready to be signed. Citigroup then announced the hiring of Robert Rubin, who resigned his post as treasury secretary in 1999. While in office, Rubin favored the dismantling of Glass-Steagall. Shortly after leaving office, he attended a function in New York where he met Weill by chance. After some long discussions, he decided to join Citigroup. Responding to an article in the *Wall Street Journal* criticizing him for taking a private sector job so quickly, Rubin wrote, " I didn't see...why I had to become a monk just because I'd spent time in public service."[30] Rumblings were heard from consumers' groups almost immediately after the announcement. They only became louder when Rubin's first-year compensation, including salary, bonuses, and stock options, was reported to be around $45 million. Although he favored H.R. 10 in principle, Rubin had not endorsed it without reservation at times while it was still on the table. In another move that would have left muckrakers from an earlier era howling, Weill was named to a three-year term on the Board of Directors of the Federal Reserve Bank of New York, beginning in 2001. Perhaps it was natural that the CEO of the country's newest and largest financial institution sit on the board, but it seemed to critics seemed that the game-keepers and the poachers had all joined the same club. Other members of the board, while well-known in industry, had much lower public profiles.

Consumer groups did not agree with the administration's idea of progress, especially after the Clinton administration supported H.R. 10 and put its weight behind it. Ralph Nader took exception to Robert Rubin's handling of H.R. 10 while he was still treasury secretary. Claiming that Rubin had attempted to work out a compromise between treasury officials and Congressmen working on the bill, Nader charged in a complaint to the government that Rubin had improperly influenced the legislation. The job at Citigroup upon leaving office only reinforced the point. The Justice Department concluded that no criminal investigation was warranted after receiving Nader's original complaint in January 2000. The response did not satisfy him, however. Writing to the Treasury, he claimed, "It is impossible to determine what facts were investigated or what witnesses were interviewed, on the basis for the conclusions by either your office or the Department of Justice."[31] The water was already under the dam, however.

The New Economy was still moving along at great speed, and the financial department store was one of its cornerstones. Providing customers with a wide range of services from under one roof was considered *de rigeur*. The "antiquated" New Deal laws, decried by most commentators and politicians, had finally given way. Glass-Steagall had been rolled back. Almost no one mentioned that it was Glass-Steagall that originally introduced deposit insurance.

The demise of Glass-Steagall and the official opening of a New Era occurred in the late fall of 1999. As President Clinton signed the new law, he stated, "This legislation is truly historic, we have done right by the American people." Senator Phil Gramm, chairman of the Senate banking committee, added a note of progress by adding, "The world changes, and Congress and the laws have to change with it."[32] Gramm was a supporter of H.R. 10 (without the references to the CRA). After his recent term in Congress was finished, he moved into the private sector. Like Rubin, he benefited from the new legislation when he was offered a job with the investment banking unit of UBS Warburg as vice chairman in 2002. The bank specialized in mergers and acquisitions (M&A), being an amalgam of the Union Bank of Switzerland and S.G. Warburg & Co., which itself earlier had merged with Dillon Read. The job was seen as a payback because it was the Gramm-Leach-Bliley Act that allowed UBS to buy securities house Paine Webber for $12 billion in 2000 in a smaller, yet significant product of the new deregulated environment.

Gramm later joked about his new job, commenting that he would have to take the appropriate securities licensing tests along with "a group of 30-year-olds" before he could settle down to work. Critics were not in so jovial a mood, however. A writer at the ever-watchful *San Francisco Chronicle* commented that it was "glad to see Wall Street is serious about cleaning up its act...the man holds a doctorate in economics from the University of Georgia, awarded during the Harding administration, I believe."[33] Seems that old memories die hard.

As Glass-Steagall passed into oblivion, there were few kind words at its funeral. *The Economist* remarked, "Nobody will mourn the passing of the Glass-Steagall Act. It was a bad act from day one." Almost every commentator, newspaper, and politician was happy to see it go without any nostalgia. After the modernization bill passed, Representative Jim Leach held a party in Washington to celebrate the passing of the act. A large cake bearing the icing message "Glass-Steagall, RIP, 1933–1999" was served along with champagne. In attendance were Alan Greenspan, Treasury Undersecretary Lawrence Summers, Comptroller of the Currency John D. Hawke, and other congressmen and lobbyists. For deregulators, the long battle was over. But whether the war also was finished was questionable.

The Market Collapse

The true test of the new financial environment would come only when a crisis developed. How well the deregulated banks fared in this environment would prove whether the years of lobbying and claims of advanced risk management techniques were valid or nothing more than hyperbole. Unfortunately, the ink was hardly dry on Gramm-Leach-Bliley before the extraordinary bull market began to fall precipitously.

Banks always had been responsible for fueling speculative bubbles in the stock market, and the 1990s were no exception. Banks loaned money both to the call money market and to the most aggressive companies trying to take advantage of advancing stock prices. With fewer restrictions than in the past, the post-1998 lending was different from past bank behavior and would have profound consequences. Traditionally, under the old banking laws, banks made short- and medium-term loans to companies while the securities firms raised long-term capital in the form of new stocks or bonds. As long as the two money providers were separate, problems at a client company were equally divided between the two. The bank was at greater risk because it was loaning its customers' money. The securities firms were only at risk until the new securities were sold to investors. They collected their underwriting fees and went on to another deal. Combining the two could be problematic, however.

In the wake of the Citigroup deal, the lines became badly blurred. If a large client fell into financial difficulties, the risk was not actually diversified but remained with the parent financial institution, which could develop exposure through both lending and underwriting. Investment banks did not consider the underwriting risk particularly serious unless they were sued for not being diligent in their activities, a situation that did not occur often in the past. But when both situations converged, the risks could be considerable. Banks began courting many corporate customers by lending them money in the first instance with an eye toward underwriting their securities at a later date. That was full-service banking. It could also spell full-service disaster.

Two particularly aggressive companies typified the bull market of the late 1990s. One was WorldCom, a telecommunications company with grand ambitions of becoming the next AT&T, run by Bernard Ebbers, The other was Enron, an energy company based in Texas, run by Kenneth Lay. Both relied heavily on their banks for funds and became prime examples of the financial abuses of the 1990s. Their subsequent problems were caused by fraud and deception, but the flames were fanned by the new banking relationships, which made money too easy to obtain.

WorldCom traced its origins to the founding of MCI, another well-known but small telephone provider. The company got its start in the 1960s as a start-up provider of long-distance services for small business customers. In the 1970s, MCI began the court challenge that eventually brought AT&T to its knees, forcing the company to agree to a breakup with the Justice Department after years of litigation. In 1983, the same year that AT&T finally agreed to its own dissolution, a group of local businessmen in Mississippi adopted the same general business plan by founding a long-distance company that would purchase wholesale long-distance service from AT&T and resell it. One of the founders was Bernard Ebbers. Born in 1941 in Alberta, Ebbers moved south to attend college in Mississippi. His first job was as a milkman. He later coached in high school before buying a motel and expanding it into a chain. The company founded humbly in a motel restaurant in 1983 would later be renamed WorldCom.

Through a series of acquisitions, Ebbers built the company into a major long-distance provider. He acquired 68 phone companies after 1983, beginning by offering long-distance services mostly to small businesses. He then branched into the local markets with the $12 billion acquisition of MFS Communications in 1996. WorldCom stock soared on the prospects, and Ebbers was presented with a golden opportunity to use it to expand even further. The apple of his eye was MCI, better known than his own company but cheaper in market terms. Clearly a buyer of other companies rather than a long-range planner, he was a prime example of the aggressive CEO of the 1990s, more interested in growth than a long-range market plan. But Wall Street initially was impressed.

In order to continue expanding, WorldCom needed to continue purchasing larger companies in the highly competitive telecommunications industry. A major competitor was GTE, which made an all-cash bid for MCI worth $28 billion. WorldCom prevailed, however, with an all-stock bid valued at $37 billion. The sheer size of the all-stock deal dumbfounded many on Wall Street. WorldCom issued an additional 760 million shares to pay for it. It outbid the British telecommunications company BT, which also was interested in expanding. The day the deal was originally announced, shock was obvious on Wall Street. "That is it, the world has finally gone mad," one investment banker remarked after hearing the terms. Another remarked, "I literally though that the WorldCom deal was the deal that would end all, or at least most, deals." But in traditional Wall Street fashion, after the shock had worn off, new deals emerged, dwarfing the older ones.

MCI WorldCom was a giant in telecommunications, with combined revenue of $30 billion and operations in 65 countries, 75,000 employees, and 22 million customers. Regulators in Europe and the United States insisted on certain divestitures, including Internet service, so that the new company would not have undue influence in emerging communications. The new entity remained the brainchild of Ebbers, and investment bankers from Lazard Freres and Salomon Smith Barney, among others, advised on the deal. True to the 1990s, the investment bankers were happy to collect their fees in the new banking environment. Within four years, they would not be happy with the decision, especially after WorldCom unraveled under massive accounting irregularities.

The investment world quickly sang WorldCom's praises. A technology magazine named it one of the 10 most powerful companies, behind only Cisco and Microsoft. After listing its virtues, the magazine went on to conclude, "MCI WorldCom will probably be a keeper on this list."[34] As for its investment virtues, they were impeccable, according to technology analyst Jack Grubman at Salomon Smith Barney. Based partially upon his recommendations, *Fortune* listed WorldCom as one of its 10 "safe harbor" stocks, those that should protect value in good times and bad. Grubman glowed: "There are few, if any, companies anywhere in the S&P 500 that are as large as WorldCom . . . that have [its] growth potential . . . this company remains the must-own large-cap stock for anyone's portfolio."[35]

Based upon projections, WorldCom indeed seemed to justify the hyperbole. Revenues for 2000 were projected to be $42 billion, and earnings were expected to reach $5.5 billion. The enormous deal was tenuous in many respects since phone services were falling in price and customers expected better services for less. Only consolidation could help some companies that otherwise would not have survived. WorldCom was always cash hungry as a result, bringing it into contact with the new muscular bank of the Citigroup era. In fact, its three main bankers were Citibank, Bank of America, and J.P. Morgan Chase. The latter was created after Morgan and Chase combined in 2000, the first significant merger after Gramm-Leach-Bliley. Also included was Deutsche Bank, giving WorldCom four of the most aggressive "new" bankers of the period. Although the company had relied on bankers throughout its short history, the convergence of commercial and investment banking made the company a prime target for banks: As it became older and more seasoned as a borrower, it would need to float new securities, bringing it into touch with the more lucrative sides of the new banking, securities underwriting and merger advice.

As part of its aggressive funding package, WorldCom used its friends in the banking business to borrow $10 billion in bonds in 2001, the third largest corporate bond deal ever packaged. The amount was so large that it rivaled a borrowing by the Treasury in the same year, although WorldCom's credit rating was considerably lower. The enormous issue was managed by J.P. Morgan Securities, Salomon Smith Barney of Citigroup, Bank of America Securities, and Deutsche Bank Alex. Brown. It was the perfect example of the new banking: A deal nurtured and conceived in banking headquarters and brought to market by the purported free-standing securities subsidiaries. The problem was that the bonds were in trouble almost from inception because of the WorldCom's financial problems, but the banks claimed that the financial position was sound when they brought them to market.

Many other research analysts other than Grubman also glowed in the 1990s. It became clear that many were bullish on stocks, always recommending that they be bought, while very few were issuing sell orders. The issue revolved around investment banking fees. Many firms expected their analysts to be bullish on the stocks of companies with which the firms wanted to establish investment banking relationships, in the hope of exacting heavy fees for underwriting and advice. The 1990s were littered with incidents of securities firms running afoul of chief executives at companies requiring capital, who fired them in favor of others whose analysts were more amenable to the healthy research report. As a result, any reputation Wall Street firms had for objectiveness fell by the wayside. In bull markets no one was asking any hard questions. All stocks were expected to rise in the New Era.

This was a far cry from the complaints made by the SEC in the 1950s concerning the release of research reports made while a new issue was in its cooling-off period. The traditional time period between the actual registration of a stock and its sale to the public had been shortened considerably in the early 1980s when Rule 415B was adopted by the SEC, allowing companies needing capital to come to market in a streamlined process.[36] In the 1990s, new issues appeared instantly on the stock exchanges, allowing almost no time for the new issues market to close in its usual slower manner. All issues were hot, and investors wanted to trade them immediately rather than hold them. When the subsequent investigation of Wall Street practices was made by New York Attorney General Eliot Spitzer, tendentious research was on the top of the list of complaints made by investors against the Street. The fines that resulted cost Citigroup $400 million because Grubman and others had been issuing research based more on a desire to court investment banking relationships than to provide investors with objective analysis that could have saved them billions.

The close connection between the two previously divorced sides of banking did not go unnoticed. When William Donaldson was named to succeed Harvey Pitt as SEC chairman, he mentioned the problem in his confirmation hearings before the Senate. The process in which underwritings followed the granting of soft loans was called "tying-in." Granting what were known as soft loans to potential investment banking clients was well known and suspected in the New Era. Soft loans were made at less than the usual interest rate to capture a corporate customer's business. Donaldson told the Senate that "making soft loans to get more profitable business is an issue that rivals the use of research as the handmaiden of banking."[37] Both practices were subtle but unknown outside Wall Street. They were used to great advantage during the bull market by many banks eager to court underwriting business.

During the course of the investigations into analysts' activities, another 1920s practice resurfaced. Many investment banks doing brisk business in initial public offerings (IPOs) in the 1990s had been allocating shares to friends and cronies. Many of the issues were extremely popular when announced, and the chance of an ordinary investor obtaining them at initial offering was very difficult, if not impossible. The investment banks instead were giving them to corporate executives, friends, and others with whom they wanted to curry favor. These investors could then sell them in the market, often at a significant profit. Small investors familiar with the 1930s remembered that the same procedure was used by J.P. Morgan and others through their preferred lists. The 70 intervening years had not put a stop to the practice.

In 2003, Sanford Weill announced that he was stepping down as chief executive of Citigroup. His hand-picked successor was Charles Prince, the architect of the two-year grace period concept that Citicorp and the Fed subscribed to several years before. Weill's remuneration for the year was $30 million, excluding stock sales and options, and Prince's total compensation was around $29 million. Robert Rubin received approximately $17 million in salary and options. Although the numbers were less than in years past, it was clear that the dismantling of Glass-Steagall was lucrative for executives if not for investors. The previous year was much less profitable, but Wall Street often had a short memory when earnings were considered to be turning around. Weill had been suspected of indirectly compensating Grubman, his star analyst of the 1990s, by donating $1 million to a New York Y so that the analyst's toddler children could attend its nursery school, into which it was more difficult to gain entry than some colleges.

Other New York institutions also felt the influence of Wall Street. In 2003, a deal was announced by Weill affecting two of

New York City's best-known cultural institutions. He and Paul Guenther, the former president of Paine Webber, announced a merger between the New York Philharmonic and Carnegie Hall. Guenther was chairman of the orchestra and Weill chairman of Carnegie. The deal planned to merge the two institutions into an even larger one that would dominate the cultural scene in the city. But shortly after the proposed deal was announced, it was revealed that not all of the directors of the Philharmonic were aware of the arrangement before it was announced. Previously, Beverly Sills, the chairwoman of the Metropolitan Opera, claimed that Weill would be a good partner for the Philharmonic. But when it became clear that the deal had been agreed to without the consent of the full board, she demurred. "I really don't believe that happened," she remarked, after hearing the details, "Nothing can be done without the approval of the full board. Not a decision like this. This is monumental."[38] The deal collapsed two months later.

Loose Banking

Of the many industries deregulated in the 1990s, utilities companies were among the last to be freed of their New Deal restrictions. The Public Utility Holding Company Act had held sway since the 1930s and remained resilient while other industries lost many of their restrictions. By the mid-1990s, energy had become a hot topic in Washington and the time was ripe for deregulation in the utilities business.

Energy was a buzzword in the New Economy. The crucial part of the Energy Policy Act of 1992 allowed sales of power between utility companies and liberalized the rules for mergers between holding companies. Excess energy had been sold between power companies for some time and was often imported via Canada as well. As a result of the law, mergers also began to occur between energy companies and utilities. The industry was being shaken by the new competitive environment. At the same time, many states were threatening to allow consumers to choose their own utility suppliers. In this environment, mergers appeared to be a valid way to achieve economies of scale and produce cheaper prices.

One aggressive energy company was Houston-based Enron Corporation. Originally a natural gas producing company, it began to expand into electrical utilities in 1997 with the acquisition of the Portland General Corporation, the Oregon-based electrical utility. The merger was the first of it kind between an energy company and a utility. It also introduced the Texas company to electricity trading, in addition to its traditional gas trading. "The proposed merger with Portland General represents an outstanding opportunity for us to create the leading energy company of the future in the North American energy markets," said Kenneth Lay, Enron's chairman and CEO.[39]

Enron was one of the most aggressive energy companies in the 1990s. Its growth was achieved through acquisition, using the merger as its chief method of research and development, preferring to buy the expertise needed rather than develop it internally. The company embarked on its aggressive business model with gusto. Soon, it acquired the knack of performing its own financial services as well. It hired its own merger specialists from Wall Street and employed them rather than pay fat fees to the usual merger houses. In a remark that was characteristic of investment banks 20 years before, the company described its new strategy. "The company is one of the most transaction-oriented non-investment bank companies in the world," one of its directors remarked. Within a short time, Enron would be more of a trading company than a traditional energy supplier, and the orientation would help lead to its downfall.

Operating like an investment bank, the company began moving away from its core businesses toward the end of the 1990s and began shopping for a buyer for Portland. The utility was not returning the 20 percent annual return that Enron required. The quest for higher and higher returns finally led to fraud and the demise of the company in 2002. But it was not

alone. Both WorldCom and Conseco, two other aggressive acquir-
ers, also found themselves in bankruptcy at the same time, providing a chilling final chapter to the strategy that made them
grow exponentially in the previous decade.

Caught up in the New Economy growth model, Enron
decided to take the low road to profitability. It created offshore
entities through special-purpose vehicles that held relatively
small amounts of assets and liabilities. These vehicles were mas-
terpieces of offshore financing, created by financial engineering
to hide poorly performing assets. They also disguised assets as
revenue, giving the misleading impression that the company was
more profitable than it actually was. Then, the stock market
began to decline, and the company's earnings and offshore vehicles began to implode. Once the seventh largest company in the
country, Enron and its accounting firm Arthur Andersen did not
survive the scandal. When the entire house of cards collapsed,
Enron became the largest bankruptcy filing in American history.
Unfortunately, it would not retain the distinction for long. A
widespread accounting fraud at WorldCom soon eclipsed it for
that distinction, finally leading to new legislation to tighten
financial control of accountants and corporate boards.

Andersen also became a victim of the fraud and was prose-
cuted for helping Enron destroy documents that it was ordered
to surrender as part of the SEC investigation that followed the
losses. Seventy years before the same firm stated, concerning
the new Securities Act of 1933, "Under this concept, the company has the original responsibility for the fairness of the financial statements, but in signing his certificate with respect to
those statements, the public accountant places his professional
opinion on the line that the statements are fair and that they
reflect accepted accounting principles." Andersen might rea-
sonably have claimed the same was true in 2002, but helping its
client destroy documents vital to the SEC investigation had little
defense. As a result, the firm began losing clients and finally dis-
integrated. A new law was not needed in this respect. Many ques-

tioned why the SEC held Andersen to such a high standard and pursued the firm when the real culprits worked at Enron, but the securities laws clearly mentioned the role of accountants in the process of assisting SEC-registered public companies. But the real question was larger than the fate of the parties involved. How had such a massive fraud been committed at a public company almost 70 years after the original securities disclosure law had been passed?

Lawsuits against Wall Street firms and banks intensified after the market collapse, with the majority of them filed over the allocation of IPO shares. The collapse of Enron and WorldCom also had a severe effect on the newly merged banking institutions. Many of the large money center banks, notably J.P. Morgan Chase and Citigroup, lost substantial amounts of money because the two companies collapsed. They loaned money to them as part of their commercial banking function while seeking investment banking business at the same time, something that the old Glass-Steagall rules prohibited. When losses came, they hit from both sides. Until the losses were incurred, the investment banking side was particularly rewarding, however. Despite its internal investment banking operations, Enron was still a major source of fees for Wall Street investment banks until its collapse, as was WorldCom. The old line of demarcation clearly had been crossed, and the bullish activities of the banks made a major contribution to the market collapse because of the inflated values many of the loans had caused.

Accounting Reform

In the 1930s, the start of Senate hearings followed the Crash by almost three years. In the early 2000s, the reaction to the corporate collapses came much more quickly. The question of accountability was clearly on the mind of Congress when it passed the Sarbanes-Oxley Act in the summer of 2002. The bill was sponsored by Senator Paul Sarbanes, a Democrat from Maryland, and

Representative Mike Oxley, a Republican from Ohio. Officially known as the Public Company Accounting Reform and Investor Protection Act, the law addressed the problem of accounting by public corporations and the responsibility of auditors to investors. The old question being raised again required tighter regulation than the admittedly loose language that the original Securities Act provided.

The problem was not new but had been exacerbated by the Enron collapse. During the 1990s, it had been brewing, and it was inevitable that an egregious case of fraud and corporate deception eventually would occur, given the fast-paced atmosphere created by the bull market. Several years earlier, the SEC chairman had already been asking questions about the relationship between company CEOs and their accountants. "What is the Financial Accounting Standards Board's great sin?" asked Arthur Levitt Jr., chairman of the SEC, speaking to the Economic Club of Detroit. He was responding to criticisms leveled by corporate executives at the Financial Accounting Standards Board. "It has asked companies to tell investors the whole truth about their financial performances including exposure from their own investments," he concluded, preempting a difficult process that would come to light with Enron several years later.[40]

The Sarbanes-Oxley law created the Public Accounting Oversight Board, which was given the broad responsibility of administering the act. Its passing demonstrated the progress made over the years in financial engineering and the uses to which it could be put by those intent on breaking the existing securities laws. Simply, the act put the onus on accountants to spot difficulties before they occurred and also put attorneys on the spot as well by requiring them to inform regulators if they spotted illegalities being committed by their clients regarding financial disclosure. Both instances proved uncomfortable, but at least zeroed in on the problems remaining even after the 1933 act was passed. Wall Street was not fond of new regulation, but publicly criticizing the new law was not political given the climate of investor unrest and potential political backlash. Some commentators were quick to point out that the new law would dissuade "entrepreneurs" from taking risks for fear of the new law. The same argument was made in the 1930s, evoking about the same amount of sympathy.

Those in favor of deregulation maintained their positions in the face of criticism that they had let the fox into the henhouse. The architects of deregulation continued to argue that they did their best to modernize an antiquated banking system and that human nature was responsible for the mess, as it had been so many times before. Representative Jim Leach, Republican from Iowa, remarked, "It has nothing to do with Gramm-Leach-Bliley," when questioned on whether the 1999 financial reform law led to the fall of Enron. Critics remained unconvinced that Wall Street was capable of reforming itself any more than it had been in the past. Self-regulation, the mantra that many firms and the NYSE espoused when defining how their activities were monitored, was clearly working only on a day-to-day level with organizations such as the NYSE and NASDAQ, but was clearly missing the larger picture. It was not, and never had been, designed to replace government-inspired regulation that imposed serious penalties and deterrents to financial fraud and malpractice. Regulators were needed and still existed, but the new financial environment provided many more opportunities for malfeasance than its predecessors. Those who normally favored regulation always feared that the liberalized environment of the 1990s bore the seeds of its own destruction. After Enron, WorldCom, and other corporate collapses induced by fraud, they could only conclude that they had been correct all along.

Corporate America and its accountants and investment bankers were not the only parties under fire. The specialist system used by the NYSE and other stock exchanges continued to come under attack during the bull market. In the late 1990s, the specialists again were accused of coming between their customers' orders in order to scalp a few cents off an order or to buy and sell before customers in a clear attempt to shave a profit from a trade. The most egregious of these practices was the one known as front running, in which the specialists acted for their own books first when seeing a customer order coming. "If you think a specialist's ability to see incoming orders gives him a built-in advantage when trading for himself, you're right," commented Arthur Levitt. "It's like being in a card game in which only one of the players gets to see everyone else's hand."

After the scandal that toppled NYSE chairman Richard Grasso in 2004 because of the size of his compensation package, a group of specialist firms settled a complaint with the SEC for an approximate $240 million over front-running allegations. The dual capacity system, discussed since the early 1930s, was still producing conflicts of interest, but the specialist community successfully had fought all attempts to change their operating procedures. After 70 years of discussion, the dual capacity system was still producing controversy with no apparent resolution in sight. Another product of the Grasso affair was that Sanford Weill withdrew his name from consideration for a spot on the NYSE board of directors. After the massive fine paid by Citigroup the previous year, it was deemed inappropriate for him to sit on the board. He already sat on the board of the New York Fed, a job once held by his predecessor Charles Mitchell.

Despite all of the reaction and counterreaction, reformers were still making inroads in deregulation even after Gramm-Leach-Bliley was passed. One of the last protections found in the Glass-Steagall Act was the prohibition against banks being owned by industrial companies. In order to avoid Japanese style *keiretsu* arrangements, where the relationships between many corporations and their bankers became blurred, the modernization act left the old law inviolate on the issue. But true to form, the assault on that part of the remaining regulation began quietly in the new century.

The issue was actually a modern version of the old state bank problem, wrestling with jurisdiction. A new bill named H.R. 1375 was introduced into the House that would allow additional banking powers to industrial loan companies, a little-known category of limited-service banking institution that could be owned by industrial companies. Congress quietly liberalized the rules for these banks so that they could offer checking accounts to customers, effectively making them consumer banks. But many of the activities were coming at the same time that the country's largest retailer, Wal-Mart, was actively shopping for a bank to buy. The coincidence of the two prompted one union leader to state, "I have what banks are about to get—the Wal-Mart experience— and it will not leave you with a smiling face. Think of me as the whistle on a train speeding down the track headed straight for America's banks."[41] He warned about the dangers of allowing a giant retailer into the banking business. What would become of banking supervision on the state level if the last remaining vestiges of Glass-Steagall were removed in favor of massive corporate organizations, that decided to move into the banking business?

Even after doubts were raised about the dismantling of regulations in the wake of the stock market collapse in 2001, reformers were intent on assaulting the last vestige of control over banks, the Bank Holding Company Act. The old idea that banks held a public trust and should be treated as unique institutions was being eroded slowly but surely, as the 1920s' idea of a financial department store reemerged in a contemporary style. Wall Street and Main Street, traditionally on the opposite sides of the political and economic spectrum, finally met in the aisles of the financial services department of a nationwide chain. How these new financial institutions would fare in the event of a serious financial crisis is hardly clear, but one lesson from the 1920s and 1930s remains. When that crisis occurs, the fallout will be widespread. More than just investors will be affected. Savers, retirees, and those who never bothered with Wall Street will be acutely aware of its presence.

POSTSCRIPT

IS DEREGULATION WORKING?

One striking fact emerged from the scandals and crises of the early 2000s as the stock market unraveled. Many of the issues raised in the 1930s were rising again after years of dormancy. Had they not been settled years before? After decades of SEC and NYSE rules and new laws, the old problems seemed to have resurfaced as if they had never been addressed to begin with.

The original flaws in language found in the Securities Act of 1933 provided space for abuse, using the "I forgot" or the "It wasn't me" defense. When investors were misled through what was supposed to be full disclosure, who exactly was to blame? Was it possible that no one in particular could be blamed because contemporary corporate organizations were too complex? If so, was this a better argument for keeping regulations in place? Clearly, the events of the late 1990s and early 2000s raised more questions than they answered.

The swings in political ideology that caused Wall Street and the banks to be regulated and then deregulated decades later provide a good microcosm of American history in the twentieth century. In the 1930s, politics prevailed. Attacks against Wall Street bankers were made by Midwest firebrands for whom the East Coast establishment might well have been from a foreign country. Its manners, attitudes, and actions were not understood by those whose strong ethic could never quite appreciate making money by trading intangible assets. Real work meant producing a product, something that could be felt and appreciated. When the New York money contingent paid any attention to those outside their domain, the attention was viewed with suspicion. The first securities laws were passed by those states that wanted to stop slick salesmen from selling a bit of the "blue sky" to their citizens.

Between World War I and the 1950s, much less was known about the economic forces that caused stock market crashes, depressions, and recessions than was known in the 1980s and 1990s. Beginning in the late 1950s, statistical and quantitative techniques were beginning to be applied that would lead many analysts and politicians to conclusions that were materially different from those made in previous decades. These new techniques were seized by think tanks and other public policy groups to help bolster their own prejudices and conclusions about the nature of regulation and deregulation. By the late 1970s, the drive had begun to drive out the last vestiges of the New Deal and return the country to a market-driven economy.

Decades and mountains of SEC and Fed regulations later, the suspicion began to return after the biggest stock market bubble in American history finally burst. Investors were angry with their brokers, their analysts, and the mutual funds that lost money in record amounts. The inevitable comparisons with 1929 were made, and indeed there were many similarities. Most remain anecdotal at best. But the true similarities were to be found in the changing nature of the financial system. The real culprit was a deregulated financial system that blurred the lines between banks and brokers on one hand and savings and investment on the other.

Regulators from the SEC to the Fed will claim that all of their liberalizing actions were made in compliance with the relevant interested parties over a period of time and that their actions were well considered. That is true, but the real problem is that all of the compliance took place between those of like mind. The big banks wanted deregulation, and they eventually got it with agreement from the Fed. Wall Street's record was somewhat better in this respect because there was always a tension between the SEC and the Street, but too often the SEC bowed to the Street's

ability to police itself through self-regulation out of sheer practicality and a limited budget. It was also in Wall Street's best oligarchic interests to keep the banks out of their business. When
the handwriting finally was on the wall that financial mergers
were inevitable, it too joined the chorus for deregulation.

The creation of Citigroup was the apex of the deregulatory
movement that began in earnest with the Reagan revolution in
1981. Wall Street banks and the Fed will claim that the new environment could have been created decades before had it not
been for a recalcitrant Congress. Some Congressmen remembered the original intent of Glass-Steagall and remained vigilant
for as long as possible before being overwhelmed by cries for
reinterpreting history.

In the new era of Wall Street banking, the past is understood
as nothing more than a series of misinterpretations about the
intent of bankers and investment bankers. In the new revisionist
view of the 1930s, the Securities Acts of 1933 and 1934 and the
Glass-Steagall Act would never have been passed had we known
then what we know today about economics and finance. This is
a persuasive argument, but it leaves one bit dangling that remains troublesome. How does one account for the stock market
debacle of 2001, Enron, WorldCom, and the host of other scandals that have emerged? The new environment allowed fraud,
deceit, false information, and outright theft to skate through
what remained of the old regulations that had prevented such
things from happening on a grand scale for 70 years.

In the years between 1933 and the early 2000s, it became
clear that the old regulations were mostly successful in controlling the behavior of financial institutions and securities dealers.
However, the advances in financial innovation, plus the determination of some to ignore the law, created a situation in which
existing regulations proved too general in the face of an onslaught of new financial products. But the moment that safeguards were removed, even prior to the Financial Services
Modernization Act, the whole financial system became vulnerable to the abuses of the past. In the brave new world of financial
services, the risks are greater than at any time since the 1920s.

BIBLIOGRAPHY

Aldrich, Winthrop W. *Proposed Banking Act of 1935.* New York: Chase National Bank, 1935.

Allen, Frederick Lewis. *Only Yesterday: An Informal History of the 1920s.* 1931. Reprint, New York: John Wiley & Sons, 1997.

Anonymous. *Washington Merry-Go-Round.* New York: Blue Ribbon Books, 1931.

Ashby, Leroy. *The Spearless Leader: Senator Borah and the Progressive Movement in the 1920s.* Urbana: University of Illinois Press, 1972.

Baldwin, Neil. *Henry Ford and the Jews: The Mass Production of Hate.* New York: Public Affairs, 2001.

Barth, James R., R. Dan Brumbaugh, and Robert E. Litan. *The Future of American Banking.* Armonk, NY: M.E. Sharpe, 1992.

Baruch, Bernard. *My Own Story.* New York: Holt, Rinehart & Winston, 1957.

Bennett, Robert A. "Inside Citicorp: The Changing World of Banking," *New York Times,* May 29, 1983.

Benston, George J. *The Separation of Commercial and Investment Banking.* New York: Oxford University Press, 1990.

Bent, Silas. *Strange Bedfellows: A Review of Politics, Personalities, and the Press.* New York: Horace Liveright, 1928.

Berle, Adolph A., and Gardiner C. Means. *The Modern Corporation and Private Property.* Revised edition, New York: Harper & Brothers, 1967.

Beschloss, Michael R. *Kennedy and Roosevelt: The Uneasy Alliance.* New York: W.W. Norton, 1980.

Celler, Emanuel. *You Never Leave Brooklyn: The Autobiography of Emanuel Celler.* New York: The John Day Company, 1953.

Chandler, Lester V. *Benjamin Strong, Central Banker.* Washington, DC: Brookings Institution, 1958.

Chernow, Ron. *The House of Morgan: An American Banking Dynasty and the Rise of Modern Corporate Finance.* New York: Simon and Schuster, 1990.

Cowing, Cedric. *Populists, Plungers, and Progressives: A Social History of Stock and Commodity Speculation, 1890–1936*. Princeton, NJ: Princeton University Press, 1965.

Dobyns, Fletcher. *The Amazing Story of Repeal*. Chicago: Willett, Clark & Co., 1940.

Douglas, William O. *Finance and Democracy*. New Haven: Yale University Press, 1940.

Fabricant, Solomon. "Toward a Firmer Basis of Economic Policy: The Founding of the National Bureau of Economic Research." National Bureau of Economic Research, 1984.

Fite, Gilbert Courtland. *Peter Norbeck: Prairie Statesman*. Columbia: University of Missouri Press, 1948.

Flynt, Wayne. *Duncan Upshaw Fletcher: Dixie's Reluctant Progressive*. Tallahassee: Florida State University Press, 1971.

Friedman, Milton, and Anna Schwartz. *A Monetary History of the United States*. Princeton, NJ: Princeton University Press, 1963.

Goldberg, Lawrence G., and Lawrence J. White. *The Deregulation of the Banking and Securities Industries*. Washington, DC: Beard Books, 1979.

Greider, William. *Secrets of the Temple: How the Federal Reserve Runs the Country*. New York: Simon & Schuster, 1987.

———. "The Education of David Stockman," *Atlantic Monthly*, December 1981.

Heatherly, Charles L., and Burton Yale Pines, editors. *Mandate for Leadership III: Policy Strategies for the 1990s*. Washington, DC: Heritage Foundation, 1989.

Heatherly, Charles L., editor. *Mandate for Leadership: Policy Management in a Conservative Administration*. Washington, DC: Heritage Foundation, 1981.

Hoover, Herbert. *American Individualism*. Garden City, NY: Doubleday Page, 1922.

———. *The Challenge to Liberty*. New York: Charles Scribner's Sons, 1934.

———. *The Memoirs of Herbert Hoover*. New York: Macmillan, 1952.

Hyman, Sidney. *Marriner S. Eccles: Private Entrepreneur and Public Servant*. Stanford, CA: Stanford University Graduate School of Business, 1976.

Institutional Investor. *The Way It Was: An Oral History of Finance 1967–1987*. New York: William Morrow, 1988.

Johnson, Claudius O. *Borah of Idaho*. New York: Longmans, Green & Co., 1936.

Kaufman, Henry. *On Money and Markets: A Wall Street Memoir*. New York: McGraw-Hill, 2000.

Kennedy, David M. *Freedom from Fear: The American People in Depression and War, 1929–1945*. New York: Oxford University Press, 1999.

Kennedy, Susan Estabrook. *The Banking Crisis of 1933*. Lexington: University Press of Kentucky, 1973.

Krainer, John. "The Separation of Banking and Commerce." *Economic Review*, Federal Reserve Bank of San Francisco, 2000.

Krooss, Herman, editor. *Documentary History of Banking and Currency in the United States*. 4 vols. New York: Chelsea House, 1983.

La Follette, Robert M. *La Follette's Autobiography: A Personal Narrative of Political Experiences.* 1911. Reprint. Madison: University of Wisconsin Press, 1963.

La Guardia, Fiorello H. *The Making of an Insurgent: An Autobiography, 1882–1919.* Philadelphia: J.B. Lippincott Co., 1948.

Langley, Monica. *Tearing Down the Walls.* New York: Simon & Schuster, 2003.

Lasser, William. *Benjamin V. Cohen: Architect of the New Deal.* New Haven: Yale University Press, 2002.

Lawrence, Joseph Stagg. *Wall Street and Washington.* Princeton, NJ: Princeton University Press, 1929.

Lebhar, Godfrey M. *Chain Stores in America 1859–1950.* New York: Chain Store Publishing Co., 1952.

Leinsdorf, David, and Donald Eltra. *Citibank: Ralph Nader's Study Group Report on First National City Bank.* New York: Grossman Publishers, 1973.

Levitt, Arthur, with Paula Dwyer. *Take on the Street.* New York: Pantheon Books, 2002.

Lundberg, Ferdinand. *America's 60 Families.* New York: Citadel Press, 1937.

McCraw, Thomas K. *Prophets of Regulation.* Cambridge, MA: Harvard University Press, 1984.

McDaniel, George William. *Smith Wildman Brookhart: Iowa's Renegade Republican.* Ames: Iowa State University Press, 1995.

McElvaine, Robert S. *The Great Depression: America 1929–1941.* New York: Times Books, 1984.

McFadden, Louis T. "Gold and Gold Requirements in Close Race." *The Magazine of Wall Street*, Vol. 47, No. 6, January 10, 1931.

Meltzer, Allan H. *A History of the Federal Reserve, 1913–1951.* Chicago: University of Chicago Press, 2003.

Meyer, Charles H. *The Securities Exchange Act of 1934 Analyzed and Explained.* New York: Francis Emory Fitch, 1934.

Morgan, J.P. & Co. *Glass-Steagall: Overdue for Repeal.* New York: privately published, 1995.

————. *Rethinking Glass-Steagall.* New York: privately published, 1984.

Neprash, Jerry A. *The Brookhart Campaigns in Iowa, 1920–1926.* New York: Columbia University Press, 1932.

Norris, George W. *Fighting Liberal: The Autobiography of George W. Norris.* New York: Macmillan, 1945.

Pecora, Ferdinand. *Wall Street Under Oath: The Story of Our Modern Moneychangers.* New York: Simon & Schuster, 1939.

Pusey, Merlo. *Eugene Meyer.* New York: Alfred A. Knopf, 1974.

Regan, Donald T. *A View from the Street.* New York: New American Library, 1972.

Ricci, David M. *The Transformation of American Politics: The New Washington and the Rise of Think Tanks.* New Haven: Yale University Press, 1993.

Rosenof, Theodore. *Economics in the Long Run: New Deal Theorists and Their Legacies, 1933–1993.* Chapel Hill: University of North Carolina Press, 1997.

Ross, Earle Dudley. *The Liberal Republican Movement.* 1910. Reprint, Seattle: University of Washington Press, 1970.

Rubin, Robert, and Jacob Weisberg. *In an Uncertain World.* New York: Random House, 2003.

Seligman, Joel. *The Transformation of Wall Street: A History of the Securities and Exchange Commission and Modern Corporate Finance.* Boston: Houghton Mifflin, 1982.

Smith, Hedrick. "Reagan's Effort to Change Course of Government," *New York Times,* October 23, 1984.

Smith, James Allen. *The Idea Brokers: Think Tanks and the Rise of the New Policy Elite.* New York: Free Press, 1991.

Sobel, Robert. *NYSE: A History of the New York Stock Exchange, 1935–1975.* New York: Weybright & Talley, 1975.

———. *Amex: A History of the American Stock Exchange, 1921–1971.* New York: Weybright & Talley, 1972.

Stockman, David. *The Triumph of Politics: The Inside Story of the Reagan Revolution.* New York: Avon Books, 1987.

Stone, Amey, and Mike Brewster. *King of Capital: Sandy Weill and the Making of Citigroup.* New York: John Wiley & Sons, 2002.

Strouse, Jean. *Morgan: American Financier.* New York: Random House, 1999.

Truman, Harry S. *Memoirs.* New York: Doubleday, 1955.

Tucker, Ray, and Frederick R. Barkley. *Sons of the Wild Jackass.* Boston: L.C. Page, 1932.

Twentieth Century Fund. *Stock Market Control.* New York: D. Appleton Century, 1934.

U.S. Senate. *Stock Exchange Practices: Report of the Committee of Banking and Currency.* 73rd Congress, 2nd session, June 6, 1934.

Watkins, T.H. *The Great Depression: America in the 1930s.* Boston: Little Brown, 1993.

Werner, M.R. *Little Napoleons and Dummy Directors: Being the Narrative of the Bank of United States.* New York: Harper & Brothers,1933.

Wicker, Elmus. *The Banking Panics of the Great Depression.* New York: Cambridge University Press, 1996.

Willis, Henry Parker. *Investment Banking.* New York: Harper Brothers, 1929.

Winkler, John K. *The First Billion: The Stillmans and the National City Bank.* Babson Park, MA: Vanguard Press, 1934.

Witte, John F. *The Politics and Development of the Federal Income Tax.* Madison: University of Wisconsin Press, 1985.

Wolfskill, George. *The Revolt of the Conservatives: A History of the American Liberty League, 1934–1940.* Boston: Houghton Mifflin, 1962.

Yergin, Daniel. *The Prize: The Epic Quest for Oil, Money, and Power.* New York: Simon & Schuster, 1991.

Zweig, Phillip L. *Wriston: Walter Wriston, Citibank, and the Rise and Fall of American Financial Supremacy.* New York: Crown Publishers, 1996.

NOTES

Chapter 1

1. Robert M. La Follette, *La Follette's Autobiography: A Personal Narrative of Political Experiences* (reprint, Madison: University of Wisconsin Press, 1963), pp. 286–87.
2. *New York Times*, January 27, 1912.
3. *Washington Post*, May 26, 1912.
4. *New York Times*, December 21, 1912.
5. Ron Chernow, *The House of Morgan: An American Banking Dynasty and the Rise of Modern Finance* (New York: Simon & Schuster, 1990), p. 158.
6. *House Report* No. 1593, 62nd Congress, 3rd Session, p. 2 ff.
7. According to an article in the *Canton (OH) Sentinel* published some years later, the original capital of the bank was $50,000 when it was founded in 1882 and increased to $100,000 in 1907. In 1901, the bank paid $48,000 in dividends to its shareholders, a sizeable amount given the limited size of its capital. The amount was almost equal to the capital at the time. See *Canton (OH) Sentinel*, November 30, 1950. Many of its records were lost in a fire during the 1940s.
8. *New York Times*, March 2, 1919.
9. In an amendment to the Federal Reserve Act passed on June 3, 1922, Congress added one more member to the Federal Reserve Board. The board now had seven members rather than six and the secretary of the treasury and the comptroller of the currency remained *ex officio* members.
10. *New York Times*, January 9, 1921.

11. Ibid., December 17, 1922.
12. Ibid., January 9, 1927.
13. Quoted in Merlo Pusey, *Eugene Meyer* (New York: Alfred A. Knopf, 1974), p. 204.
14. *New York Times*, March 27, 1930.
15. Ray Tucker and Frederick R. Barkley, *Sons of the Wild Jackass* (Boston: L.C. Page and Co., 1932), p. 179.
16. Jerry A. Neprash, *The Brookhart Campaigns in Iowa 1920–1926* (New York: Columbia University Press, 1932), p. 30.
17. *New York Times*, January 14, 1923.
18. Quoted in Joseph Stagg Lawrence, *Wall Street and Washington* (Princeton: Princeton University Press, 1929), p. 310.
19. Speech by Frank Godfrey quoted in the *Edwardsville (IL) Intelligencer*, March 13, 1929.
20. Anonymous, *Washington Merry-Go-Round* (New York: Blue Ribbon Books, 1931), p. 200.
21. Originally, Brookhart claimed Loomis was a partner of J.P. Morgan & Co., which was not true at the time.
22. Ray Tucker and Frederick R. Barkley, *Sons of the Wild Jackass*, p. 346.
23. George William McDaniel, *Smith Wildman Brookhart, Iowa's Renegade Republican* (Ames: Iowa State University Press, 1995), p. 251.
24. Quoted in Leroy Ashby, *The Spearless Leader: Senator Borah and the Progressive Movement in the 1920s* (Urbana: University of Illinois Press, 1972), p. 282.
25. *New York Times*, October 4, 1924.
26. Ibid., June 9, 1926.
27. Ibid., November 9, 1929.
28. Ibid., November 11, 1929.
29. Fiorello H. LaGuardia, *The Making of an Insurgent: An Autobiography 1882–1919* (Philadelphia: J.B. Lippincott Co, 1948), p. 60.
30. Ray Tucker and Frederick Bartley, *Sons of the Wild Jackass*, p. 372.
31. See George Wolfskill, *The Revolt of the Conservatives: A History of the American Liberty League, 1934–1940* (Boston: Houghton Mifflin, 1962).
32. *New York Times*, September 14, 1931.
33. *Bismarck (ND) Daily Tribune*, November 8, 1920.
34. *Sheboygan (WI) Press*, March 2, 1933.
35. Ray Tucker and Frederick Bartley, *Sons of the Wild Jackass*, p. 1.
36. Emanuel Celler, *You Never Leave Brooklyn: The Autobiography of Emanuel Celler* (New York: The John Day Company, 1953), p. 8.

Chapter 2

1. *Brooklyn Daily Eagle*, October 24, 1929.
2. Speech in the House of Representatives, February 26, 1930. HR 9683, *Congressional Record*, p. 4323 ff. The Bank for International Settlements

was being organized to establish a system of German war reparations to be made to the allies of World War I.

3. Speech in the House of Representatives, December 20, 1930. *Congressional Record*, p. 1320 ff.
4. See Charles R. Geisst, *Wheels of Fortune: The History of Speculation from Scandal to Respectability* (New York: John Wiley & Sons, 2002), especially Chapters 1 and 2.
5. *New York Times*, September 21, 1930.
6. Louis T. McFadden, "Gold and Gold Requirements in Close Race," *The Magazine of Wall Street*, January 1931, p. 350.
7. Anonymous, *The Mirrors of Wall Street* (New York: G.P. Putnam's Sons, 1933), p. 255. One of several *Mirrors* books written by Clinton Gilbert and published anonymously.
8. *New York Times*, April 21, 1932.
9. Ibid., April 13, 1932.
10. Ibid., April 21, 1932.
11. Speech in the House of Representatives, December 13, 1932. *Congressional Record*, p. 399 ff.
12. *Salamanca (NY) Republican-Press*, December 15, 1932.
13. *Helena (MT) Daily Independent*, June 16, 1933.
14. *New York Times*, February 1, 1933.
15. Wayne Flint, *Duncan Upshaw Fletcher: Dixie's Reluctant Progressive* (Tallahassee: Florida State University Press, 1971), p. 171.
16. *Wisconsin Rapids Daily Tribune*, March 10, 1933.
17. *New York Times*, April 1, 1933.
18. Ibid., May 21, 1933.
19. Ibid., June 4, 1933.
20. *The Magazine of Wall Street*, January 6, 1934.
21. Quoted in Joel Seligman, *The Transformation of Wall Street: A History of the Securities and Exchange Commission and Modern Corporate Finance* (Boston: Houghton Mifflin, 1982), p. 71.
22. Quoted in *The First Sixty Years 1913–1973* (Chicago: Arthur Andersen & Co., 1974), p. 22.
23. Ibid.
24. *Helena (MT) Daily Independent*, June 16, 1933.
25. *New York Times*, July 9, 1933.
26. Quoted in Tomas K. McCraw, *Prophets of Regulation* (Cambridge, MA: Harvard University Press, 1984), p. 175.
27. George William McDaniel, *Smith Wildman Brookhart: Iowa's Renegade Republican* (Ames: Iowa State University Press, 1995), p. 246.
28. *The Mirrors of Wall Street*, pp. 227–228.
29. Speech in the House of Representatives, May 29, 1933. *Congressional Record*, p. 4540.
30. *Edwardsville (IL) Intelligencer*, August 13, 1934.
31. *Jerusalem Post*, May 29, 2000.

32. M.R. Werner, *Little Napoleons and Dummy Directors: Being the Narrative of the Bank of United States* (New York: Harper & Brothers, 1933), p. 203.
33. *New York Times,* May 27, 1933.
34. Quoted in Ron Chernow, *The House of Morgan* (New York: Simon & Schuster, 1990), p. 372.
35. *New York Times,* May 29, 1933.
36. The original deposit insurance provided by Glass-Steagall was for accounts of $2,500 until July 1, 1934, when it was increased to $10,000. For these accounts, all of the deposit was insured. On larger amounts, the percentage dropped to less than 100 percent.
37. *New York Times,* June 22, 1933.
38. *Helena (MT) Daily Independent,* July 2, 1933.
39. Speech before the New York Bankers' Association, Lake George, New York, June 27, 1933.
40. U.S. Senate Committee on Banking and Currency, *Stock Exchange Practices.* 73rd Congress, 2nd Session, June 1934, p. 113.
41. Ibid., p. 185.
42. *Helena (MT) Daily Independent,* August 3, 1933.
43. *New York Times,* July 2, 1933.
44. U.S. Senate Committee on Banking and Currency, *Stock Exchange Practices.* 73rd Congress, 2nd Session, June 1934, p. 176.
45. Ferdinand Pecora, *Wall Street Under Oath: The Story of Our Modern Money Changers* (New York: Simon & Schuster, 1939), p. 135.
46. *New York Times,* July 9, 1933.
47. Speech given by Frank M. Gordon, president of the Investment Bankers Association, to the National Association of Security Commissioners, Milwaukee, Wisconsin, September 18, 1933.
48. *New York Times,* December 7, 1933.
49. Ibid.
50. Ibid., January 18, 1934.
51. *The Mirrors of Wall Street,* p. 129.

Chapter 3

1. *New York Times,* December 9, 1934.
2. Joel Seligman, *The Transformation of Wall Street: A History of the Securities and Exchange Commission and Modern Corporate Finance* (Boston: Houghton Mifflin, 1982), p. 82.
3. *New York Times,* February 25, 1934.
4. *Today,* April 21, 1934.
5. *New York Times,* February 22, 1934.
6. Wayne Flint, *Duncan Upshaw Fletcher: Dixie's Reluctant Progressive* (Tallahassee: Florida State University Press, 1971), p. 176.
7. *New York Times,* March 1, 1934.

8. Adolph A. Berle and Gardiner C. Means, *The Modern Corporation and Private Property* (revised edition, New York: Harper & Brothers, 1967), p. 18.
9. U.S. Senate Committee on Banking and Currency, *Stock Exchange Practices*. 73rd Congress, 2nd Session, June 1934, pp. 382–383.
10. *New York Times*, March 21, 1934.
11. Quoted in the *Nevada State Journal*, March 12, 1935.
12. Twentieth Century Fund, *Stock Market Control* (New York: Appleton-Century Corp., 1934), p. 189.
13. *New York Times*, July 7, 1934.
14. Michael Beschloss, *Kennedy and Roosevelt: The Uneasy Alliance* (New York: W.W. Norton & Co., 1980), p. 85.
15. Harold L. Ickes, *The Secret Diary of Harold L. Ickes: The First Thousand Days, 1933–1936* (New York: Simon & Schuster, 1953), p. 172.
16. Speech by Joseph P. Kennedy before the National Press Club, Washington, D.C., July 25, 1934.
17. *The Magazine of Wall Street*, September 29, 1934.
18. Quoted in Arthur Schlesinger Jr., *The Politics of Upheaval* (Boston: Houghton Mifflin, 1960), p. 280.
19. Quoted in George Wolfskill, *The Revolt of the Conservatives: A History of the American Liberty League* (Boston: Houghton Mifflin, 1962), p. 152.
20. *Sheboygan (WI) Press*, February 28, 1936.
21. Ibid., January 30, 1934.
22. *New York Times*, November 11, 1934.
23. Quoted in the *Helena (MT) Daily Independent*, April 11, 1935.
24. Statement by Winthrop W. Aldrich, "Proposed Banking Act of 1935," before the Subcommittee of the United States Senate Committee on Banking and Currency, May 15, 1935.
25. Quoted in the *Oshkosh (WI) Northwestern*, November 22, 1935.
26. Wayne Flint, *Duncan Upshaw Fletcher*, p. 178.
27. Ron Chernow, *The House of Morgan: An American Banking Dynasty and the Rise of Modern Finance* (New York: Simon & Schuster, 1990), p. 384.
28. Quoted in the *Chronicle-Telegram* (Ohio), August 14, 1935.
29. *Philadelphia Inquirer*, March 3, 1935.
30. *New York Times*, February 8, 1935.
31. George William McDaniel, *Smith Wildman Brookhart: Iowa's Renegade Republican* (Ames: Iowa State University Press, 1995), pp. 292–293.
32. *New York Times*, July 5, 1935.
33. Quoted in T.H. Watkins, *The Great Depression: America in the 1930s* (Boston: Little Brown, 1993), p. 101.
34. Quoted in the *Gettysburg (PA) Times*, December 24, 1932.
35. A summary of many newspaper editorials concerning the Bonus March was reprinted in the *Daily Northwestern* (Wisconsin), July 29, 1932,
36. Quoted in the *Nevada State Journal*, April 27, 1936.
37. *New York Times*, March 28, 1937.

38. *Helena (MT) Daily Independent,* April 10, 1937.
39. *New York Times,* September 29, 1937.

Chapter 4

1. Quoted in the *New York Times,* February 9, 1958.
2. *Nevada State Journal,* March 6, 1934.
3. Quoted in the *New York Times,* April 2, 1952.
4. Ibid., January 8, 1957.
5. The decision was actually part of three decisions by the court in one day, all relating to the same banking topic.
6. Solomon Fabricant, "Toward a Firmer Basis of Economic Policy: The Founding of the National Bureau of Economic Research." National Bureau of Economic Research, 1984.
7. See David M. Kennedy, *Freedom from Fear: The American People in Depression and War 1929–1945* (New York: Oxford University Press, 1999), Chapter 2.
8. *Council Bluffs (IA) Nonpareil,* June 17, 1955.
9. *New York Times,* March 3, 1955.
10. Quoted in the *Council Bluffs (IA) Nonpareil,* March 17, 1955.
11. Speech to the Economic Club of New York, April 28, 1955.
12. Quoted in the *New York Times,* March 5, 1955.
13. *New York Times,* March 5, 1955.
14. Ibid., March 17, 1955.
15. Quoted in *Stevens Point (WI) Journal,* June 25, 1962.
16. Revenue bonds are not based upon a community's general taxing power but on a particular revenue stream from the project it is borrowing money to fund.
17. Joel Seligman, *The Transformation of Wall Street: A History of the Securities and Exchange Commission and Modern Corporate Finance* (Boston: Houghton Mifflin, 1982), p. 350.
18. *New York Times,* October 7, 1968.
19. Donald T. Regan, *A View from the Street* (New York: New American Library, 1972), p. 154.
20. David Leinsdorf and Donald Eltra, *Citibank: Ralph Nader's Study Group Report on First National City Bank* (New York: Grossman Publishers, 1973), pp. 306–307.
21. Cary's suggestions were originally contained in an article published months before. See William L. Cary and Walter Werner, "Outlook for Securities Markets," *Harvard Business Review,* July-August, 1971.
22. *New York Times,* May 23, 1975.
23. *Barron's,* February 5, 1962.
24. Quoted in the *Chronicle-Telegram* (Ohio), September 14, 1969.
25. Harvey A. Rowen, "The Intersection of the Banking and Securities Industries and Future Deregulation," in Lawrence G. Goldberg and

Lawrence J. White, editors, *The Deregulation of the Banking and Securities Industries* (New York: Beard Books, 1979), p. 317.

Chapter 5

1. Speech before the American Bankers' Association, White Sulphur Springs, West Virginia, April 25, 1973.
2. *New York Times*, July 10, 1977.
3. Federal Reserve *Statistical Release*, Money Stock Measures, February 4, 2004.
4. *The Post* (Maryland), September 1, 1979.
5. *New York Times*, October 7, 1979.
6. Quoted in *The Post* (Maryland), February 21, 1980.
7. William Greider, *Secrets of the Temple: How the Federal Reserve Runs the Country* (New York: Simon and Schuster, 1987), p. 155.
8. The phaseout of Regulation Q was intended to occur over a six-year period and be presided over by a deregulation committee. However, by the time the Garn-St. Germain Act was passed, rates were effectively deregulated.
9. *New York Times*, April 14, 1980.
10. Ibid., February 8, 1981.
11. David M. Ricci, *The Transformation of American Politics: The New Washington and the Rise of Think Tanks* (New Haven: Yale University Press, 1993), p. 162.
12. Quoted in James Allen Smith, *The Idea Brokers: Think Tanks and the Rise of the New Policy Elite* (New York: Free Press, 1991), p. 195.
13. Robert Knabel, "Securities and Exchange Commission" in Charles L. Heatherly, editor *Mandate for Leadership: Policy Management in a Conservative Administration* (Washington: Heritage Foundation, 1981), pp. 808–811.
14. William Greider, "The Education of David Stockman," *Atlantic Monthly*, December 1981.
15. *Mountain Democrat* (California), December 4, 1981.
16. *New York Times*, February 11, 1982.
17. *The Post* (Maryland), October 18, 1982.
18. Quoted in Hedrick Smith, "Reagan's Effort to Change Course of Government," *New York Times*, October 23, 1984.
19. Robert A. Bennett, "Inside Citicorp: The Changing World of Banking," *New York Times*, May 29, 1983.
20. James W. Stevens, "The Intersection of the Banking and Securities Industries and Future Deregulation," in Lawrence G. Goldberg and Lawrence J. White, editors, *The Deregulation of the Banking and Securities Industries* (New York: Beard Books, 1979), p. 298.
21. *New York Times*, July 3, 1983.
22. Ibid., July 27, 1984.
23. *Frederick (MD) Post*, June 28, 1984.

24. *New York Times*, November 12, 1987.
25. *American Banker*, December 28, 1984
26. Quoted in the *American Banker*, February 9, 1987.
27. *New York Times*, May 1, 1987.
28. *The Frederick (MD) Post*, November 28, 1987.
29. *Mountain Democrat* (California), November 30, 1987.
30. *New York Times*, July 11, 1987.
31. Quoted in the *Washington Post*, July 22, 1987.
32. *New York Times*, August 26, 1987.
33. *Clarke v. Securities Industry Association*, No. 85-971, 479 US 388. The court held that a brokerage operation was not a core operation of national banks and thus not a branch so the separate operations established by banks did not violate the McFadden Act.
34. *New York Times*, November 19, 1987.
35. Ibid.
36. *Washington Post*, May 13, 1988.
37. The new rules were the result of an effort by the Federal Reserve and the Bank of England to raise the capital requirements on banks uniformly. As a result of an accord signed at the Bank for International Settlements in 1988, all banks in member countries were required to have a new capital ratio of 8 percent, primary equity as a percentage of outstanding loans.
38. *New York Times*, July 23, 1988.

Chapter Six

1. Charles L. Heatherly and Burton Yale Pines, editors, *Mandate for Leadership III: Policy Strategies for the 1990s* (Washington: Heritage Foundation, 1989), p. 455.
2. *New York Times*, January 10, 1988.
3. Ibid., October 26, 1988.
4. Jiji Press Ticker Service, January 19, 1989.
5. *American Banker*, January 25, 1989.
6. Ibid., January 25, 1989.
7. *St. Louis Post Dispatch*, June 15, 1989.
8. *New York Times*, September 22, 1990.
9. Ibid.
10. *Wall Street Journal*, September 24, 1990.
11. *Los Angeles Times*, September 23, 1990.
12. *New York Times*, November 1, 1991.
13. *Institutional Investor*, September 1998.
14. *New York Times*, May 9, 1995.
15. Quoted in the *Times-Picayune* (Louisiana), March 7, 1995.

16. Monica Langley, *Tearing Down the Walls* (New York: Simon & Schuster, 2003), pp. 258–259.
17. "Reforming Glass-Steagall in the Public Interest." J.P. Morgan & Co., April 1995.
18. *New York Times*, April 8, 1998.
19. Testimony of Federal Reserve Governor Susan M. Phillips, "Restrictions on Securities Underwriting and Dealing," Subcommittee on Financial Institutions and Regulatory Relief of the Committee on Banking, Housing, and Urban Affairs, U.S. Senate, March 20, 1997.
20. *American Banker*, June 25, 1998.
21. *Journal of Commerce*, September 1998.
22. *Bond Buyer*, June 11, 1998.
23. Associated Press, March 3, 1999.
24. Amey Stone and Mike Brewster, *King of Capital* (New York: John Wiley & Sons, 2002), p. 230.
25. Federal Reserve press release, September 23, 1998.
26. *Multinational Monitor*, November 1998.
27. Testimony of Federal Reserve Chairman Alan Greenspan, "H.R. 10, the Financial Services Competitiveness Act of 1997," Committee on Banking and Financial Services, U.S. House of Representatives, May 22, 1997.
28. Testimony of Federal Reserve Chairman Alan Greenspan, "H.R. 10, the Financial Services Act of 1998," Committee on Banking, Housing, and Urban Affairs, U.S. Senate, June 17, 1998.
29. Testimony of Federal Reserve Governor Laurence H. Meyer, "Mergers and Acquisitions in Banking and Other Financial Services," Committee on the Judiciary, U.S. House of Representatives, June 3, 1998.
30. Robert E. Rubin and Jacob Weisberg, *In an Uncertain World* (New York: Random House, 2003), p. 305.
31. *American Banker*, December 28, 2000.
32. *New York Times*, November 12, 1999.
33. Alan T. Saracevic, "So Much for Wall Street Cleaning Up Its Act," *San Francisco Chronicle*, October 13, 2002.
34. *Network World*, December 28, 1998.
35. *Fortune*, December 21, 1998.
36. This was called "shelf registration." Companies would file their applications and financial documents with the SEC in advance of the actual sale. When market conditions were conducive, they could quickly freshen up the documents and proceed with the sale of new securities quickly.
37. *American Banker*, February 6, 2003.
38. *New York Times*, August 12, 2003.
39. *Financial Times*, July 23, 1996.
40. *Journal of Accountancy*, August 1997, p. 11.
41. *American Banker*, May 2, 2003.

INDEX

Father Coughlin. *See* Coughlin, Charles
Fed watchers, 200
Federal Deposit Insurance
    Corporation, 266
Federal Reserve Act, 27, 28, 93
    major architect of, 36, 77
Federal Reserve Bank of New York, 75,
    270. *See also* New York Fed
Federal Reserve Bill, 61
Federal Reserve Board, 2, 29, 112, 223
    Crash of 1929 and, 61
    creation of, 13, 105
    criticism, 66
    fixing, 128–133, 201–203
        early attempts, 128
    influence, in 1920s, 15
    McFadden's opposition, 32
    opponents, 30
    pre-1929 criticism of, 49
    problems as 1920s' bull market
        continued, 62
    reconstitution of, Brookhart
        proposal to, 43
    state banks join, 37
Federal Securities Act, 98.
    See also Glass-Steagall Act
Federal Trade Commission, 42, 81
    call for examination of chains by, 38
    function, 83–84
    utilities study, 134
Filene, Edward A., 121
Finance capitalism, 8
Financial department store, 216
Financial Institutions Reconstruction,
    Recovery, and Enforcement Act,
    247
Financial Services Modernization Act,
    2, 7, 233, 270, 290
First National City, 179
First Union National Bank, 199
Fletcher, Duncan, 53–54, 137, 142
    as chairman of Senate Banking and
        Currency Committee, 71–72, 76
    FDR influence, 76
    role in passage of Eccles Act, 132
Fletcher-Rayburn bill, 115, 116
    aim, 117
    criticism of, 130

deliberations over, 122
Ford, Gerald, 206
Ford, Henry, 18, 71, 86
Frank, Barney, 245, 246
Frankfurter, Felix, 82
Frew, Walter, 27
Fulbright, J. William, 165
Fulbright Committee
    investigations, 166
    political nature, 169
    view of market, 169
Funston, Keith, 172
Futures Trading Act (1921), 55

G
Galbraith, John Kenneth, 198
Garn, Jake, 210, 212, 222
Garn-St Germain Act, 212, 228, 251,
    252
    S&L crisis and, 241
Gary, Judge Elbert, 42
General Electric, 187
Germany, 192
Giannini, A. P., 151, 157
Gilbert, Clinton, 66, 106
Gingrich, Newt, 255, 258
Glass, Carter, 36, 37, 61, 106
    as architect of Federal Reserve Act, 77
    as member of Senate Banking and
        Currency Committee, 76, 77
    opposition to Eccles Act, 130
    as Secretary of Treasury under
        Wilson, 77
Glass Banking Act, 102
Glass-Steagall Act, 2, 66, 92–94, 180, 210
    advocacy for repeal under Clinton
        administration, 253
    banking as defined by, 94
    Citicorp attack, 243–248
    compliance with, 132
    criticism of, 104
    demise, 269–272
    deposit insurance provision, 93
    effectiveness, 111
    FDR response to, 94
    J. P. Morgan & Co.'s attack, 262
    McFadden opposition to, 93
    opposition to, 3, 199